LAWNS AND GROUND COVERS

How to Select, Grow and Enjoy

Michael MacCaskey

HPBooks

Executive Producer: Richard Ray
Contributing Editor:
   Susan Chamberlin
Photography: Michael Landis

Produced by Horticultural Publishing Co., Inc.:
Art Director: Richard Baker
Associate Editor: Lance Walheim
Research Editor: David Loring
Production Editor: Kathleen Parker
Design: Judith Hemmerich, Lingke Oei
Typography: Linda Encinas
Illustration: Roy Jones
Staff Photographer: William Aplin
Additional Photography: American
   Phytopathological Society; Max E. Badgley;
   Derek Fell; Michael MacCaskey; Scott Millard;
   Dr. Harry Niemczyk; Dr. Michael Parella
Photographic Assistant: Richard B. Ray

Published by HPBooks
a division of Price Stern Sloan, Inc.
11150 Olympic Boulevard
Los Angeles, California 90064
ISBN: 0-89586-099-6
Library of Congress
Catalog Card Number: 81-82133
© 1982 Price Stern Sloan, Inc.
Printed in U.S.A.
14 13 12 11 10 9

Cover photo: Michael Landis
Ground cover planting features *Lonicera Japonica* 'Halliana'. The lawn is St. Augustinegrass overseeded with annual ryegrass.

The Garden Floor 3

Lawn or Ground Cover? *4*, Choosing a Lawn or Ground Cover *5*, Low-Maintenance Landscapes *6*, Alternatives *8*.

Lawns 13

Lawn Regions *14*, Lawn Grasses *15*, Specialty Grasses *30*.

Planting a Lawn 33

Prepare Soil *34*, Underground Sprinkler Systems *37*, Installing an Underground Irrigation System *42*, Sowing Seed *44*, Installing Sod *45*.

Caring for Your Lawn 47

Water *48*, Mow *50*, Fertilize *52*, Lawn Troubles *54*, Winter Overseeding and Renovation *66*, Calendar *68*.

Ground Covers 73

Ground Cover Basics *74*, Erosion Control *78*, Ground Cover Selection Guide *80*, Encyclopedia of Ground Covers *84*.

Glossary *172*, Mail Order Sources *174*, Acknowledgments *174*, Index *175*.

The Garden Floor

Every garden has a floor. It may be nonliving such as brick, wood decking, cement paving or a mulch of tree bark, pine needles or gravel. It may be a grass lawn or ground cover. Many garden floors are a combination of the two.

Each kind of ground cover has advantages and disadvantages. Paving materials are the most expensive to install but are the best surfaces for patios and walkways. They last for many years and require little maintenance except for an occasional cleaning.

Lawns usually require the most maintenance, which varies according to grass type. For most grasses, regular watering, mowing and fertilizing are in order. Lawns are generally adapted to most soils and situations. Green grass is a pleasing, complementary color and one of the softest, most resilient surfaces for play.

If lawns are generally adapted, ground covers are specialists. There is a ground cover for nearly every landscape use, but few for every situation. Ground covers also range from high maintenance to low maintenance, depending on the plant and the situation. Many demand little care once they are established.

Mulches, too, are quite varied. If installed properly, they can be maintenance-free for many years. Organic mulches decompose to benefit the soil. Some kinds must be replaced periodically, because they tend to be washed or knocked out of their boundaries.

A matter of function—Deciding which ground covering plant or material to use as the floor of your garden is an essential part of landscaping. The garden floor is usually the most extensive feature of a home landscape, helping to establish its character.

Whether starting from scratch or upgrading an existing landscape, consider the *function* you want a ground cover to fill. In some cases, decking can perform the same duties as a living ground cover. The same is true for brick and concrete paving. But if you have a slope to protect, plants are by far the best choice. Consider, too, the natural beauty of plants versus inert materials. Plants are frequently the best possible option.

The garden floor may be grass, rock, wood or any other material that appropriately serves its function. This lawn is Kentucky bluegrass. Pebble rock imitates a stream bed.

Lawn or Ground Cover?

A lawn of Kentucky bluegrass, ryegrass or bermudagrass has a place in nearly every landscape. No other ground cover plant is as readily planted, maintained and enjoyed. A grass lawn is unsurpassed as a recreational surface, whether in a football stadium or in a child's yard. The color, texture and evenly cropped height of a grass lawn complements, enlarges and enhances the landscape.

But large expanses of grass lawn can be expensive and difficult to maintain—especially in these days of water shortages. The large, rolling grass lawn as an American institution and status symbol is giving way to more practical, economical alternatives. This means smaller lawns or sections of grass integrated with other ground covers.

Instead of *only* lawn, you need to be aware of the many ground cover options. Along with the nonliving ground covers mentioned before, there are hundreds of low, spreading plants that cover the ground effectively and economically. More than 200 are described in this book.

Here are a few ideas to help you select the floor for your landscape:
• Alter patterns and planting areas of older landscapes to create different moods and capture a unique quality. Fine-textured, low surfaces such as grass lawns lend a sense of spaciousness to the landscape.
• Consider the effects of various colors. Light yellow-green is bold. Medium green and blue-green are more discreet. Large expanses of bright flower colors attract the eye.
• Complex patterns and coarse textures reduce the sense of space. They may become distracting and irritating. Aim for simplicity.

Precisely clipped driveway border of boxwood is complemented by equally meticulous lawn. Regular maintenance is required, and the effect is formal.

Informality and much less maintenance generally characterize gardens that feature ground covers. This ground cover is *Pachysandra terminalis.*

Choosing a Lawn or Ground Cover

Making the final choice of one plant over another can be the most agonizing part of landscaping. Consider your experience and the information in this book, plus all the advice you can collect from friends, neighbors and local nurserymen.

It is a good idea to make notes of what plants you have, need or want. Putting thoughts in writing will help crystalize your objectives. It is then easy to compare your data with plant descriptions and landscape plans. To give you some idea of how this process might occur, here are some notes made by a gardener living in Pasadena, California.

Lawn areas for play do not have to be large to be effective. Dichondra is sometimes difficult to maintain in large plantings, but works well as a soft, safe outdoor surface on a small scale.

One Gardener's Notes

Maximum and minimum temperatures—Called local nursery and airport. Minimum around 27F (−3C). Maximum rarely to 113F (44C).

Recommended lawn grasses—Warm-season grasses include bermuda, zoysia and dichondra. Ryegrasses are the best cool-season grasses.

Water—Summer drought is certain with occasional winter drought. Nurseryman says local water is "salty."

Soil—Fairly heavy clay type. Hard to work. Lawn will need organic amendment.

Outdoor spaces needed—Need fenced play yard for children. Some space for vegetables and fruit trees.

Full sun areas—Front yard faces south, gets most of sun. Perhaps vegetables should go here.

Shade areas—Heavy shade under trees in back yard. No grass there. Entire back yard faces north.

Slope areas—East side of lot is steep slope. Need ground cover for erosion control.

Garden maintenance—Vacations and business require a landscape that has some degree of self-sufficiency.

SOME CHOICES

After comparing notes with available plants and other data, the Pasadena gardener made these selections:
• Plant dichondra in back yard. This grass takes shade and thrives on high heat.
• Campanula, ferns or liriope should grow in shade of deciduous tree.

• Remove weeds and control slope erosion with *Convolvulus cneorum* and *Cistus* species shrubs, surrounded by African daisies or *Baccharis pilularis*. For more color, plant one of the small varieties of ice plant. Install permanent drip watering system with automatic timer.

Low-Maintenance Landscapes

Ground covers other than grass have traditionally been associated with low maintenance. This assumption needs some clarification. In specialized situations, a ground cover planting may be low maintenance from the beginning. Seeding native grasses on a hillside is an example. But ground covers usually demand regular care the first few years, with particular attention paid to weed control. Gradually, maintenance diminishes, but only after careful attention in the beginning.

Here are some specifics to keep in mind if a low-maintenance landscape is your goal:

Reduce lawn size—Reducing the size of lawn increases its visual impact. Smaller lawns become more of an accent and less anonymous. Your efforts to maintain a beautiful lawn are concentrated over a smaller area, making an attractive lawn more attainable.

Confine lawn to specific areas—Small, numerous patches of grass, each requiring watering, mowing and edging, are very time consuming. Usually, lawns of this type happen by accident. Without planning, your landscape soon becomes dominated by grass.

Make lawn accessible—Do not surround lawn completely with shrubs or flower beds. Lawns should be used for play and recreation. Design lawn areas so you can get mower to and from them easily. Avoid having to carry a heavy mower from front to back yard.

Use ground cover alternatives—Ground covers exist for every situation around your home. Some will serve in place of a lawn. They are most useful in heavy shade, on steep slopes and in excessively wet or dry soils where grass will not grow.

Install a mowing strip—A firm, narrow edging at the right height guides the mower's wheels and reduces the amount of time it takes to hand trim. See illustration at right.

Consider installing a drip irrigation system, low-precipitation spray heads and an automatic clock—Consult a professional irrigation specialist for advice if landscape is complicated, or if a slope or hillside is involved. Quality counts when installing an irrigation system. Photos and text describing how to install your own system are shown on pages 37 to 43. A cut-rate system will often cost you more over a period of time due to failure of materials and inefficient, wasteful watering.

Improve soil, if necessary—Choose plants that will thrive in the existing soil, or thoroughly amend soil to accommodate the plants you want. Plants forced to struggle where not adapted are less attractive, grow more slowly and are more prone to problems.

Learn how to water—Many troubles result from poor watering habits. Get to know the specific needs of the plants in your landscape. When you water, be certain to wet soil to the depth of the roots. Wait for first signs of water stress—drooping, wilting, lackluster leaves—before watering again. See page 48.

Use a mulch—Mulch around new ground cover plantings in summer to prevent infestations of weeds, cool the soil and save water through reduced evaporation. Winter mulches protect plants from cold and prevent damage caused by alternate freezing and thawing of the soil.

Garden with the natural rhythms of the seasons—Time feeding, mowing, watering and pruning to seasonal cycles—not calendar dates. Feed lawns in fall when roots will store energy. Increase mowing frequency when grass is growing fastest.

Create wide tree basins—Surround lawn trees with a wide circle of mulch or ground cover. The tree is relieved of competition from grass, aided by mulch and protected from mower damage. At the same time, lawn area is reduced. Thin, weedy lawn in dense shade of tree is also eliminated.

Make comfortable paths—Where easy flow of pedestrian traffic is important, paths should be wide enough for two people to walk abreast. Be practical—determine width of utility paths by measuring distance between wheelbarrow handles.

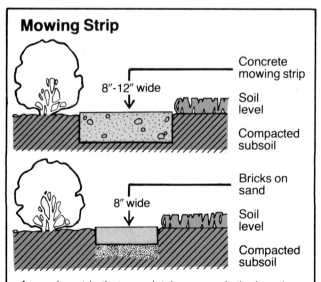

Mowing Strip

8"-12" wide

Concrete mowing strip

Soil level

Compacted subsoil

8" wide

Bricks on sand

Soil level

Compacted subsoil

A mowing strip that completely surrounds the lawn is a standard feature of low-maintenance landscapes. Consider installing sprinkler heads down center of concrete strip. Heads are protected from edger or mower damage and trimming is eliminated. Place sleeve of 2-inch-diameter plastic pipe around heads to depth of concrete.

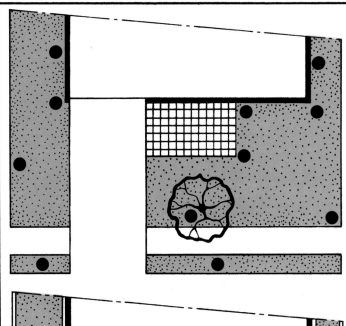

High, Medium and Low Maintenance

High Maintenance

A black spot ● indicates problem areas in this typical garden design. The lawn between the sidewalk and street is difficult to mow and water. Numerous stops and starts slow mowing. The tree in the lawn needs special protection from the mower, necessitating hand trimming. Edges along the house and property line must also be trimmed by hand.

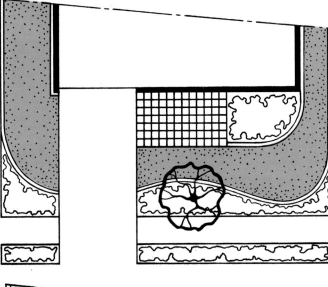

Medium Maintenance

A combination of lawn and ground cover makes mowing and watering jobs easier. Sweeping curves and a mowing strip speed mowing. Problem areas of lawn are reduced. Ground cover is used around the tree, at the entry and in the strip between sidewalk and street.

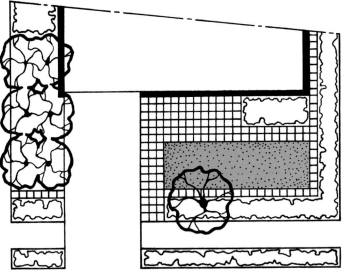

Low Maintenance

Mowing this lawn is now easy. Lawn area is reduced and bordered by a mowing strip. Ground covers fill odd spots. Side lawn area has been replaced by a small orchard of dwarf fruit trees.

Alternatives

Most landscapes look best with a combination of ground covers. Curving lines of rock mulch for tree basin is attractive, accents the grass lawn and benefits tree's health.

Many gardeners are experimenting with ground covers that are distinctly different from traditional plantings. Low maintenance and water and energy conservation characterize each. Here are five that might interest you.

ROCKSCAPING

Landscaping with rock, or *rockscaping,* has many practical virtues. A rockscape is best and most commonly used to *reduce* lawn and ground cover areas, not eliminate them. When properly planned, a rockscape is attractive and requires little maintenance. A rockscape is especially appropriate with natural settings and Spanish or western architecture. In the desert Southwest, a rockscape can connect your home to the natural landscape. Realize, however, that even a rockscape is not completely maintenance-free. If not installed properly, it could require more weeding and raking maintenance than a lawn. To ensure success, follow these steps.

1. Eliminate all perennial weeds and grass in the area to be covered with rock. These include nutgrass, bermudagrass, Johnsongrass and ground morning glory. If necessary, use glyphosate herbicide or a soil fumigant. See page 57.

2. Level and roll all surfaces to be covered until firm. Position any large boulders you intend to use at this time. Spread and level 1 inch of sharp, 20 grit concrete sand over soil. Sand is necessary—it acts as a cushion for the plastic cover to come. Without sand, gravel will cut through the plastic, allowing weed growth.

3. Cover sand with black plastic that is at least 4 millimeters thick. Be sure to overlap edges sufficiently or weeds will grow through. Lay rocks at the corners to hold in place until gravel is spread. Cut 2-foot-diameter holes in plastic for plants.

4. Spread a 4-inch layer of 1-inch-diameter gravel over the plastic for a "ground cover." This size gravel has a texture and effect similar to low-growing, connecting plants.

5. Spread 4 inches of pea gravel or finely decomposed granite rock, 5/8-inch diameter or less, over the plastic in the "lawn" area. Rock this size has a visual texture similar to a grass lawn.

6. Bury steppingstones or boards in the rock for walkways. Without some kind of pathway, you'll eventually ruin your shoes walking over the crushed rock.

Design principles—Effective design using rocks in the landscape is the same as designing with plants: You want an attractive landscape using compatible materials placed in a natural way. Here are some tips:

• Situate boulders and large stones where you would typically place shrubs and hedges.
• Use fewer sizes of stones in a rockscape than you would different kinds of plants in a landscape.
• Bury one-fourth to one-third of large rocks below soil surface. This is how they would be found in nature.
• Position large sedimentary stones on a horizontal plane for accent.
• Use rock and gravel of similar texture or related origin. Avoid combining volcanic rock with granite or stream-bed rock.
• Use pea gravel to simulate the effect of lawn.
• Use 1-inch-diameter gravel or washed pebbles for ground cover effect.
• Use 2- to 4-inch stones for low border effect.
• Red and black volcanic rock combine well.
• Use native or adapted plants to accent rockscape.
• Use sedums and bulbs around large boulders.

MULCHES OF BARK OR WOOD CHIPS

A wide variety of organic mulches is available and varies by locality. All are beneficial in many ways. They reduce water evaporation, modify soil temperatures and

Carefully placed stream-bed rocks accent shape and emphasize character of mature oak. Moisture, which can cause disease, does not accumulate around tree's crown. Adjacent planting of ivy is blocked from spreading to, and up, tree.

Where lawn is difficult to grow, such as under and around trees and driveway borders, a mulch or live ground cover is a good alternative.

help control weeds. Some of the best organic mulches include bark and wood products.

Fir bark pebbles or chunks are very attractive. They are rich, reddish brown when first placed in the garden, gradually aging to a pleasing gray. Garden centers offer many grades of fir bark in bags. If a large quantity is needed, you will save money by buying through a supplier of bulk garden materials. Many companies will sell materials by the yard or by the pickup truckload.

Shredded bark has the same rich color as fir bark but is variable in size and shape. Tree chips are irregular in shape and come in many colors. In many areas, tree chips are available at nominal cost from the city maintenance department or private tree care companies.

These kinds of ground covers are very effective in natural, low-maintenance landscapes. They act as a forest floor. The primary disadvantage is need of replenishment. Every year or two, fresh bark must be added to compensate for the amount that decomposes or washes away. Bark must be bordered or confined to prevent excessive loss from water runoff or pedestrian traffic.

If weeds are a problem, a bark cover is best applied in a 3- to 4-inch layer. To cover 1,000 square feet to this depth requires 10 cubic yards. Where weeds are not a major problem or where slow-growing ground cover plants will eventually fill in an area, a layer 1 to 2 inches thick will be sufficient. You can reduce cost by using the least-expensive mulch for the bottom layer, covering this with a thin layer of the most attractive material.

NATIVE MOSS

Native mosses are outstanding, low-maintenance ground covers and lawn substitutes. But these are not plants you buy at the nursery. Rather, you encourage them where they grow naturally. A moss lawn requires moist, well-drained acid soil, preferably with some clay. It does well in shade, such as on a north-facing slope.

David Benner, a horticulturist who lives in New Hope, Pennsylvania, has experimented with a lawn of native moss for the last dozen years. He reports:

"I have found moss to be an outstanding lawn substitute. My moss lawn is now 12 years old and has never been mowed, fertilized or sprayed. If given moisture, it is green all year. During extended drought, it browns but does not die. It becomes green again within minutes after a rain.

"I simply encouraged the moss at the expense of my former grass lawn. Grass prefers a soil pH of 6.5, whereas moss prefers a pH of 5.5 or less. Instead of liming to raise the pH to encourage grass, I applied 4 pounds of soil sulfur per 100 square feet. Within a few months, the soil pH had dropped from 6.5 to about 5, and the moss began to thrive. Over the next three or four years, the grass continued to give way to the moss until the lawn turned entirely to moss.

"Moss can be transplanted. Try it in early spring when the weather is cool and the soil is moist. Most important, leave no air spaces between soil and transplanted clumps of moss. You must sprinkle them frequently the next several weeks until they are established.

"Moss lawns need very little care until fall. Leaves falling on moss from deciduous trees must be removed before winter. If leaves are not removed, the moss will rot and die. I wait until after the first hard freeze. The moss is frozen to the ground and less likely pulled loose by a rake.

"The only maintenance is occasional weeding. Dandelion, thistle, oxalis and veronica are sometimes problems. I try to pull them out by the roots before they set seed.

"One interesting advantage of a moss lawn is that it is an ideal germination medium for all kinds of rare and normally hard-to-grow wildflowers. Right now I have seedlings of *Shortia galacifolia* as well as seedling rhododendrons, azaleas, *Pieris, Leucothoe, Chrysogonum, Lobelia* and *Houstonia.*"

PRAIRIE GRASS

Just a century ago, a huge sea of prairie grass covered most of the arid Midwest and the northern section of the United States. The sight must have been impressive to the pioneers. On the plains of the Illinois, Des Moines and Wabash rivers, the prairie stretched as far as the eye could see. Full height in the fall was an incredible 10 to 12 feet.

There are three basic kinds of natural prairie grass. *Shortgrass prairie* is mostly western wheatgrass, buffalograss and blue grama. It survives on as little as 20 inches of rain a year. *Midgrass prairie* of the Dakotas, Nebraska, Kansas and Oklahoma produces 1-1/2- to 2-foot-tall side oats grama, split beard bluestem, little bluestem, needle-and-thread, prairie dropseed and others with about 30 inches of rain. *Tallgrass prairie* thrives the farthest east where rainfall averages 40 inches or more a year. Grasses there include big bluestem, switchgrass and Indiangrass.

Prairie grass is one of the most outstanding landscape features of North America. However, most

Bark mulch covers soil between conifers to reduce weeds, cool soil and conserve water. Bark gradually decomposes and improves soil. Replenish mulch each spring by spreading one-third of the quantity originally required.

stands were gradually sacrificed to farming over the last century. Now many architects, designers, ecologists and gardeners are re-establishing prairie grass for low-maintenance landscapes. Where the setting is appropriate, prairie grass is attractive, interesting and maintenance-free once established.

Seed or plants of prairie grass are commercially available. Obtaining seed from a commercial source is advised. The supplier will also provide good advice for planting your particular site. It is important that you plant seed adapted to your climate and soil area. Consult your local county agricultural adviser or the Soil Conservation Service for further help.

Establishing prairie grass requires effort and patience. Allow three seasons—the first for preparing the seedbed, the second for planting and the third for watching prairie grass take off.

First season:
Prepare soil—Make seedbed reasonably weed-free by repeated tilling at monthly intervals through the season. Fertilizer and amendment are not necessary. Roll until soil is packed fairly hard.

Seed—A typical mix includes three kinds of grasses and six flowering plants. Fast-growing grasses such as needlegrass, Junegrass, Canadian wild rye, bee balm, yellow coneflower and black-eyed Susan are often included in mixes. Use big bluestem, Indiangrass or switchgrass in moist, heavy soil. Rely on side oats grama, needle-and-thread, western wheatgrass and Junegrass in dry, sandy soil.

Second season:
Planting—Sow in spring. Mix tiny grass seed with sand for easier spreading. Sow flower seed in bunches so new plants will not be overrun by faster-growing grass. Cover with 3/8-inch layer of soil or mulch. Roll to ensure good seed-to-soil contact. Start some flower seed in flats for later use as fill-in transplants.

Mow—Mow first and second month after planting with a rotary mower set to cut 4 to 8 inches high. Mowing retards growth of fastest-growing weeds and plants and encourages slower-growing prairie grasses.

Patience—Prairie grass plants show little aboveground activity the first year. Deep and strong root systems are developing underground.

Fill-in—Transplant plants grown from flats or nursery-grown plants to thin areas. Plant prairie flowers in clumps.

Third season:
Mow—Mow 2 to 3 inches high with rotary mower early in spring. No mowing required thereafter.

Enjoy—Growth will be fast and strong from now on. Your own landscape of prairie grass will give you some idea of the texture and beauty of America's prairie 200 years ago.

Thymus pseudolanuginosus, woolly thyme, is one of the best ground cover herbs. It grows low—usually less than 1 inch high. It spreads fast, is cold hardy and drought tolerant.

HERB LAWN

Herbs such as creeping thyme, chamomile and yarrow make the toughest, most traffic-resistant ground covers. Make a lawn using one or all three of these. Adding seed of legumes such as white clover or birdsfoot trefoil makes a wonderful, wild, grow-what-will lawn.

Herb lawns need mowing, weeding, watering and fertilizing just as typical grass lawns, but less of each. Their fragrance and texture is also a pleasure.

A lawn of creeping thyme (*Thymus praecox arcticus*) is extremely beautiful. It is hardy and tolerant, but also needs regular weeding. Even when a planting of thyme is completely filled in, grassy weeds invade easily. Best way to start a thyme lawn is with plugs planted about 12 inches apart. There's more about creeping thyme on page 167.

Chamomile (*Chamaemelum* species) is the traditional English lawn substitute. Plant perennial Roman chamomile, not the taller, annual chamomile used for tea. Roman chamomile can be kept low by mowing with a reel mower, and is fairly resistant to weed invasions. Start with plugs planted 12 inches apart. See page 104.

Yarrow (*Achillea* species) is particularly tolerant of drought and infertile soil, even compared to other herbs. There are several species. *Achillea tomentosa* is the common, low ornamental. Some recommend *A. millefolium* for use as a lawn. It is well adapted as a lawn, evidenced by the vigor with which it invades and overtakes some grass lawns. Nurseries sell yarrow in 1-gallon containers. Set these large clumps about 18 inches apart. See page 85.

Before planting, prepare the soil by making it as weed-free as possible. Sow legume seed after planting herbs, then mulch and water.

Lawns

A lawn has many virtues. Color, texture and feel of grass pleases the senses. Grass cools and freshens the air, traps dust and reduces glare. A neatly clipped and trimmed grass lawn lends a consistency and order to the landscape. Above all, there is no more versatile outdoor surface than a lawn. Lawn is relatively inexpensive, clean and safe for outdoor activities and tumbling children. No other ground cover possesses these combinations of utility and beauty.

GRASS SELECTION GUIDE

Lawn grasses are classified as either *cool season* or *warm season*. Cool-season grasses grow best during cool periods of spring and fall. Most are tolerant of cold winters, so are used in the northern latitudes. Cool-season grasses include Kentucky bluegrass, fine fescues, ryegrasses and bentgrasses.

Warm-season grasses grow best in areas with high summer temperatures. Most become dormant to some degree when temperatures drop below freezing. Most are killed by cold northern winters. Warm-season grasses include bahia, bermuda, centipede, St. Augustine and zoysia.

About the grass descriptions—In the following section, each grass is pictured close-up and in the landscape. These photos give you some idea of texture, color and overall appearance of each grass. The accompanying map shows the area of the United States and Canada where each grass is best adapted. Keep in mind that these adaptation zones are general guides. Local conditions vary considerably. Also, many grasses do well beyond their typical range, though they may require pampering to grow well. Some gardeners want to grow a specific grass and are willing to provide the extra care necessary for it to thrive.

Relative tolerances to heat, cold, salt, diseases, pests, drought, shade and wear for each grass are indicated by the chart at the top of each description. These ratings, like the zones of adaptation, serve only as useful guides. Those listed primarily in the "high tolerance" column are the low-maintenance grasses. Those frequently rated "low" in tolerance will likely require extra care.

The glossary beginning on page 172 explains the different terms discussed in this book.

A "perfect" lawn, such as this one in Richardson, Texas, begins by choosing a well-adapted grass. This is 'Tifway' hybrid bermuda.

Lawn Regions

The map below outlines the basic lawn grass zones of the United States and Canada. Use the map as a guide and compare it to descriptions of individual grasses and specific climate adaptations. Much lawn seed is sold as *mixes*—combinations of several grasses. These combine strengths and compensate for weaknesses. A typical mix of cool-season grasses includes Kentucky bluegrass, fine fescue and perennial rye. Perennial ryegrass combined with common bermudagrass tolerates summer heat and stress and remains green in winter.

PACIFIC NORTHWEST AND COASTAL BRITISH COLUMBIA

Climate of this zone is generally cool and humid. This region is the center of cool-season grass-seed production. Adapted grasses are Kentucky bluegrass, fine fescue, bentgrass and ryegrasses.

SOUTHERN CALIFORNIA

Many kinds of grasses are planted in this zone. Common bermudagrass, *Paspalum* species and zoysiagrass are low maintenance. Kentucky bluegrass, mixed with improved perennial ryegrass for disease resistance, is popular. Tall fescue is also grown here. Use annual and perennial ryegrass to overseed dormant bermudagrass.

SOUTHWEST

Summer heat is intense here. Soils are dry and water is precious. Lawns are best planted small and oasislike. Common and improved bermudagrass are best bets. Overseed them with ryegrass for winter. Zoysiagrass and St. Augustinegrass are options.

MOUNTAIN, NORTHERN GREAT PLAINS AND CANADIAN CENTRAL PLAINS

Climate is dry and semiarid. Rainfall varies between 10 and 25 inches annually. Daily temperature range is extremely wide. Kentucky bluegrass and fine fescues are most common. Hardy varieties of improved perennial ryegrass and tall fescue are sometimes used. Bermudagrass and zoysiagrass are occasionally planted in the southern part of the region. Use crested wheatgrass, buffalograss or blue grama for low-maintenance lawns.

GREAT LAKES, NORTHEASTERN STATES AND EASTERN CANADA

Rainfall is abundant, averaging up to 45 inches. Kentucky bluegrass, fine fescues and improved perennial ryegrasses are common and well adapted. Hardy bermudgrasses, page 16, and zoysiagrass, page 29, are sometimes planted in coastal areas.

MOUNTAIN, PIEDMONT AND THE CENTRAL SOUTH

Climate is warm and humid with rainfall ranging between 40 and 70 inches per year. Bermudagrass and zoysiagrass are common. Tall fescue is well adapted. Kentucky bluegrass, fine fescues and perennial ryegrass are frequently grown. Use improved perennial or annual ryegrass over dormant bermudagrass.

GULF COAST AND FLORIDA

Climate is tropical, with a year-round growing season. St. Augustinegrass is the most important lawn grass of Florida. Zoysiagrass is widely recommended. Bahiagrass, centipedegrass and tall fescue are commonly grown. Due to the longer growing season, all grasses need more mowing and more fertilizer.

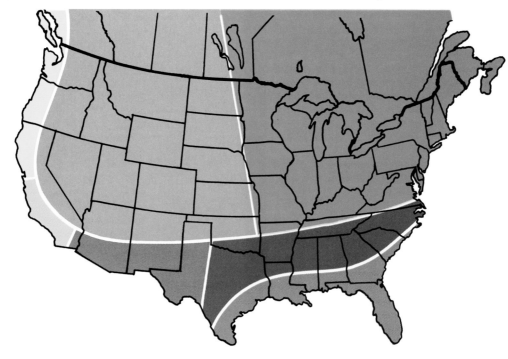

Bahiagrass
Paspalum notatum

To Plant: Sow 8 to 10 pounds of seed per 1,000 square feet in spring. Germinates in 20 to 40 days.
Water: Moderate.
Fertilizer: 2 to 4 pounds actual nitrogen per 1,000 square feet per year.
Mowing: Frequent mowing required to remove seedheads. Adjust rotary mower to about 2-1/2 inches high.

Bahiagrass was introduced to the United States from Brazil around 1913. It is well adapted to coastal areas from central North Carolina to eastern Texas, especially where soils are sandy and infertile. A coarse-textured grass, it spreads aggressively with short, thick rhizomes. Drought tolerance is above average, but bahiagrass is best where rainfall is abundant and evenly distributed throughout the year. Mole cricket is a common pest.

VARIETIES

'Argentine'—Leaves are more narrow than common bahiagrass but wider than 'Pensacola'. Medium cold tolerance. Sometimes used for home lawns.
'Paraguay'—Coarse texture, tough leaves. Used along roadsides for erosion control.
'Pensacola'—Narrow, upright leaves. Tolerant of low temperatures. Good response to fertilizer. Best bahiagrass for home lawns.

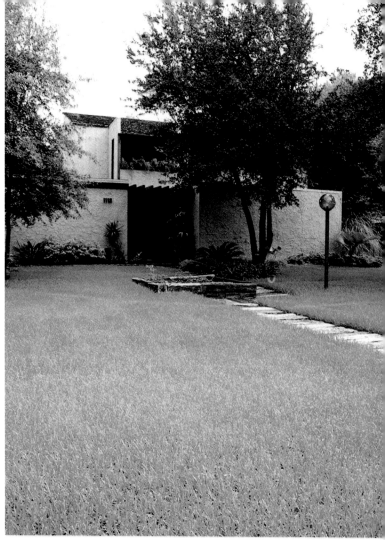
Bahiagrass

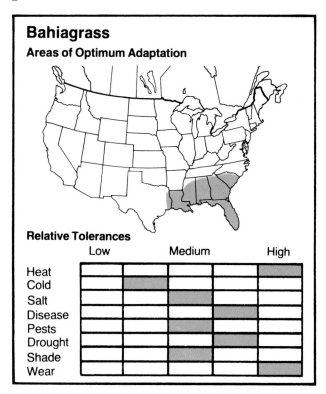

Bahiagrass
Areas of Optimum Adaptation

Relative Tolerances

	Low		Medium		High
Heat					■
Cold		■			
Salt			■		
Disease				■	
Pests			■		
Drought				■	
Shade			■		
Wear					■

Bahiagrass

Common bermudagrass

Common bermudagrass

Bermudagrass, Common

Cynodon dactylon

To Plant: Sow 1 to 2 pounds of seed per 1,000 square feet. Germinates in 10 to 30 days.

Water: Moderate.

Fertilizer: 2 to 6 pounds of actual nitrogen per 1,000 square feet per year. Use higher rate for improved appearance and where growing season is long.

Mowing: Cut at 3/4 to 1-1/2 inches high with reel or rotary mower.

A tough, low-maintenance lawn that can be attractive if watered and fertilized regularly. Overseed with ryegrass or fine fescue for winter lawn. Control invasiveness with glyphosate chemical spray.

Bermudagrass Hybrids and Varieties

Cynodon species

To Plant: Use sod, plugs or sprigs. Seed of hybrid bermudagrass is sterile. If you plant sprigs, spread 2 bushels per 1,000 square feet, late spring to midsummer.

Water: Moderate.

Fertilizer: Use 6 to 10 pounds actual nitrogen per 1,000 square feet per year. Use higher rates when maintenance is intensive and growing season is long. Use complete fertilizer with minor elements depending on soil conditions.

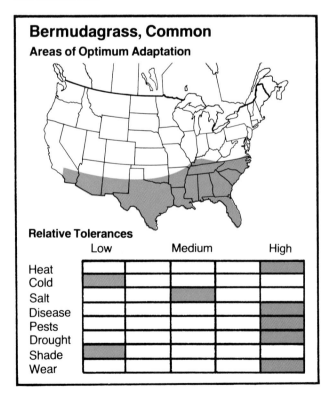

Bermudagrass, Common
Areas of Optimum Adaptation

Relative Tolerances

	Low		Medium		High
Heat					■
Cold	■				
Salt			■		
Disease					■
Pests					■
Drought					■
Shade	■				
Wear					■

Mowing: Use reel mower adjusted to cut 1 inch high.

Tif series bermudagrass hybrids are dwarf and fine textured compared to common bermudagrass. Some are used as substitutes for creeping bentgrass in the South.

HYBRIDS AND VARIETIES

'Midiron'—Dark green, medium texture. Vigorous. Excellent cold tolerance. Wears well in winter.

'Midway'—Dark green, medium texture. Excellent cold tolerance. Minimum thatch buildup.

'Pee Dee'—Dark green, medium texture. Good cold tolerance. Relatively high maintenance.

'Santa Ana'—Dark green, fine texture. Developed in southern California. Features short dormant season and high air-pollution tolerance. Very dense growing. Needs periodic thinning and dethatching.

'Sunturf'—Dark green, very fine texture. Good cold tolerance.

'Tifdwarf'—Dark green, fine texture. High maintenance. Tolerates exceptionally low mowing. Normally used for golf greens and lawn bowling—rarely for home lawns.

'Tifgreen'—Medium green, fine texture. One of the best for golf greens—accepts heavy wear and close, 1/8-inch cut.

'Tifway'—Dark green, fine texture. Best of the Tif series for home lawns. Does not require ultra-low mowing and generally needs less maintenance.

Hybrid bermudagrass

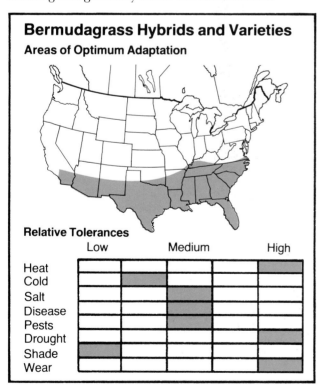

Bermudagrass Hybrids and Varieties
Areas of Optimum Adaptation

Relative Tolerances

	Low		Medium		High
Heat					■
Cold		■			
Salt			■		
Disease			■		
Pests			■		
Drought					■
Shade	■				
Wear					■

'Tifgreen' hybrid bermudagrass

Bentgrass

Bentgrass
Agrostis species

To Plant: Sow 1/2 to 1 pound per 1,000 square feet of 'Penncross', 'Emerald', 'Seaside' and 'Penneagle'. For 'Cohansey', 'Congressional' and 'Toronto', use 2 bushels of sprigs per 1,000 square feet. Seed germinates in 6 to 20 days.
Water: Needs large amount.
Fertilizer: 4 to 6 pounds of actual nitrogen per 1,000 square feet per year. Might require a complete fertilizer including minor elements, depending on soil conditions.
Mowing: Use reel mower adjusted to cut 1/4 inch to 1 inch high.

SPECIES AND VARIETIES
A. canina, Velvet bentgrass—Tolerant of low soil fertility. Aggressive if mowed close and often. High-quality lawn for home, bowling green or putting green. Sometimes used in seed mixes.
A. gigantea, Redtop—Prefers clay soils of low pH and low fertility. Rarely included in seed mixes because it tends to be short-lived and weedy.
A. stolonifera, Creeping bentgrass—High-quality lawn for putting or bowling greens. Mow low—1/4 inch— with a reel mower. Established by either seed or vegetative means. See varieties listed under "To Plant" above.
A. tenuis, Colonial bentgrass—Aggressive, usually dominant grass if planted in a mix. Varieties include 'Astoria', Exeter', 'Highland' and 'Holfior'.

'Seaside' bentgrass

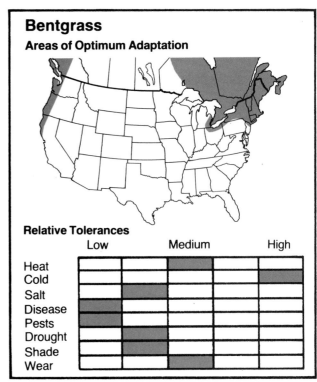

Bentgrass
Areas of Optimum Adaptation

Relative Tolerances

	Low		Medium		High
Heat			▓		▓
Cold					▓
Salt		▓			
Disease	▓				
Pests	▓				
Drought		▓			
Shade		▓			
Wear			▓		

Centipedegrass
Eremochloa ophiurides

To Plant: Sow 1 to 2 pounds of 'Centi-Seed' per 1,000 square feet. Germinates in about 20 days. Requires two seasons to establish. Or spread 5 to 6 bushels of sprigs per 1,000 square feet.

Water: Medium.

Fertilizer: Provide 1 to 2 pounds actual nitrogen per 1,000 square feet per year. Use low, 12 to 15 percent nitrogen fertilizer. Apply phosphorus and potassium only during the dormant season.

Mowing: Cut 1 to 1-1/2 inches high with reel or rotary mower.

Centipedegrass was introduced to the United States from southern Asia in 1916. It is well adapted to infertile, acid soils common to many regions of the Southeast. It tolerates less cold than bermudagrass, but more than St. Augustinegrass. Too much nitrogen promotes tender growth, which can be severely damaged by winter cold. Seedheads develop but are low and inconspicuous compared to bermudagrass or bahiagrass. Not as fine textured as bermudagrass so it will not develop a manicured look. Subject to iron chlorosis, especially after nitrogen fertilization. Correct with iron sulfate.

'Oklawn' is the only variety available. Released by Oklahoma Agricultural Experiment Station in 1965, it features improved drought and cold tolerance compared to common centipedegrass.

Centipedegrass

Centipedegrass
Areas of Optimum Adaptation

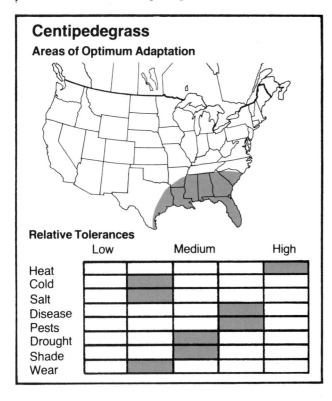

Relative Tolerances

	Low		Medium		High
Heat					▨
Cold		▨			
Salt		▨			
Disease				▨	
Pests				▨	
Drought			▨		
Shade			▨		
Wear		▨			

Centipedegrass

Creeping fescue

Fescue, Fine

Festuca rubra, F. longifolia

To Plant: Sow 5 pounds of seed per 1,000 square feet. Germinates in 7 to 14 days.
Water: Drought tolerant. Moderate.
Fertilizer: Low—1 to 3 pounds per 1,000 square feet per year. Dies out if overfertilized.
Mowing: Use reel or rotary mower adjusted to cut 2 inches high. Keep mower sharp. Hard fescues, *F. longifolia*, are relatively difficult to cut. Dull mowers shred leaf tips, giving lawn a brownish cast.

Three kinds of fine fescue are included here. Creeping red fescue and chewings fescue are subspecies of *F. rubra*. Red fescue spreads by underground runners called *rhizomes*. Chewings fescue is a clump-forming, nonspreading type. Hard fescue, *F. longifolia*, grows in clumps like chewing fescue, but has more heat and drought tolerance. In outward appearance, all three are virtually indistinguishable.

Fine fescues mix well with other grasses. They frequently comprise about 20 percent of a mix along with Kentucky bluegrass and improved perennial ryegrasses. In general, fine fescues add shade and drought tolerance to such a mix. Fine fescues are also useful for overseeding dormant bermudagrass.

'Fortress' creeping fescue

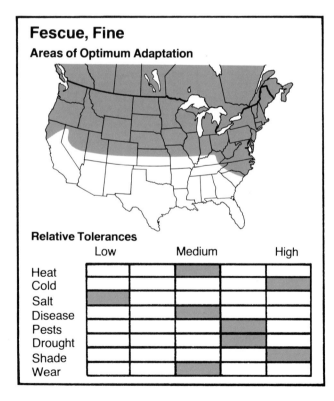

Fescue, Fine
Areas of Optimum Adaptation

Relative Tolerances

	Low	Medium	High
Heat		▓	
Cold			▓
Salt	▓		
Disease		▓	
Pests			▓
Drought		▓	
Shade			▓
Wear		▓	

VARIETIES OF CHEWING FESCUE

'Banner'—Dark green. Tolerates low mowing. Disease resistant but occasionally susceptible to powdery mildew.

'Highlight'—Medium green, very fine texture. Very aggressive in mixtures. Tolerates low mowing.

'Jamestown'—Medium to dark green. Dense and vigorous. Tolerates low mowing. Susceptible to powdery mildew.

'Shadow'—Dark green. Dense and vigorous. Improved disease resistance. Resists powdery mildew in shade.

VARIETIES OF CREEPING FESCUE

'Dawson'—Medium dark green, slender. Good for overseeding dormant bermudagrass. Tolerates low mowing. Susceptible to dollar spot.

'Fortress'—Dark green color blends well with Kentucky bluegrass and improved perennial ryegrasses. Strong spreader. Resists powdery mildew and has relatively good heat tolerance.

'Pennlawn'—A blend of fescue types, but primarily red fescue. Dark green with dense growth habit. Commonly mixed with Kentucky bluegrasses and improved perennial ryegrasses. Most commonly available fine fescue.

'Ruby'—Dark green color. Medium texture and density.

VARIETIES OF HARD FESCUE

'Scaldis'—Medium dark green. Improved heat and drought tolerance. Low maintenance.

'Waldina'—Medium dark green. Improved disease, heat and drought tolerance.

Left, 'Alta' fescue. Right, creeping fescue.

Fescue, Tall
Festuca arundinacea

To Plant: Sow 10 to 20 pounds of seed per 1,000 square feet. Seedlings are vigorous and fast growing. Germinates in 7 to 15 days.

Water: Moderate.

Fertilizer: 2 to 6 pounds of actual nitrogen per 1,000 square feet per year.

Mowing: Adjust rotary mower to cut about 2 inches high.

Tall fescue is a low-maintenance lawn grass. Most commercially available varieties were developed for forage qualities. Their utility has made them popular for home lawns in some areas. Generally, they do not perform well and make low-quality lawns. Tall fescue does not form a dense sod and tends to retreat into clumps, especially if not seeded at high rates. In many lawns, it is a coarse, fast-growing weed.

Despite these disadvantages, tall fescue is being used more frequently as a grass for home lawns. Several new "turf-type" tall fescues are available. They are new and have not yet been evaluated over the long term. But they promise to combine the heat, drought and wear tolerance and low-fertility requirements of forage types with other desirable characteristics. Look for varieties that have better color, finer texture, good mowing characteristics and improved disease resistance.

VARIETIES OF TURF-TYPE TALL FESCUE

'Falcon'—Medium dark green, medium leaf texture and turf density. Moderately low growing. Good heat and drought tolerance. Moderately resistant to leaf spot and brown patch.

'Houndog'—Medium dark green, medium leaf texture. Medium to low turf density. Semiprostrate growth habit. Good heat and drought tolerance. Moderate resistance to brown patch and *Helminthosporium* net blotch.

'Olympic'—Dark green, medium leaf texture and medium turf density. Somewhat lower growing than other varieties. Moderate shade adaptation. Less prone to develop iron chlorosis. Improved resistance to crown rust and *Helminthosporium* net blotch. Moderate resistance to brown patch. Maintains good green color with low soil fertility.

'Rebel'—Medium dark green, medium leaf texture and medium turf density. Good heat and shade tolerance. Moderate resistance to *Helminthosporium* net blotch. Somewhat susceptible to brown patch. Persists well with close mowing compared to other varieties.

'Alta' fescue

'Shannon'—Medium dark green, medium to coarse leaf texture. Medium turf density. Slower vertical growth rate than other varieties. Good drought and shade tolerance. Improved cold tolerance compared to common tall fescues. Moderate resistance to brown patch and *Helminthosporium* net blotch. Good mowing qualities.

VARIETIES OF FORAGE-TYPE TALL FESCUE

'Alta'—Medium green, coarse leaf texture and medium to low turf density. Upright growth habit. Good drought tolerance, poor cold tolerance. Susceptible to *Helminthosporium* net blotch and brown patch.

'Fawn'—Light green, coarse texture and low turf density. Well adapted to heavy clay soils. Poor heat and cold tolerance. Very susceptible to *Helminthosporium* net blotch, brown patch and crown rust.

'Goar'—Medium green, medium to coarse texture and medium to low turf density. Upright growth habit. Improved heat tolerance, but poor cold tolerance. Tolerant of salinity and high pH. Susceptible to *Helminthosporium* net blotch and brown patch. Slow to establish.

'Kentucky 31'—Medium green, coarse texture, medium to low turf density. Slightly prostrate growth habit. Good heat tolerance but poor cold tolerance. Good shade tolerance. Susceptible to *Helminthosporium* net blotch. Well adapted to transition zone. Forms medium-textured turf under shaded conditions in warm, humid climates.

Tall fescue

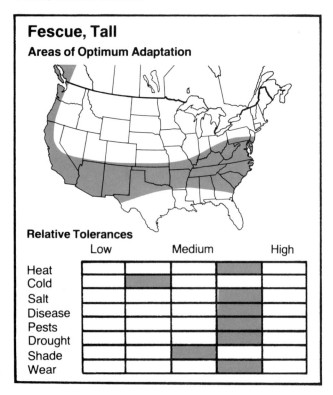

Fescue, Tall
Areas of Optimum Adaptation

Relative Tolerances

	Low		Medium		High
Heat					
Cold					
Salt					
Disease					
Pests					
Drought					
Shade					
Wear					

Kentucky Bluegrass

Poa pratensis

To Plant: Sow 1 to 2 pounds of seed per 1,000 square feet. Germinates in 14 to 30 days. Commonly available as sod.

Water: Medium to large amount.

Fertilizer: Apply 4 to 6 pounds actual nitrogen per 1,000 square feet per year. Use a complete fertilizer including minor elements depending on soil conditions.

Mowing: Varieties differ, but few should be cut below 1-1/2 inches high. Dwarf, low-growing varieties can be cut as close as 3/4 inch. Common Kentucky bluegrass should be cut higher, approximately 2-1/2 inches.

Kentucky bluegrass is widely adapted, attractive and hardy. It is the most widely planted grass in northern latitudes. It is the standard of color, texture, feel and maintenance against which other grasses are measured. Plants spread by strong, underground rhizomes, ultimately forming a dense sod.

In most areas, Kentucky bluegrass requires supplemental irrigation to maintain healthy growth during periods of drought. Without irrigation, leaves brown and cease to grow. Growth resumes with rains or renewed irrigation.

VARIETIES

'Adelphi'—Dark green, medium texture. Dense and low growing. Very good low-temperature color. Greens

Kentucky bluegrass

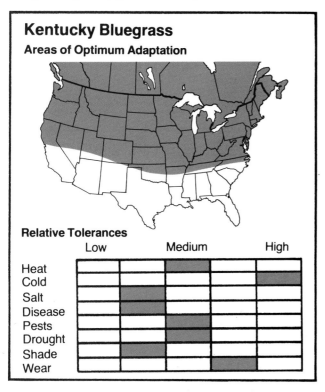

Kentucky Bluegrass
Areas of Optimum Adaptation

Relative Tolerances

	Low		Medium		High
Heat			■		
Cold					■
Salt		■			
Disease		■			
Pests			■		
Drought			■		
Shade		■			
Wear			■		

Kentucky bluegrass

Kentucky bluegrass

up fast in spring. Resistant to leaf spot, stripe smut and *Fusarium* blight.

'America'—Dark green, fine texture. Dense and low growing. Slow vertical growth rate. Moderate shade tolerance. Resistant to leaf spot, stripe smut, striped rust and *Fusarium* blight. Tolerates low nitrogen levels.

'Aquilla'—Medium dark green, medium to fine texture. Dense and fairly low growing. Good low-temperature color and spring green-up. Accepts low nitrogen levels.

'Baron'—Dark green, medium to coarse texture. Dense and low growing. Good low-temperature color. Moderately slow to green up in spring. Good seedling vigor—establishes rapidly. Moderate resistance to leaf spot and stripe smut.

'Bensun' (A-34)—Medium green, medium texture. Very dense and low growing. Tolerant of shade and low mowing. Very aggressive and competitive. Good wear resistance and spring green-up. Resists stripe smut. Moderately resistant to leaf spot.

'Birka'—Dark green, medium to fine texture. Dense and low growing. Moderately slow to green up in spring. Moderately tolerant of shade and low mowing. Resistant to leaf spot, stripe smut and powdery mildew.

'Bonnieblue'—Medium dark green, medium texture. Dense and low growing. Excellent low-temperature color. Greens up quickly in spring. Establishes fairly fast. Tolerates low mowing. Resists leaf spot and stripe smut.

'Bristol'—Dark green, medium texture. Dense and low growing. Excellent low-temperature color. Greens up quickly in spring. Recommended for shady sites. Moderate tolerance of low mowing.

'Cheri'—Dark green, medium texture. Dense and low growing. Accepts low mowing. Fair color at low temperatures. Vigorous seedlings establish fast.

'Columbia'—Medium dark green, medium texture and density. Low growing. Excellent color at low temperatures. Greens up quickly in spring. Good heat tolerance. Establishes fast. Moderately tolerant of low mowing. Resists leaf spot, stripe smut and *Fusarium* blight.

'Eclipse'—Dark green, medium texture and density. Very low growing. Good low-temperature color and spring green-up. Excellent cold tolerance. Tolerant of heat, drought and shade.

'Enmundi'—Dark green, medium texture and density. Very low growing. Tolerant of heat, drought and low mowing. Limited seed availability.

'Fylking'—Dark green, medium to fine texture. Dense and low growing. Good low-temperature color and spring green-up. Tolerant of cold and drought. Establishes fast and accepts low mowing. Makes a strong sod. Resistant to leaf spot. Some resistance to stripe smut. Highly susceptible to *Fusarium* blight.

'Glade'—Dark green, medium texture. Dense and low growing. Moderately good color at low temperatures. Good for shady sites. Slow vertical shoot growth. Moderately competitive. Resistant to stripe smut and powdery mildew. Moderate resistance to leaf spot.

'Majestic'—Dark green, medium texture. Dense, low, semiprostrate growth habit. Excellent low-temperature color. Greens up quickly in spring. Establishes fast. Accepts low mowing. Good resistance to leaf spot. Moderate resistance to stripe smut.

Kentucky bluegrass

'Merion'—Dark green, medium to coarse texture. Dense and low growing. Relatively poor color at low temperatures. Slow to green up in spring. Cold and drought tolerant. Slow to establish from seed. Fast to root when planted as sod in summer. Resists leaf spot. Susceptible to stripe smut, powdery mildew and rust. Not recommended for shady sites.

'Nugget'—Dark green, medium to fine texture. Dense and low growing. Cold hardy but very poor color at low temperatures. Slow to green up in spring. Excellent shade tolerance—recommended for shady sites. Resists leaf spot and powdery mildew. Susceptible to dollar spot.

'Parade'—Medium dark green, medium texture and density. Low growing. Very good low-temperature color. Fast to green up in spring. Establishes fairly fast and wears well. Resists leaf spot, stripe smut and *Fusarium* blight.

'Plush'—Medium green, medium texture and density. Low growing. Good low-temperature color and spring green-up. Establishes fast, moderately aggressive. Wears well.

'Ram I'—Dark green, medium to fine texture. Dense and low growing. Resistant to powdery mildew. Slow vertical shoot growth rate.

'Rugby'—Medium dark green, medium texture. Dense and low growing. Good low-temperature color and spring green-up. Medium heat and drought tolerance. Establishes rapidly. Very tolerant of low mowing. Good disease resistance. Tolerant of low fertility.

'Scenic'—Dark green, medium texture and density. Low growing. Attractive color with low fertility. Drought tolerant. Spreads fast. Resists pink snow

mold, snow scald, powdery mildew and leaf spot diseases. Susceptible to stripe smut.

'Shasta'—Medium dark green, medium texture and density. Excellent resistance to stripe rust in Pacific Northwest and northern California. Resistant to leaf spot and stripe smut.

'Sydsport'—Medium dark green, medium texture. Dense and low growing. Fairly good spring green-up. Widely adapted variety. Establishes fast and wears well. Aggressive and competitive. Forms dense sod. Resistant to leaf spot, stripe smut, *Fusarium* blight and powdery mildew.

'Touchdown'—Medium green, medium to fine texture and density. Erect growth habit. Greens up fast in spring. Shade tolerance better than most. Aggressive and competitive. Tends to develop thatch. Resists leaf spot, stripe smut and powdery mildew. Very susceptible to stripe smut.

'Vantage'—Medium green, medium to fine texture and density. Erect growth habit. Excellent heat and drought tolerance and good spring green-up. Use for a low-maintenance lawn. Looks acceptable with little care, but is susceptible to stem rust.

'Victa'—Dark green, medium to coarse texture. Dense and low growing. Moderately slow to green up in spring. Establishes fast. Moderately resistant to leaf spot and stripe smut.

'Windsor'—Medium dark green, medium to fine texture. Fairly dense and low growing. Good spring green-up and medium cold tolerance. Looks and grows best with high levels of nitrogen. Moderately resistant to leaf spot. Susceptible to stripe smut.

Annual ryegrass

Ryegrass, Annual
Lolium multiflorum

To Plant: Sow 5 to 10 pounds of seed per 1,000 square feet. Apply heavier rates in poor soils where low germination is expected, or when dense, fine-textured winter lawn is desired. Germinates in 5 to 14 days.
Water: Medium.
Fertilizer: Grows best with moderate fertility. Provide approximately 4 pounds actual nitrogen per 1,000 square feet per year.
Mowing: About 1-1/2 to 2 inches high with reel or rotary mower.

Huge quantities of annual ryegrass are sown over winter-dormant lawns each fall. For a brief period—fall to late spring—they are an attractive alternative to a dormant, brown lawn. Individual plants that survive into the following season become coarse-textured, fast-growing, weedy clumps. Most overseeded annual ryegrass dies out with heat. To encourage the permanent, dormant lawn, mow ryegrass lawn low in late spring.

An improvement over annual ryegrass for winter overseeding is called *Oregon intermediate ryegrass*. Its botanical name is *Lolium x hybridum*. It was developed from a cross between a low-growing annual ryegrass and 'Manhattan' perennial ryegrass. Oregon intermediate ryegrass is much lower growing, more disease resistant and has better heat and cold tolerance than annual ryegrass.

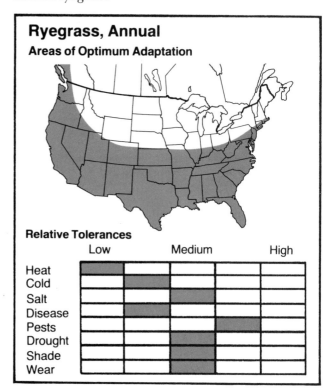

Ryegrass, Annual
Areas of Optimum Adaptation

Relative Tolerances

	Low	Medium	High	
Heat	■				
Cold		■			
Salt			■		
Disease		■			
Pests				■	
Drought			■		
Shade			■		
Wear			■		

Annual ryegrass

Ryegrass, Perennial
Lolium perenne

To Plant: Sow 5 to 10 pounds of seed per 1,000 square feet. In a mix, limit improved perennial ryegrasses to 20 percent by weight of mix. Germinates in 3 to 10 days.
Water: Medium.
Fertilizer: Apply 4 to 5 pounds actual nitrogen per 1,000 square feet per year.
Mowing: Cut 1-1/2 inches high. Some varieties will tolerate consistent mowing at 3/4 inch.

Common perennial ryegrass is short-lived and has poor heat tolerance. Leaves are very fibrous so they tear rather than cut cleanly. Common perennial ryegrass grows rapidly and vigorously, making a usable lawn in as little as three weeks. "Improved" or "turf-type" perennial ryegrasses are equally rapid growers. In addition, they are more disease resistant, more heat and cold tolerant, have better color and texture and live longer. Improved ryegrasses also mow more cleanly and easily.

VARIETIES OF PERENNIAL RYEGRASS

'Birdie'—Medium green, dense, fine texture. Good heat tolerance. Resists brown patch, usually resistant to crown rust. Mows cleanly.

'Blazer'—Moderately dark green, dense, fine texture. Moderately good heat and cold tolerance. Resists leafspot and brown patch. Good mowing quality.

'Citation'—Dark green, dense, fine texture. Heat tolerant. Resists brown patch and usually red thread disease. Mows well.

'Delray'—Medium dark green, dense, fine texture. Moderately good heat, cold and brown patch resistance.

'Derby'—Medium dark green, good texture and density. Medium heat and cold tolerance. Mows well and resists brown patch disease.

'Diplomat'—Medium dark green, very dense with fine texture. Medium heat and cold tolerance. Mows well and resists brown patch.

'Fiesta'—Moderately dark green, dense, fine texture. Moderately good heat and cold tolerance. Resists brown patch.

'Omega'—Medium dark green, dense, fine texture. Medium heat and cold tolerance. Mows well. Resists brown blight and brown patch.

'Pennant'—Moderately dark green, fine texture. Good heat and drought tolerance. Good brown patch and sod webworm resistance.

'Pennfine'—Medium dark green, dense, fine texture. Resists brown patch. Good mowing quality.

'Regal'—Dark green, dense, fine texture. Medium heat tolerance. Mows well. Resists brown patch.

'Yorktown II'—Dark green, fine texture. Very dense. Medium-to-good heat and cold tolerance. Mows very well. Resists brown patch and crown rust.

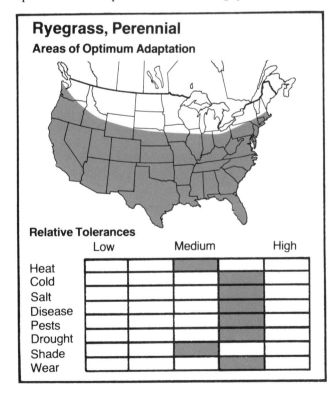

Ryegrass, Perennial
Areas of Optimum Adaptation

Relative Tolerances

	Low	Medium	High
Heat		■	
Cold			■
Salt			■
Disease			■
Pests			■
Drought			■
Shade		■	
Wear			■

'Derby' perennial ryegrass

'Bitter Blue' St. Augustinegrass

St. Augustinegrass

St. Augustinegrass
Stenotaphrum secundatum

To Plant: Frequently started with plugs planted on 12- to 18-inch centers. Widely available as sod.
Water: Large amount.
Fertilizer: Use 4 to 5 pounds actual nitrogen per 1,000 square feet per year. Use a complete fertilizer. May require minor elements if soil is depleted.
Mowing: Mow 1-1/2 to 2 inches high. Use a reel mower if possible. A rotary mower allows thatch to develop.

St. Augustine is an aggressive grass, crowding out most weeds. Particularly well adapted to soils of the Florida Everglades. Pests include brown patch, gray leafspot, chinch bugs and St. Augustine Decline (SAD) virus. The best defense against pests is to plant resistant varieties.

VARIETIES

'Bitter Blue'—Blue-green, medium density. Frost tolerant. Does not wear well.
'Floratam'—Dark green, good density. Resists SAD virus and chinch bugs. Poor tolerance to cold.
'Floratine'—Dense, horizontal growth habit. Accepts low mowing—to 1/2 inch. Overall cold hardiness is fair. Low-temperature color retention is good.
'Seville'—Dark green, dense, more tolerant of shade and cold than other St. Augustines. Resists SAD virus and gray leafspot disease. Susceptible to chinch bugs.

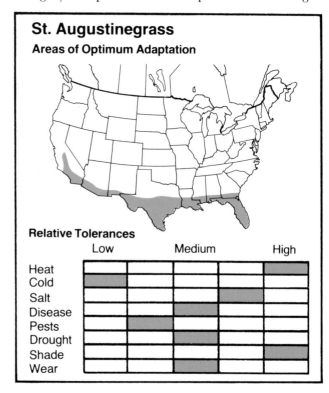

St. Augustinegrass
Areas of Optimum Adaptation

Relative Tolerances

	Low		Medium		High
Heat					■
Cold	■				
Salt				■	
Disease			■		
Pests		■			
Drought			■		
Shade				■	
Wear		■			

Zoysiagrass

Zoysia species

To Plant: Use sprigs, plugs or sod. Five cubic feet of sprigs will cover 1,000 square feet. Space 3-inch-diameter plugs on 12-inch centers.

Water: Little, once established.

Fertilizer: Apply 4 pounds actual nitrogen per 1,000 square feet per year.

Mowing: Mow 1-1/2 to 2 inches high with a reel or rotary mower.

Zoysiagrass is highly tolerant of drought and pests. Two disadvantages prevent it from being the most popular southern lawn grass: Winter dormant period is long and overseeding is difficult due to the turf density. Also, the rate of establishment is slow, sometimes requiring two full growing seasons.

VARIETIES

'Emerald'—Dark green, medium texture. Dense and slow growing. As attractive as hybrid bermudagrass. Developed in Georgia and introduced in 1955.

'Jade'—Dark green, medium texture. Dense and slow growing. Developed in southern California and introduced in 1980. Establishes in one season from sprigs. Retains winter color in warmest areas of Southwest.

'Meyer' or **'Z-52'**—Dark green, relatively coarse texture. Poor winter color, but greater cold hardiness than 'Emerald' or 'Jade.' Introduced in 1951.

'Emerald' zoysiagrass

Zoysiagrass
Areas of Optimum Adaptation

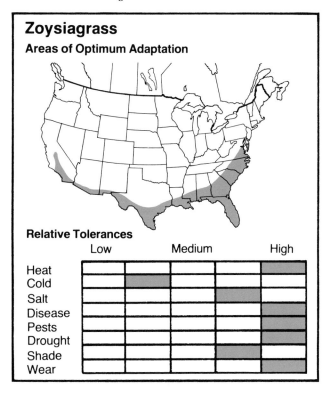

Relative Tolerances

	Low	Medium	High
Heat			■
Cold	■		
Salt		■	
Disease			■
Pests			■
Drought			■
Shade		■	
Wear			■

'Jade' zoysiagrass

Specialty Grasses

Blue Grama
Bouteoua gracilis

This native of the North American Great Plains is adapted to typical, arid-alkaline conditions found in these regions. It is also highly tolerant of heat and drought. Blue grama is a gray-green, low-growing bunching grass with a medium to fine texture. It is basically a warm-season grass but is hardy to −40F (−40C). It is somewhat resistant to wear.

Blue grama is easy to start from seed. Sow 1 to 2 pounds of seed per 1,000 square feet. Use a thick, 1/2 to 1 inch deep mulch and then roll until seedbed is firm. Plant in fall or early spring and water deeply if rainfall is light. Germinates in about 30 days. Mow occasionally at about 2 to 3 inches high. Fertilizer is not absolutely necessary. Applying 1/2 to 1 pound actual nitrogen per 1,000 square feet per year helps maintain good health and growth.

Buffalograss
Buchloe dactyloides

This is one of the dominant grasses of western, short-grass prairies. It is particularly suited to the heavy soils of western Louisiana, north-central Texas, eastern Colorado, western Kansas and Nebraska and Oklahoma. It is very tolerant of heat and is cold hardy to −20F (−29C). Texture is relatively fine and color is gray-green. Spreads with above- and below-ground runners.

Buffalograss starts easily from seed that is *treated* to aid germination. Treatment involves soaking in a mild acid solution. Untreated seed germinate irregularly. Sow about 2 pounds per 1,000 square feet in the fall or early spring. Plant seed no deeper than 1 inch. Germinates within 7 days. Water deeply if rainfall is light. After it is established, buffalograss requires as little as 12 inches of rain or irrigation a year. Mowing is optional. Mow 1 inch high with a rotary mower, or allow it to reach natural height of 3 to 4 inches.

Several varieties of buffalograss are available. 'Treated Sharp's Improved' is recommended for a home lawn.

Carpetgrass
Axonopus affinis

Carpetgrass is a warm-season, tropical grass. It is adapted to the wet soils of the southern Coastal Plain from southern Virginia to Mexico, north as far as central Mississippi and Alabama. It is occasionally grown in Florida. Color is light green, texture is coarse and growth is very dense. It spreads with creeping, somewhat flattened stolons. It has poor tolerance to shade and wear.

Start carpetgrass lawn from seed, sowing about 6 pounds per 1,000 square feet. Grass develops numerous seedheads throughout the summer, requiring weekly mowing with a rotary mower. Mowing height is 1-1/2 to 2-1/2 inches. Little fertilizer is required. Between 1 and 2 pounds of actual nitrogen per 1,000 square feet per year is adequate.

Fairway Crested Wheatgrass
Agropyron cristatum

Fairway crested wheatgrass is an excellent, cold-resistant, cool-season, bunching grass for the high plains of Canada, the Northern Arid Plains of the United States and the low-rainfall areas of the northern Intermountain regions of the United States and Canada. Color is light bluish green with medium texture. It is tolerant of extended drought and accepts heavy use. Most growth is in spring and fall. Dormant during summer.

Establish wheatgrass lawn from seed. Sow 2 pounds per 1,000 square feet in very early fall. Cover with inch of soil or mulch. Germination is slightly irregular, but most seedlings will be up within 30 days. If soil is dry, water deeply before seeding and continue to water as necessary. Mow to about 2 inches high. Fertilizer is not necessary, but appearance of lawn will be improved by applying 1 to 3 pounds of actual nitrogen per 1,000 square feet per year.

Dichondra
Dichondra micrantha

Dichondra is a low, creeping ground cover. It is a popular lawn substitute in southern California and other mild-winter regions. Small, round leaves make a soft, dark green carpet. Fertilizer and water requirement is higher than with many lawns—about the same as Kentucky bluegrass. Dichondra is tolerant of heat but is hardy to only 25F (−4C). Plants spread by seed and by underground roots.

Dichondra lawns are established by seed, plugs or sod. In late spring, sow 2 to 4 pounds of seed per 1,000 square feet in well-prepared soil. Set plugs about 12 inches on centers for a solid cover in one season. Roots are not very strong and are usually shallow, so lawns need frequent watering. Fertilizer requirement is high—3/4 pound actual nitrogen per 1,000 square feet *per month*. Chinch bugs, cutworms, flea beetles, snails and slugs are common pests.

Healthiest, best-looking dichondra lawns are mowed fairly low—to about 3/4 inch—with reel mowers. Many dichondra lawns are cut to 1-1/2 inches with a rotary mower. Some gardeners do not mow at all. Unmowed height is 4 to 6 inches, but individual leaves are larger and weeds invade more easily. Be careful to avoid *scalping* the lawn—removing most of the leaves. Lawn will recover but exposed stems will sunburn and brown. Reduce height of tall dichondra lawn very gradually.

Kikuyugrass
Pennisetum clandestinum

Kikuyugrass is a vigorous, spreading grass common to coastal regions of California from San Francisco to Mexico. It is native to eastern Africa and was introduced to California in the 1920s for erosion control.

Leaves are yellowish green with a coarse texture. They may grow several inches long, terminating in a sharp point. Perhaps the most characteristic feature of kikuyugrass is its white, pencil-thick stolons. They enable the grass to spread rapidly. It is common to see kikuyugrass growing 1 or 2 feet up shrubs, tree trunks, telephone poles and fences.

Because of its color, texture, feel and invasiveness, kikuyugrass is generally considered the worst kind of weed. Where well adapted, even bermudagrass gives way to it. The advantages of kikuyugrass are year-round green color and low maintenance. In fact, most maintenance practices are oriented toward restraining rather than encouraging it. Mow at 1/2 or 3/4 inch with a sharp reel mower. Water and fertilize sparingly.

Paspalum 'Sweet Adalayd'
Paspalum vaginatum

This is an attractive, low-maintenance bermudagrass substitute for southern California. An Australian native, it spreads like bermudagrass, by both above- and below-ground runners. Leaves are medium to dark green with a fine texture. Green color holds through mild winters. Otherwise, dormancy is about the same or slightly longer than 'Santa Ana' bermudagrass. Average fertilizer requirement is 4 to 6 pounds actual nitrogen per 1,000 square feet per year. Grass is heat and drought tolerant. Salt tolerance is very high. Thatch is not usually a problem.

Establish *Paspalum* lawns by spreading 3 bushels of stolons over 1,000 square feet. Best time to plant is late spring or summer. Allow 2 to 3 months for a complete cover. Mowing height can vary between 1/4 and 1-1/2 inches.

Roughstalk Bluegrass
Poa trivialis

This Kentucky bluegrass relative is noted for high tolerance of moist soils and shade. Color is glossy, yellow-green. Grass is soft, has a fine texture and is very cold hardy. It has minimal tolerance of heat and drought. Spreads by above-ground runners. An excellent component in a grass seed mix to cover difficult areas such as heavy shade or wet soils. It is invasive in good soil with full sun.

An improved variety of roughstalk bluegrass, 'Sabre,' is an excellent choice for moist, shady sites. It is included in seed mixes intended for such locations.

Carpetgrass

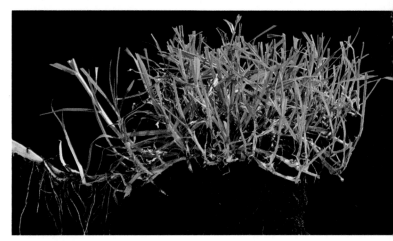

Fairway crested wheatgrass

Kikuyugrass

Paspalum 'Sweet Adalayd'

Planting a Lawn

The following pages detail the fundamentals of planting a lawn with seed, sod, stolons and sprigs. The method you choose and the sequence of operations you follow will vary with site, grass type and your own judgment. But the basics are the same.

Should you plant seed, sod, stolons or sprigs? Seed is least expensive, and more kinds of grasses, custom blends and mixes are available. If you choose to start your lawn with seed, use the highest-quality seed available. The label should show that it contains "0" crop and "0" weed seed. Buying bargain-basement seed saves a few dollars initially, but promises a future of weed pulling and eventual renovation.

The exact mix of seed you plant may be designed for beauty, or practical quality such as tolerance of shade, drought or wear. Seed mixes also vary by climate region. But rather than attempt a technical analysis that accounts for all these factors, the best advice is to rely on a reputable, high-quality seed company.

Sod produces a finished lawn as soon as it is installed. But surprising to some, a sod lawn requires the same degree of soil preparation and frequent watering as a seed lawn the first few months. Quality of sod, sprigs and plugs is equally important. However, the lawns from which these come are usually grown locally under controlled conditions. Quality is normally very high.

Many southern grasses—notably hybrid bermudas, centipede and zoysia—are planted by *sprigs*, individual stems or pieces of stems.

Keep in mind that sod, sprigs and plugs are living plants and plant parts. Plant as soon as they are delivered and keep them watered after they are planted—just as with a new seed lawn.

Use the preceding chapter on Lawns to help determine the best grass for you. Plant at the most favorable time of year. Early fall is best for cool-season lawns from seed and bentgrass sprigs. Late spring is the best time to plant seed, sod and plugs of warm-season grasses.

Rich, loose, weed-free soil can make the difference between a beautiful, easy-care lawn and a mediocre, troublesome one. But given an ideal soil, lawns are more robust, more vigorous, less demanding and easier to maintain.

If the planting area is prepared beforehand, sod lawns are easy to install. Pallets of sod were delivered to this site about one hour ago and the job will be complete, including cleanup, in another hour.

Prepare Soil

The appearance of your lawn and how you care for it largely depends on soil quality. Lawns will grow only as well as the roots grow. For this reason, well-prepared soil is an important key to a healthy, attractive lawn. You can follow many different procedures in preparing the soil for a lawn planting. Here are the essentials.

TEST SOIL

Fertilizers, lime, sulfur and gypsum frequently are recommended additions to new lawns. But they are not always necessary. If added incorrectly without directives provided by a soil test, they might be wasted or cause harm. The only sure way to know if nutrients and soil pH are correct is by a *soil test*.

With the exceptions of California and Illinois, your nearest county extension office or state university will provide soil sample containers, information and soil analysis. In California and Illinois, look in the Yellow Pages for "Soil Testing Laboratories."

When you collect soil for a test, gather it from various parts of the area to be planted. The laboratory test will then represent the general soil condition of the site. Collect soil by taking small cores of soil from five locations for each sampling area.

Each area of a home lot should be sampled separately. For example, the front lawn area will be one sample, the back lawn area another, and so on. Areas in shade should be sampled separately from sunny areas. Slopes should be sampled separately from low spots.

A soil coring tube is the easiest way to collect samples. When pushed into damp soil, this tube pulls a 3/4-inch-wide and 12-inch-long plug of soil. Place the middle 2 or 3 inches of soil plug in a bucket. You can also take a sample with a trowel or shovel as long as soil is collected from a depth of 4 to 6 inches. Be sure the trowel or shovel is clean and does not have any chemicals or other residues that might affect the sample.

Mix the soil samples from the five locations in a bucket. Place 1 or 2 cups of this mixed soil in the container provided by the laboratory.

CLEAN AND GRADE SOIL

Remove all debris, including large stones, roots, stumps and construction materials. Do not bury debris under the future lawn.

Eliminate any perennial weedy grasses such as quackgrass, bermudagrass and creeping bentgrass. Spray with glyphosate herbicide when weeds are actively growing. Water weeds before spraying. Wait 7 to 10 days before removing weeds to be sure they are completely dead. For more on weed killers, see page 57.

If extensive grading is necessary, scrape away and retain topsoil. Eliminate low areas that may become basins for standing water. Contour soil surface so water will run off. A slight, 1 percent grade sloping away from buildings is recommended. Steeper grades make lawn establishment and maintenance more difficult. Contours can be used to add interest and blend with natural or created landscape features.

Redistribute topsoil after rough grade is established. Allow soil to settle before planting. Uneven settling around buildings and over water and sewer trenches is common. Several deep waterings will aid settling.

AMEND SOIL

Poor soil is a major cause of lawn problems. The only time soil can be significantly improved is before planting. Improving soil under an existing lawn is possible but it is a gradual and difficult process.

If the composition of your soil is largely clay or sand, mix organic material—composted sawdust, fir or redwood bark or peat moss—into the top 4 to 6 inches. Water a day or two before finishing the soil preparation. This will help eliminate large, hard clods.

Fertilizer—Phosphorus and potassium applications should be based on soil test information. As a rule, do not apply more than 2 pounds of actual nitrogen per 1,000 square feet before seeding or sodding. If a soil test is not possible, the general recommendation calls for 15 to 20 pounds of 10-10-10 fertilizer per 1,000 square feet. Thoroughly mix the fertilizer into the soil.

Lime—Use lime only if the soil test indicates the pH is below 6.0. Excessive lime causes problems, especially in sandy soil. Thoroughly incorporate ground limestone into the top 4 to 6 inches of soil during one of the initial cultivations.

Sulfur—If soil pH is above 7.5, lower it by applying elemental sulfur. See the chart on page 35 for a guide to sulfur and lime application amounts.

Gypsum—This amendment is often recommended to improve clay soils. But gypsum definitely does not loosen heavy clay soils unless sodium content is excessive. Benefits are neglible unless addition is specifically recommended by a soil test laboratory. Use gypsum if soil is high in "exchangable sodium percentage," which means it is high in sodium salt. Gypsum is also recommended if pH is acceptable and either calcium or sulfate is low.

PREPARE SEEDBED AND ELIMINATE WEEDS

Level, roll and rake the weed-free seedbed before planting. Use a roller half-filled with water to firm

Adjusting pH

To raise pH to 6.5, apply ground limestone

	Pounds to apply per 1,000 square feet	
if pH is	Sandy Soil	Clay Soil
5.5-5.9	25-50	50-100
5.0-5.5	50-100	75-150
4.5-5.0	75-150	100-200

To lower pH to 6.5, apply elemental sulfur

	Pounds to apply per 1,000 square feet	
if pH is	Sandy Soil	Clay Soil
7.5	10-25	20-25
8.0	25-35	35-50
8.5	35-50	40-50

Adding Soil Amendment

Cubic yards of material to apply

Square feet of area	Amendment thickness over area		
	2 inches	3 inches	4 inches
	*1/4 by volume	1/3 by volume	1/2 by volume
250	1.56	2.34	3.12
500	3.12	4.68	6.24
1,000	6.24	9.36	12.48
1,500	9.36	14.04	18.72

*Assuming the amendment is tilled into soil to 8-inch depth.

seedbed. Rollers are available from nurseries and rental yards. Your footsteps will indicate the proper firmness. If steps leave an impression more than 1/2 inch deep, roll again. Rolling will also reveal those slightly high or low areas that need further leveling.

If you plan to install an underground sprinkler system, do so at this stage. See pages 37 to 43.

If sod is your choice, planting can follow immediately after final preparation of soil. Be sure that all perennial weeds are controlled. Soil level should be 1/2 to 1 inch below final grade, to accommodate sod thickness. Turn to page 45 for step-by-step details.

If weeds are present and you plan to sow seed or plant sprigs, stolons or plugs, make another effort to control weeds now. You have already cleared the lawn area of existing perennial weeds and grasses. Now you must reduce the number of weed seeds waiting on the soil surface. Once you plant and begin watering, the weeds will germinate and compete with your lawn grass. Sod covers these weed seeds and prevents their growth.

There are three ways to reduce the number of weeds at this time: *fumigation, pre-emergent herbicides* and *fallowing*. Fumigation is an involved process using potent chemicals, and is best performed by landscape maintenance professionals. Consider it if you anticipate a particularly severe weed problem. Soil fumigants useful to home gardeners are listed on page 57.

An alternative is to use a pre-emergent herbicide. Many kinds are compatible with newly planted plugs. A few might be used with newly planted stolons and sprigs—check labels, cooperative extension agents and manufacturers. Siduron, which is sold under the trade name Tupersan, prevents the growth of many weeds such as crabgrass and bermudagrass without affecting the grass seed that you sow. Do not use it on newly seeded bermudagrass or bentgrass lawns. Siduron is also recommended when reseeding renovated lawns.

Fallowing is the third alternative. Basically, this means to wait out the weeds. This will take 6 weeks at least, sometimes longer. Water the prepared seedbed just as if seed is sown. In a few days, weed growth appears. Eliminate them with a spray of cacodylic acid herbicide. Repeat this cycle until no new weed growth appears after you water. Rather than using herbicide, you can lightly cultivate to eliminate weeds. However, each time soil surface is disturbed, previously buried weed seed are brought to the surface. More time is then required to make the bed relatively weed-free.

SOWING SEED

Early fall is the best time to establish a cool-season lawn from seed. Early spring is an acceptable alternative, but cool, often excessively wet soil and severe competition from annual weeds are significant problems. Late spring is the best time to establish a warm-season lawn from seed. Midsummer plantings are more difficult with either type because of high temperatures, lack of rainfall and weed competition.

Sow seed at the recommended rate. Evenly sow one half of the total amount in one direction and the remaining half in the crisscross direction. Use a spinning, *centrifugal* spreader for large areas, or the more common and more controllable *drop* spreader for moderate-size lawns. After seeding, rake very lightly with a stiff, narrow-pronged rake. You do not want to move seed, just cover it slightly. An alternative to raking soil over seed is to cover the seedbed with a mulch of peat moss, composted fir bark or similar light organic material. Mulch should not be more than 1/4 inch thick. Finally, lightly roll mulch and seed with a roller *half-filled* with water to ensure good contact between seed and soil.

Watering—Perhaps the most important step to a new lawn from seed is regular watering. If soil is very dry, water deeply before planting. The soil surface must be kept moist at all times after planting. Young seedlings

Soil Preparation

1. Distribute amendment evenly over entire area intended for lawn. Also spread half the recommended amount of starter fertilizer and lime or sulfur as recommended by a soil test report.

2. Approximately 6 cubic yards of organic amendment spread over this area will make a layer about 2 inches thick.

3. Incorporate amendments 6 to 8 inches deep by tilling. Tillers of different sizes and types are available through local rental agencies.

4. Soil is light and fluffy after tilling. Level with rake.

5. Water to help settle and firm soil. Install underground irrigation system at this point.

6. Level and roll seedbed until firm. A gauge of proper firmness is depth of footprint—if more than 1/2 inch, continue rolling. Soil is now ready to accept seed, sod, sprigs, stolons or plugs.

die within hours if deprived of moisture. Light sprinklings every morning, noon and evening are recommended. Greater frequency is necessary if weather is particularly hot, dry and windy. Avoid puddles and washing of soil. Use a sprinkler that applies water as slowly and gently as possible. Run sprinkler until puddles begin to form. Shut off sprinkler until the puddles soak in, then run sprinkler again until watering is complete. Follow these watering procedures for about 3 to 6 weeks—until root system is established.

INSTALLING SOD

Sod of cool- or warm-season grasses can be installed any time during the growing season. The area to be planted is prepared the same as for seed, but is graded 1/2 to 1 inch lower to allow for the sod thickness. Soil must be moist at time of planting to allow rapid rooting.

Prepare planting bed for sod *before* the sod is delivered or before you bring it home. After the sod arrives, cover with moist burlap sacks, and keep it moist until installation time.

Lay sod in a bricklike pattern, staggering ends of sod pieces. Avoid stretching or overlapping. Stretched sod shrinks as it dries and develops cracks. Once in place, roll with roller half-filled with water to ensure soil and root contact. Roots will dry out fast if suspended over an air pocket. Water to a depth of at least 6 inches as soon as possible after installation. Daily irrigation is required during the next 2 to 3 weeks or until the sod roots.

PLANTING SPRIGS, STOLONS AND PLUGS

Sprigs—These are individual sections of stems, runners and roots. They are spread over the soil like seed and kept moist until they develop roots. Space sprigs according to the rate of growth of the grass. Bermudagrass, St. Augustinegrass and centipedegrass sprigs are normally spaced on 12-inch centers. Zoysiagrass is much slower growing and is spaced on 6-inch centers.

Sprigs are planted many ways. For large areas, scatter and cultivate into the soil, then cover with a thin layer of mulch. If the area is small, plant sprigs in shallow furrows, cover with soil and firm into place.

Stolons—Stolons are like sprigs and handled similarly. They are shredded fragments of *grass stolons*—aboveground runners. Bermudagrass and some bentgrasses are typically stolonized.

Plugs—Plugging and strip sodding are similar. They are ways to make a given amount of sod spread over a larger area. Plugging is often used to patch poor areas of a lawn, or to introduce other more dominant grasses into an established lawn. Plugging is also used to establish some kinds of zoysiagrass.

Plugs of most grasses are normally spaced on 12-inch centers. Zoysiagrass is spaced on 6-inch centers if the ground is bare, more widely if plugging into an existing lawn. Plant plugs with a trowel, small shovel or special tool designed specifically for plugging. Firmly press plugs into soil to ensure good contact. Keep plugs moist for the next 2 to 3 weeks.

As with sod, keep sprigs, stolons and plugs moist and in a shaded location until planting time. Never allow these living plants to dry.

Underground Sprinkler Systems

The best time to install an underground sprinkler system is after the soil is prepared and before planting. A properly designed system is a good investment and increases property value. It makes growing a lawn or ground cover much easier and saves both time and water.

MAKING A PLAN

Before you do the installation, you need a plan. Draw a plot plan of your property on a sheet of graph paper. Indicate lawn area, ground cover area, existing trees and shrubs, structures, prevailing winds and any other influencing factors. Never use the same sprinkler circuit to water different kinds of plants, lawn and ground cover. Likewise, consider the differences of lawn on a slope and lawn in shade. You also have to know water sources for convenient hookup, available pressure and flow rate in *gallons per minute* (GPM).

Designing an involved sprinkler system requires knowledge of latest products, use of charts and graphs and some calculations. If you don't think you are up to the task, hire a professional irrigation systems designer. Many are listed in the Yellow Pages under "Irrigation Consultants" or "Sprinklers—Garden and Lawn." A professional is best prepared to tailor an efficient, accurate system to your property. A good irrigation plan is essential and cost is relatively low—about 10 percent of a contractor's installation fee.

On the other hand, many do-it-yourselfers have succeeded at design and installation of an underground sprinkler system. If you design your own system, use manufacturers' catalogs or a reference book such as *Turf Irrigation Manual* by James A. Watkins. Also consult equipment manufacturers and their representatives.

It is important that high-quality design standards be met. A poorly designed system, no matter how well it is installed, is difficult and expensive to work with or correct.

SPRINKLER SYSTEM COMPONENTS

Circuits—Sprinkler systems are a combination of heads, pipes and valves arranged in circuits. One circuit includes as many heads as water flow will allow, or are necessary. Each circuit is operated by one valve. An average system contains several circuits, each one operated individually, according to available water flow in GPM.

Heads—The best sprinkler heads for lawns remain at soil level below mower height when not in use. They pop up when in operation. A pop-up height of 2 inches is minimum for high-cut, cool-season grass lawns. Note illustration below.

Heads normally cover full-, half- or quarter-circle areas. Some kinds adjust to a wide variety of shapes and portions of circles. Plastic heads are generally better than metal because they do not corrode.

A new type of sprinkler head intended specifically for medium- to large-size residential lawns is the *impact rotor pop-up*. It covers a wide area, reducing the number of heads and piping necessary. It operates with low pressure and provides a slow application of water, which reduces runoff.

Valves—Different valves perform different jobs in an irrigation system. A group of valves located together is the *manifold*. There are four different kinds of valves:

Antisiphon device, which breaks vacuums or prevents backflow, is essential to keeping system water from being drawn back into the main line. Water drawn from the lawn system into main system could contaminate the water supply. Install antisiphon devices 8 inches apart, above ground. Many city building codes require them. The antisiphon device, also known as *atmospheric vacuum breaker,* is always on the discharge or low-pressure side of the system. A *pressure vacuum breaker* is always on the pressure or input of the system. Use one pressure vacuum breaker to serve in place of several atmospheric vacuum breakers.

A shutoff gate valve is installed between the antisiphon device and the water supply connection. This valve will turn off the complete system without losing water supply to house.

Circuit valves are the basic control valves for each circuit. They are operated manually, electrically or hydraulically. They are usually located in a convenient place or hidden beyond the sprinkler spray area, and are combined with the antisiphon valve.

Drain valves are essential wherever the ground freezes to the depth of the pipes. Installed underground at a low point, they automatically drain water from the circuit, preventing damage to the pipes from freezing water.

Pipe—The best pipe for sprinkler systems is PVC, *polyvinyl chloride.* It lasts longer than galvanized, brass or copper pipe, is less expensive and is much easier to work with. PVC pipe and fittings are bonded together by a solvent that causes the two pieces to melt into one strong pipe.

There are many grades, classes and strength designations of PVC pipe. Use strong pipe—*schedule 40* or perhaps *class 315*—for system lines that will hold pressure. Use thinner, less expensive pipe—*class 200* or

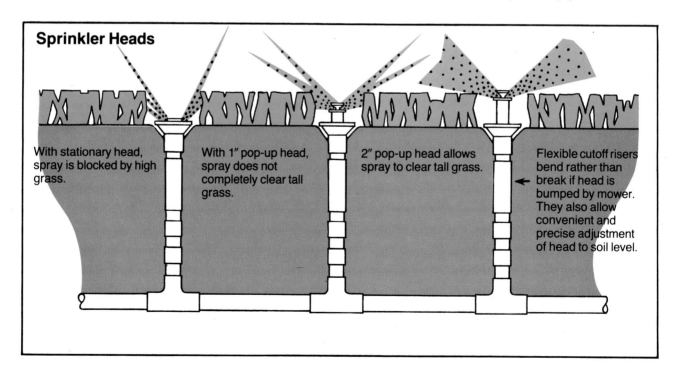

Sprinkler Heads

With stationary head, spray is blocked by high grass.

With 1" pop-up head, spray does not completely clear tall grass.

2" pop-up head allows spray to clear tall grass.

Flexible cutoff risers bend rather than break if head is bumped by mower. They also allow convenient and precise adjustment of head to soil level.

160—for lines that will hold no pressure. Size and strength of pipe must match the system's requirements.

AUTOMATIC SPRINKLER SYSTEMS

Automating your sprinkler system adds expense but saves water and time. The essential component is an electric or hydraulic valve that turns the sprinklers on and off. Each circuit's automatic valve is managed by the *controller*, a specialized kind of clock. Elaborate, automatic systems include *moisture-sensing* devices that can override the controller during periods of rain or unseasonably cool weather.

Controller—This is the brain of an automatic system. Those designed specifically for home sprinkler systems operate on low voltage, supplied by a transformer connected to a typical 110-120-volt outlet. Battery-operated kinds are available. They generally are less expensive and easier to install, but will not work when batteries fail. You program the controllers to signal the valves when to begin and end watering.

Moisture sensors—There are two basic kinds—*mechanical* and *electrical*. Mechanical sensors are called *tensiometers* because they respond to moisture tension in the soil. They have a porous ceramic tip and a water-filled tube. Water in the tube is pulled out through the porous tip into dry soil, creating suction measured on a gauge. A switch on the gauge provides the electrical connection, allowing the controller to open valves.

The electrical type operates on the principle that wet soil conducts electricity better than dry soil. Electrical units are less expensive but somewhat less exact in their measurements.

INSTALLATION NOTES

The following two pages detail the installation process. Charts and diagrams will help you interpret your plan. Make a list of all the components and quantities of each you will need to buy. It is handy to have the plan with you at the time of purchase for reference. Buy the exact brands and models specified on the plan.

Pipes and fittings should be buried deep enough to prevent damage from heavy equipment rolling over the soil. Pipe under areas to be paved should be sleeved in metal pipe before concrete is poured. Dig under or drill through existing paving. Work with short, add-on pipe sections. If you have the option, lay pipe under bricks or pavers laid on sand. They are easy to lift and the pipe can be replaced if the need should arise.

Cut into the supply line after the main water supply is shut off. The illustrations on page 41 show typical connections. Hose bib connections are usually easiest for manually operated valves.

Ask your supplier about filters if you live in a "dirty water" area. Consult your water company about this. A filter will prevent troublesome clogging. If your water comes from a private well, consult an irrigation specialist.

Use separate circuits for every area that might require different amounts of water. Examples are front and back yards, lawn and ground cover areas, sunny and shaded areas, sloping and flat areas.

Install pop-up heads and valve boxes flush with finished soil level.

Controller wire connections must be water-proofed and cleanly spliced.

EXISTING LAWN INSTALLATION

The process for installing a system in an existing lawn is the same as the one illustrated on pages 42 and 43. Care should be taken to damage the lawn as little as possible. Remove strips of sod where pipe is to be installed and store in a shady location. Water these sod strips daily. Pile dirt dug from trenches on tarps or plastic sheets. When the job is completed, return soil to the trenches and replace sod. Use a roller to press sod back into place if it is higher than the original turf level.

TROUBLESHOOTING AN EXISTING SYSTEM

If you are having trouble with your existing system, visualize where the problem might be: in the sprinkler heads, pipes, valves or controller. A common problem is sprinkler head clogging caused by dirty water or mineral deposits. Electrical problems are common to automatic systems. Check batteries of battery-powered controllers first.

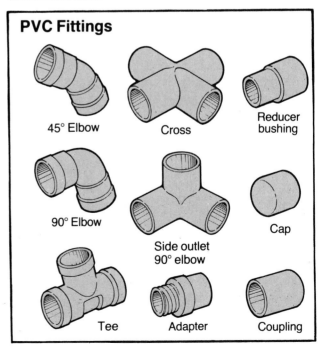

PVC Fittings

45° Elbow   Cross   Reducer bushing

90° Elbow   Side outlet 90° elbow   Cap

Tee   Adapter   Coupling

Interpreting an Irrigation Plan

An irrigation designer begins with a conceptual plan. This sketch illustrates circular spray patterns for a small front yard and a parking strip. Fully adjustable heads allow complete control and no misplaced spray. In this sample plan, three types of heads have been used.

Note equilateral triangular spacing and spray overlap. Overlap may be greater than indicated here but should not be less than 60 percent.

Half-circle heads along edges. ➤

Full-circle heads for large areas. ➤

Quarter-circle heads at corners. ➤

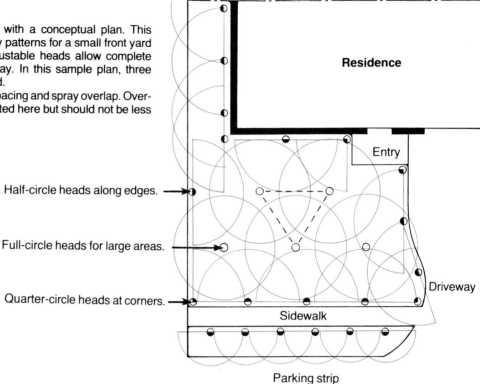

This sample system is manually operated. Automatic systems often have simpler layouts. The side yard and back yard (not shown) operate off the back-yard circuit. Water supply hook-up is at a hose bib. Pipe size—1/2″, 3/4″, 1″—indicates the diameter of each section of pipe in each circuit. Note how the pipes connect to the heads in the actual plan.

Solid circles represent circuit valves. Here valve size is indicated as 1″ to match 1″ pipe circuits. Half-circles (‿) indicate that pipes cross but do not join. Lay these pipes in the same trench.

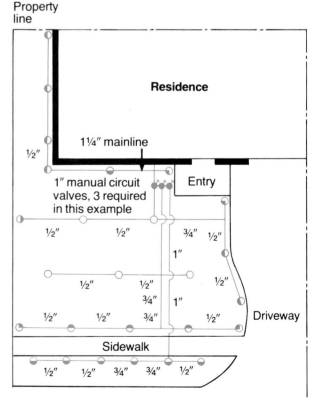

Cutting into Water Supply

Turn off water supply before you begin. Study the hookup diagrams. Choose the method that is best for your situation. If you have a well, consult an irrigation specialist.

Make the connection ahead of any pressure regulators. Remove a small pipe section, about 1-1/2 inches in length, and insert a slip-type compression tee. Install a shutoff gate valve and PVC pipe to antisiphon control valves or to electric valves and vacuum breaker. Space valves 8 inches apart. Flush antisiphon valves one by one when glue has set. Repair any leaks before connecting the rest of the system.

Meter Hookup

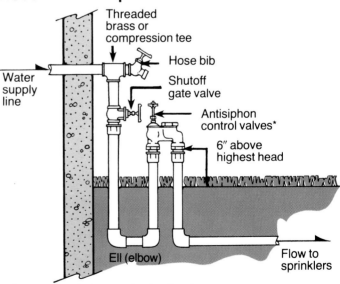

Compression tee
Shutoff ball check valve
Valve box
Water meter
Service line from meter
Shutoff gate valve
To antisiphon control valves
Pea gravel
Shutoff valve

Basement Hookup

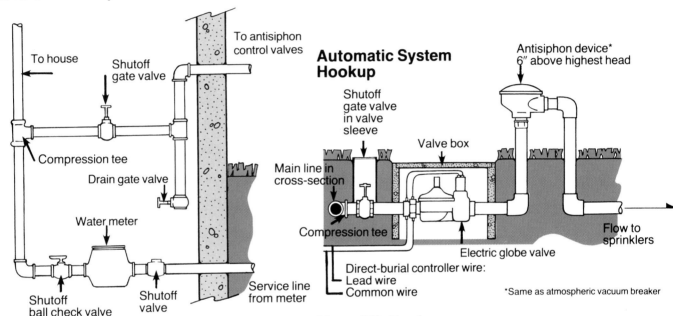

To house
Shutoff gate valve
To antisiphon control valves
Compression tee
Drain gate valve
Water meter
Shutoff ball check valve
Shutoff valve
Service line from meter

Automatic System Hookup

Shutoff gate valve in valve sleeve
Valve box
Antisiphon device* 6″ above highest head
Main line in cross-section
Compression tee
Electric globe valve
Flow to sprinklers
Direct-burial controller wire:
Lead wire
Common wire
*Same as atmospheric vacuum breaker

Main Line Compression Tee Hookup

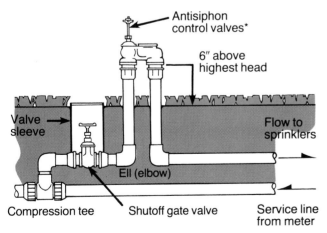

Antisiphon control valves*
6″ above highest head
Valve sleeve
Flow to sprinklers
Compression tee
Shutoff gate valve
Ell (elbow)
Service line from meter

*Same as atmospheric vacuum breaker plus valve

Hose Bib Hookup

Threaded brass or compression tee
Hose bib
Water supply line
Shutoff gate valve
Antisiphon control valves*
6″ above highest head
Ell (elbow)
Flow to sprinklers

*Same as atmospheric vacuum breaker plus valve

Installing an Underground Irrigation System

1. Study the plan. Buy pipe, fittings, valves, heads, glue and tools you will need. Borrow or rent specialized tools. You might need risers, a controller and wire for an automatic system.

2. Turn off water supply. Cut into supply where convenient to suit plan. Here, connection is made at a hose bib. See page 41. Note antisiphon valves—they prevent sprinkler backflow from contaminating main water supply. Place them 6 inches above the highest head in circuit. After valve hookup, remove heads, flush valves of dirt and check for leaks.

3. If your system is automatic, install the controlling time clock at this step. This is one type.

7. Lay pipe 2 or 3 inches from paved edges to prevent damage of heads by lawn edger.

8. Install risers if required. After joints have set, flush dirt from pipes. Open or remove riserless heads. Check for leaks. Hook up controller wires before flushing. Heads shown are screw-in type.

9. Check coverage and adjust spray patterns. Add heads as necessary to ensure complete coverage of area.

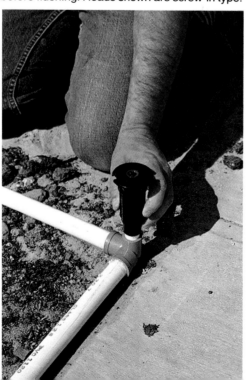

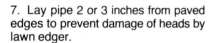

4. Lay out pipe. Make a pattern with stakes representing heads, and strings representing pipe.

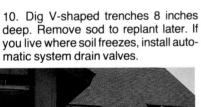

A

B

C

D

5. Glue PVC pipe with solvent.
A. Determine fitting and length of pipe.
B. Cut pipe squarely with a hacksaw. Clean cut edge with knife and cloth.
C. Put glue on inside of fitting and outside of pipe.
D. Insert pipe into fitting with a twisting motion to distribute glue. Align pipe and wipe away excess glue. *Hold* pipe until set.

6. Note the fittings that join pipe: elbows (ells) for corners, tees for straight sections, adapters for pipe size changes. Pipe under paving should be laid first.

10. Dig V-shaped trenches 8 inches deep. Remove sod to replant later. If you live where soil freezes, install automatic system drain valves.

11. Pop-up heads—when not in use—should be flush with finished *soil* level.

12. Backfill with soil. Note lines of two circuits crossing here. Water thoroughly to settle soil and fill low spots. Wet again. Clean up. Plant.

Sowing Seed

1. Hand-held broadcast spreaders are inexpensive, light-weight and easy to use. They hold about 3 pounds of seed or fertilizers, and cover a 6- to 10-foot swath with each pass.

2. How vigorously you turn the crank of broadcast spreader determines distance seed is spread, but walking rows 4 feet apart is about right. Spread half the seed walking one direction and half walking the crisscross direction. Apply starter fertilizer and siduron pre-emergent weed control now if necessary.

3. Rent peat moss spreader, also called squirrel cage, from a nursery or rental agency. Some spilling is inevitable. Fill away from new lawn rather than directly over seeded area.

4. Apply mulch layer about 1/4 inch thick. Larger seeds, such as rye and fescue grasses, can be covered deeper. Cover small seeds—bermuda, bent and bluegrasses—slightly less deeply.

5. Firmly press seed into soil with final rolling. Rolling often makes the difference between good and poor seed germination. If more than half-filled with water, the roller's weight makes handling difficult and soil is needlessly compacted.

6. Light watering until new lawn is established is crucial. Many organic topdressings, particularly peat moss, are difficult to wet thoroughly without use of a wetting agent. See page 49.

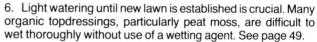

Installing Sod

1. Remove existing lawn with a *sod cutter,* available at rental agencies. Prepare soil according to steps 1-5 on page 36.

2. Level and firm soil with rake and roller half-filled with water. Finished grade should be 1/2 to 1 inch below walks, patios and driveway to accommodate sod thickness. Apply starter fertilizer now if necessary. Water thoroughly.

3. Start laying sod at longest straight boundary of area. If soil is soft or wet, work from a piece of plywood to distribute your weight. Tightly butt edges and ends together. Stagger strips as if laying a brick wall. Avoid overlapping edges.

4. Use a sharp knife to cut and fit sod around corners and irregular shapes. Work from bottom to top on steep slopes. Secure strips with wooden stakes if necessary.

5. If laying a large area, do not wait until installation is complete before watering. As soon as about 200 square feet are laid, sprinkle to prevent drying, especially during warm weather. Continue sprinkling until all sod is laid.

6. Roll with roller to ensure firm soil-to-root contact. Mound soil around exposed edges to prevent drying. Water until sod is spongy-wet to foot pressure. Soil should be moist to about 6 to 8 inches. Water frequently and heavily for 2 to 3 weeks until sod is firmly rooted.

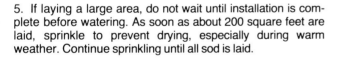

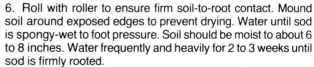

Caring for Your Lawn

To be successful at growing a healthy, attractive lawn, you should be aware of a few, practical "rules" of lawn care. Knowing the rules doesn't guarantee success, but following them simplifies the process of caring for your lawn—a complicated, mysterious procedure to many lawn growers.

The first rule of lawn care is to plant high-quality, weed-free seed or sod in deep, fertile, well-prepared, weed-free soil. This is probably the most important step you can take to ensure success. If you bypass this fundamental, attaining an attractive lawn will be difficult at best.

The second rule is to apply sufficient water to the lawn, but not too much. Overwatering encourages some diseases and is wasteful. Frequent, light watering promotes shallow roots that are quick to dry out when conditions become warm or windy. Water until the root zone—the top 4 to 8 inches of soil—is throughly moistened. Wait until the grass shows signs of needing water before watering again. Amounts and frequency are highly variable and depend on the grass, soil, climate and weather.

The third rule is to mow at the recommended height with a sharp mower. Cut the grass as frequently as possible, removing a small amount of the grass blade each time. Cool-season grasses grow fastest in spring and fall. Warm-season grasses grow fastest in midsummer.

The fourth rule is to apply recommended amounts of fertilizer at optimum times. Feed cool-season grasses throughout the year as necessary, but apply *three-fourths* of the total amount required in the *fall and winter* months. In fall, roots build energy reserves that last well into the next season. Feed warm-season grasses primarily in late spring and fall.

The fifth rule is to make positive identification of lawn pests and diseases, then closely follow the prescribed course of treatment. Pests and diseases are rarely serious concerns if you follow the first four rules, but problems sometime occur. Likewise, follow the same course with weeds and their control.

Mowing is commonly associated with lawn care. It is the garden ritual lawn owners of many continents share.

Water

Thorough and consistent watering is the single most important aspect of lawn care. The trick is to know both your lawn and watering system so water is supplied in correct amounts when needed.

Tailor your watering program to the particular requirements of your lawn. Every lawn is different. Each type of grass has its own water requirements. Soil may drain rapidly or slowly. Climates vary, depending on rainfall, sunlight and drying winds or humidity. Despite all of these variables, one guide is constant: *Wet the entire root zone with each watering.* Specifically, this means wetting the top 4 to 8 inches of soil. Apply the water at a rate the soil can absorb. You want the water to reach the roots instead of the street or gutter.

A rule of thumb is to apply 1 inch of water per week throughout the growing season. To find out how long it will take to apply this much water, place a rain gauge or container on the lawn and measure the water. Most sprinklers will apply 1 inch of water in 1 hour. If the water is applied to the point of runoff before applying 1 inch, simply turn sprinklers off, wait until water soaks in, then turn them on again. If soil is sandy and drains quickly, 1/2 inch of water may wet soil to the proper depth. In this case you will need to water more frequently.

Most soils can become compacted, which makes water penetration difficult. Often, patches of lawn seem to dry more quickly. *Thatch,* a strawlike layer of dead plant parts that accumulates at the soil level, makes it difficult for water to penetrate. A *wetting agent* can be useful. This is a chemical that helps water penetrate into thatch or compacted soil. Aeration and dethatching significantly improve water penetration. See Winter Overseeding and Renovation, page 66.

Test soil moisture—The amount of water a lawn needs is determined by the moisture in the soil. Supplying 1 inch of water a week by irrigation might be too much if available moisture in the soil is high. Water needs vary primarily with the season and weather, as well as soil type.

The easiest way to check soil moisture is also the most direct: Dig into the soil with a trowel and feel it. Tools are available that remove cores from the root zone. Or you can remove larger, replaceable plugs with a small shovel. Either way, check occasionally to see and feel if you are watering deeply enough.

Time of day to water—The best time to water is near dawn. Evaporation rates and wind are at lowest levels. Early in the morning water has a better opportunity to go where it is needed—into the soil. In addition, water pressure is highest during this period.

Know Sprinkler Habits

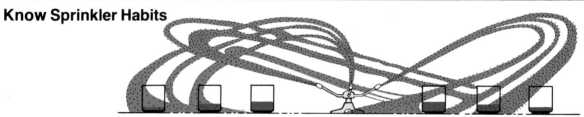

Observe pattern of sprinkler. Time how long it takes to apply 1 inch of sprinkled water in measuring cans. Sprinklers vary greatly by type and manufacturer. Generally, whirling types distribute more water close to the sprinkler head. Wave-arm types distribute more water at extreme ends of cycle. Impact heads are fairly uniform but apply water quickly. Coverage is influenced by wind. Stationary fan sprinklers distribute little water close to head.

How Much Water? How Long?

  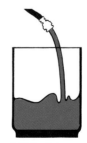

3/4-inch hose   5/8-inch hose   1/2-inch hose

Garden hoses deliver various amounts of water according to their diameter. At average water pressure in one hour, a 1/2-inch hose delivers 630 gallons, a 5/8-inch hose delivers 1,020 gallons and a 3/4-inch hose delivers 1,860 gallons. To apply 1 inch of water over 1,000 square feet requires 624 gallons.

Deep Watering Equals Deep Roots

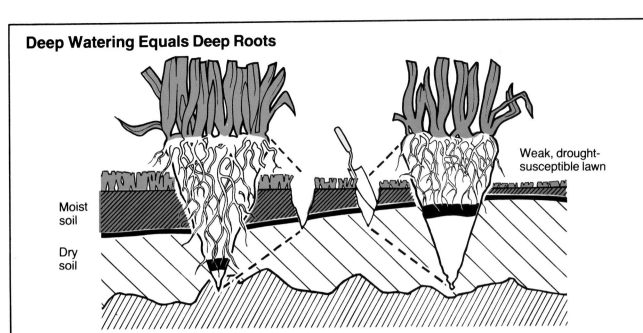

Weak, drought-susceptible lawn

Moist soil

Dry soil

Roots grow only where soil is moist. Deep watering allows roots to grow deep. Check for soil moisture at 4- to 8-inch level with soil-coring device or by removing a plug of soil.

Water Needs Vary

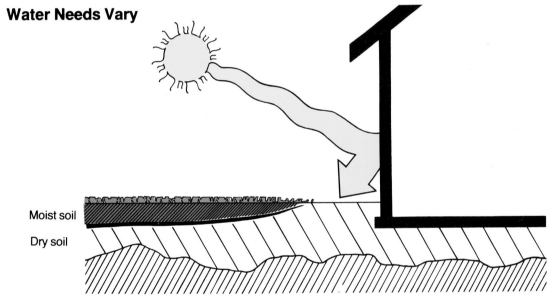

Moist soil

Dry soil

Roof overhang cuts off rainfall and reflected heat dries soil. Grass here likely needs additional water. Another solution is to plant a drought-tolerant ground cover in this area.

When Water Won't Sink In

Water beads on surface and does not penetrate.

Wetting agent breaks cohesive force of water, allowing it to slip into soil through small channels.

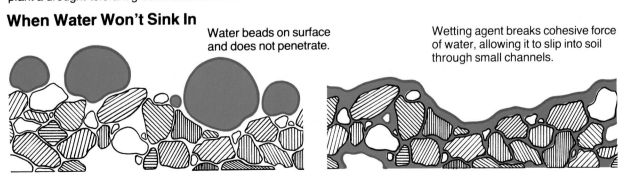

Mow

Lawn growers usually have three basic questions about mowing: *What type of mower should I use? How high should I cut? How often should I mow?*

There are many kinds of mowers, but most home gardeners rely on either a reel or rotary type. *Reel mowers* cut with a spinning reel of curved blades, which scissor-cuts grass against a stationary bed-knife. When properly adjusted, reel mowers make the neatest, cleanest cut. They are most suited to well-kept grasses that are mowed close such as bermudagrass or bentgrass.

Rotary mowers are much simpler. The motor is directly connected to a spinning blade that cuts just about everything in its path on impact. Its cut is not as clean as a reel mower. Tall, less rigorously maintained lawns are often better served by rotaries. Other characteristics of each type mower are noted in the next sections.

No matter which mower you choose, look for a good machine. Its size and power should be appropriate to the type and size of your lawn. Mowing wet grass requires more horsepower, an important consideration if that situation is common. If you have a lawn in the 20,000-square-foot range, consider a riding mower. A well-built mower will do a better job for a longer time. More importantly, it will convert a monotonous, burdensome chore into enjoyable time spent in your yard.

REEL OR ROTARY MOWER?

Cutting quality is the big difference between reel and rotary mowers. The scissor action of a well-adjusted reel mower makes the cleanest cut. Rotaries cut by impact, virtually tearing the grass tips off. Lawns cut with a rotary mower often take on a brownish cast shortly after mowing because of frayed leaf tips.

Mowing height is determined by the grass type. Rotaries have the advantage with tall-cut lawns. Reels have the advantage with low-cut lawns. Well-designed rotary mowers actually pull grass up into the cutting chamber. Most rotary mowers have simple cutting height adjustments, from 3/4 inch to 4 inches.

Maintenance of reel mowers is more demanding. Sharpening a reel mower must be done on a special machine. A rotary mower blade is easily sharpened at home with a file.

Versatility of rotary mowers is greater. Reel mowers tend to be heavier, more awkward and less adapted to trimming edges. Rotary mowers, especially the air-cushion kinds, are lightweight and easier to maneuver between garage and front and back yards.

Scalping potential of reel mowers is less than with rotary mowers. Because reel-types have a cutting edge between two wheels, scalps occur only if a sharp rise passes between the wheels. Rotaries cut on a level plane over four wheels. Grass is cut higher over dips, shorter over humps.

Power rotary mowers are most popular today. They are best for high-cut lawns, are relatively lightweight and simple to operate.

The simple, human-powered reel mower is best for small lawns. If blades are kept sharp, reel mowers make a precision cut.

OTHER MOWERS

Air-cushion mowers are lightweight and convenient to use. They mulch clippings. Height is adjustable between 3/4 and 2-1/2 inches by raising or lowering blade with spacers.

Flail and sickle bar mowers are designed especially for tall weeds and grasses in areas mowed infrequently. Stones, bottles and trash are not thrown.

Electric nylon line mowers operate on a rotary principle. They are the safest of all mower types.

HEIGHT OF CUT

The proper height to cut grass is determined by the type of grass. Low and spreading kinds such as bermudagrass are cut lower. Upright, vertical kinds such as tall fescue are cut higher. Recommended cutting heights are listed for each of the grasses on pages 15 to 29.

Lawns composed of a mix of grasses are mowed at the height that favors the most desirable grass. Kentucky bluegrass, fescue and perennial ryegrass are frequently combined in mixes. They all have the same optimum mowing height of 1-1/2 to 2 inches. A mix of cool- and warm-season grasses, such as bermudagrass and perennial ryegrass, is popular in transitional areas where neither is ideally adapted. These lawns are cut high to favor the less-aggressive cool-season grass.

Cut high for low maintenance—Root depth is directly proportional to mowing height. A higher cut allows for deeper roots. Deep roots are more efficient in obtaining water and nutrients. A deep-rooted lawn becomes more drought tolerant and is able to go longer between waterings. Less-frequent watering discourages many weeds and *leaches*, or washes away, less fertilizer from the root zone.

Adjust height with the season—Cut grass higher during periods of stress. Cut lower just prior to peak growth periods. Cut cool-season grasses lower in early spring and early fall—higher through summer. Low cut has a rejuvenating effect during the most favorable spring and fall seasons. High cut increases tolerance of drought, heat and stress.

The aim is to remove as little grass as possible with each mowing and still maintain proper height. Remove no more than one-third of the total grass height at one time. For example, a grass with a mowing height of 2 inches shouldn't be allowed to grow any higher than 3 inches before it is mowed.

FREQUENCY OF CUT

Weekly mowing is generally recommended. This frequency is convenient for most people and works well for most lawns. However, frequent cuts of small amounts are more beneficial to the grass. When growth is fast due to optimum climate and nutrients, mowing every three days may be necessary.

MOW SAFELY

Wounds caused by mower blades or by objects propelled from these blades occur too frequently. Common sense will reduce the likelihood of accidents. Follow the advice of the product manufacturer. Be sure that everyone who uses mowing equipment knows how to operate it and is familiar with rules of safe operation.

Follow these safety reminders:

• Make a habit of checking the lawn for wires, cans, rocks, twigs or other debris before mowing.
• Keep children and pets away from the area when operating any power equipment.
• Wear heavy shoes to protect feet and to maintain sure footing. Wear long pants to protect your legs from muffler or engine burns and propelled objects.
• Never remove safety guards or other original equipment from mowers.
• Use gas can with appropriate filling and pouring attachments to avoid spills.
• Wipe up or wash away gasoline spills immediately. Fill mower on a paved area to avoid killing the grass with gasoline.
• Push walking mowers forward rather than pulling them backward.
• Mow slopes sideways with a walk-behind mower. Do not mow extremely steep hills.
• Always turn off mower and disconnect spark plug wire or electric cord before unclogging, refueling or adjusting machine.
• Allow engine to cool for 10 minutes before refilling gas tank.
• Stop engine when leaving it unattended or when crossing a driveway or gravel walk.
• Check all nuts and bolts regularly to be sure they are tight.

LEAVE CLIPPINGS AND SAVE FERTILIZER

University tests have established that lawns with their clippings removed need up to two extra pounds of nitrogen per 1,000 square feet per year. This means lawns need 20 to 30 percent more fertilizer if clippings are removed. Some tests have indicated as much as 50 percent of the lawn's nitrogen requirement is met by allowing clippings to remain after mowing.

If ideal mowing frequency is impossible, clipping might be too thick to leave on the lawn. A heavy mat of clippings blocks sunlight, air and water from the growing lawn.

Lawn clippings are 75 to 80 percent water, 3 to 6 percent nitrogen, 1/2 to 1 percent phosphorus and 1 to 3 percent potassium, the same as an approximate 4-1-3 ratio fertilizer (N-P-K). Because clippings contain little woody tissue, they do not contribute to thatch.

Fertilize

A complete fertilizer contains nitrogen (N), phosphorus (P) and potassium (K). For most lawns, the ratio between these nutrients should be 3-1-2. Examples are fertilizers with formulas of 15-5-10, 21-7-14 and 30-10-20. Nitrogen is the most important nutrient.

Depending on the type of grass, length of growing season and level of maintenance, a lawn requires between 2 and 12 pounds of *actual nitrogen* each year. To determine the actual nitrogen in a bag of fertilizer, multiply the first number of the three-number formula, the percentage of nitrogen, by the number of pounds in a bag. For example, a 100-pound bag of 10-10-10 would contain 10 pounds of actual nitrogen (.10 x 100). The chart on this page shows the amount of different percent-nitrogen fertilizers to apply.

FAST- OR SLOW-RELEASE FERTILIZER

You have a choice between slow- or fast-release nitrogen fertilizers. Both have advantages and disadvantages, as indicated in the chart. Some commonly available lawn fertilizers are 50 percent slow-release (water-insoluble) nitrogen. For example, a 24-4-8 fertilizer with 12 percent water-insoluble nitrogen—one-half of 24—is 50 percent slow-release nitrogen.

Fertilizer burn is rare with slow-release fertilizers. Grasses burn when the mineral salt content of the soil is high. Excess salt literally pulls water out of grass, leaves and roots, resulting in burn. Sprinkle table salt over a raw carrot to see the principle in action.

Soil salts are naturally high where rainfall is low. Water from the Colorado River in the West is notoriously high in salt content. Slow-release fertilizers are recommended in these areas. Fast-release kinds release their total salt content to the soil at one time, increasing the chance of burn. Slow-release fertilizers are also recommended in areas when there is a possibility of ground water contamination.

FERTILIZER TIPS

Timing—Lawns, especially those composed of cool-season grasses, should receive 75 percent of their yearly nitrogen during the fall and winter seasons. Supply warm-season grasses with approximately half of their yearly nitrogen in late spring and half in fall. This is the key to best results with lawn fertilizers. During fall, grass roots are building food reserves that last through the next summer. Fertilizing in summer promotes top growth at the expense of food reserves.

Exact scheduling of fertilizer applications is dependent upon many variables, including the type of fertilizer, type of lawn and maintenance level. Be sure to read the directions on the fertilizer bag.

Leave clippings—If you allow clippings to remain on the lawn, you will reduce the necessary annual nitrogen need by 20 to 50 percent. For example, if you normally apply 6 pounds of actual nitrogen to your lawn annually and have removed clippings, you need apply only 3 to 5 pounds if you leave clippings. If you mow frequently, clippings will not usually become unsightly or become thick enough to mat.

Lime and sulfur—Grasses grow best when soil pH is about 6.5. When soil is adjusted to this slightly acid condition, fertilizers are most effective. Where rainfall is heavy, soils are typically acid. This condition can be corrected with lime, usually in the form of ground limestone.

Where rainfall is light, soils are usually alkaline. That condition is corrected with fertilizers that contain ammonium, iron sulfate or elemental sulfur. Check with your nursery, county agent, USDA Soil Conservation Service or nearby university soil science department to learn about soil conditions in your area.

AMOUNT OF FERTILIZER TO APPLY

Most kinds of fertilizer can be used on lawns. Generally, those with a 3-1-2 ratio such as 30-10-20 are best. They replace nutrients in the same ratio lawns use them.

Lawn fertilizers that blend equal amounts of water-soluble (fast-release) and water-insoluble (slow-release) nitrogen are recommended. They can be applied at rates of up to 2 pounds of actual nitrogen per 1,000 square feet. Limit a single application of soluble fertilizer to 1 pound of actual nitrogen per 1,000 square feet if you water it in after application. Limit application to 1/2 pound per 1,000 square feet if you do *not* water it in. Slow-release fertilizers such as UF, IBDU and SCU, explained in the chart opposite, can be applied at rates exceeding 4 pounds actual nitrogen per 1,000 square feet.

Organic fertilizers and manures are relatively expensive and have to be applied in greatest quantity, but they do provide many soil-improving benefits.

POUNDS OF FERTILIZER REQUIRED TO EQUAL 1 POUND ACTUAL NITROGEN				
	Square feet of lawn			
% Nitrogen	500	1,000	1,500	2,000
40	1.3	2.5	3.8	5
30	1.7	3.5	5	6.6
25	2	4	6	8
20	2.5	5	7.5	10
15	3.3	6.6	10	13
10	5	10	15	20
7 (Cottonseed meal)*	7	14	21.5	29
6 (Milorganite)*	8.5	17	25.5	34
2 (Steer manure)*	25	50	75	100

*Examples of common organic fertilizers within this nutrient range.

A CLOSE LOOK AT A FERTILIZER LABEL

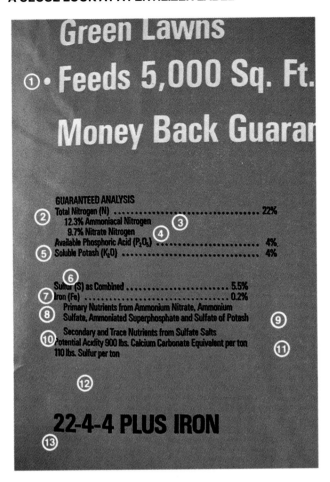

1. Bag weighs 23 pounds (not shown) of which 22 percent is nitrogen. Therefore, bag contains 5 pounds *actual* nitrogen, enough for 5,000 square feet at recommended rate of 1 pound actual nitrogen per 1,000 square feet.

2. The total amount of *elemental* nitrogen. Determined by sum of nitrogen from various sources.

3. The percentage nitrogen in ammonium form. There are many kinds of fertilizers that contain ammonium and all are categorized as *ammoniacal.* Ammoniacal nitrogen does not readily leach from the soil. Because it is ammonia-based, it reduces soil pH.

4. The percentage of nitrogen in *nitrate* form. Nitrate nitrogen availability is not temperature dependent. It is the fastest-acting form of nitrogen. Nitrate nitrogen leaches rapidly and does not affect soil pH.

5. Phosphorus is most important to new lawns. It is usually quite insoluble so a small amount lasts a long time. Does not affect soil pH.

6. Potash (potassium) is very soluble so soil needs periodic replenishment. Sufficient supply of potash is associated with improved winter hardiness and disease resistance. Does not affect soil pH.

7. Sulfur-deficient lawns develop a yellow cast that nitrogen fertilizer cannot correct. Elemental sulfur lowers soil pH. Most fertilizer sulfur, except sulfur-coated urea, is in sulfate form, which does not affect pH.

8. Iron, although typically abundant in western soils, is frequently unavailable to plants because of high pH (alkalinity). Iron deficiency causes a yellowing that appears worse after nitrogen fertilization.

9. Listing of *incomplete* primary fertilizers from which this *complete* fertilizer is made. See chart below.

10. Indicates that sulfur is in sulfate form, that is, ammonium *sulfate* and iron *sulfate.*

11. This is an *acid-forming fertilizer,* an advantage if soil pH is naturally high. See glossary, page 172. Calcium carbonate is standardized lime. If 900 pounds neutralizes one ton, then approximately 10 pounds neutralizes acid potential of this quantity.

12. Equals 1-1/4 pounds of elemental sulfur in this bag.

13. 22 percent elemental nitrogen, 4 percent phosphorus and 4 percent potassium is the *grade* of this fertilizer. Abbreviated N-P-K, these percentages are always listed in this same sequence.

COMMON NITROGEN FERTILIZERS FOR LAWNS

These fertilizers are commercial-grade sources of nitrogen. They are *incomplete* in that they supply nitrogen only. Often, two of these nitrogen fertilizers are combined with phosphorus and potassium to make one, nitrogen-balanced, *complete* fertilizer. For convenience, some complete fertilizers are combined with insecticides and herbicides.

NAME	APPROX. NITROGEN %	REMARKS
Fast Release		
Ammonium nitrate	33	Effective for rapid green-up and growth when soil temperature is below 55F to 60F (13C to 16C). Has very high salt content and is strongly acidifying.
Ammonium sulfate	21	Strongly acidifying, has high salt content.
Urea	45	Relatively low in salt.
Slow Release		
Ureaformaldehyde (UF)	38	Dependent on soil microorganisms for nitrogen release, so it is not effective below 55F to 60F (13C to 16C). Low burn potential and little effect on soil pH. Often combined with fast-release types. Cost is approximately 3 to 4 times that of urea.
Isobutylidene Diurea (IBDU)	30	Rate of nitrogen release dependent on soil pH, temperature, particle size and moisture. If pH is low, below 5, release is fast. If pH is high, above 8, release is slow. Most nitrogen is released within 2 months. Moist soils promote nitrogen release. Little effect on soil pH or salt content. Low burn potential. Cost is approximately 3 to 4 times that of urea.
Sulfur-Coated Urea (SCU)	32	Granules of urea are coated with sulfur and wax. Nitrogen release is promoted by microbial attack of sulfur coating. High temperatures, moist soil and neutral pH speed nitrogen availability. Granules may be broken by spreader or mower—speeding release rate. Sulfur coating acts to gradually reduce soil pH. Cost is approximately 1-1/2 times that of urea.

Close observation, hands-and-knees style, is the diagnostican's most useful tool. In this case, the glass magnifies characteristic pustules of stripped rust disease.

Lawn Troubles

Significant lawn troubles can be avoided by following certain basics such as planting adapted grasses and by watering, fertilizing and mowing properly. If problems do develop, the first task is to identify the cause and change any maintenance habits that contribute to the problem. Common problems are listed with the specific pests on the following pages. To completely solve the problem, it may be necessary to use appropriate pesticides.

PESTICIDES

All pesticides are toxic in some degree to plants, animals and man. The pesticides recommended here are commonly available and considered safe if used according to directions and at prescribed levels. But always be cautious when using chemical sprays.

There are three basic kinds of pesticides. *Herbicides* kill weeds. *Insecticides* kill insects. *Fungicides* kill disease-causing fungus organisms.

Toxicity of pesticides is indicated by key words on product label. "Danger," "Poison" and the skull-and-crossbones symbol all mean highly toxic. Such sprays are rarely recommended or used by home gardeners. "Warning" means moderately toxic. The common insecticide diazinon is in this category. "Caution" means slightly toxic.

These pointers will help you apply pesticides more safely and successfully.

• Follow label directions carefully and exactly. This advice is elementary and often repeated but still important. No matter how many times you have used a particular pesticide, review label information before use.
• Use the correct pesticide. Identify the pest you seek to control and be sure the product you use is recommended for that pest and for use on lawns.
• Use directed amounts. Extra pesticide, "just to be sure," does not make the treatment more effective. It may add to lawn problems rather than reduce them—and costs you money.
• Use at directed time of year, time of day and temperature. Pesticides vary, but some are safe and effective only within narrow limits.
• Proper and timely irrigation before or after treatment is important for insect control. When to irrigate depends upon the pest to be controlled.

WEEDS

Some weeds, English daisy for instance, are not terribly aggressive and may add to the lawn's charm. Others, such as white clover, blend with the lawn so they are hardly noticed. But some are distinctly different in texture and growth habit. Their persistent, aggressive growth spoils the lawn's appearance and makes gardeners want to eliminate them.

Overwatering and underwatering, mowing too short, low fertility, excessive wear, disease, insects and shade create stress that allows weeds to invade lawns. If the situation is severe and weeds have established a foothold, consider complete renovation of the lawn. This may include planting a stronger or more adapted grass, installing a good watering system or correcting other serious problems.

Regular care of lawns will prevent most weed problems. There are also many ways to eliminate weeds. Hand pulling is the oldest method, and an excellent, outdoor exercise. But herbicides may be necessary to reclaim a weed-dominated lawn. Knowing the differences in basic weed types and herbicides is necessary for proper weed control.

Narrowleaf or broadleaf weeds—Grassy weeds such as crabgrass, tall fescue and annual bluegrass are *narrowleaf* weeds. The veins of their leaves are parallel. Dandelion, oxalis and burclover are *broadleaf* weeds. Their leaves have netted veins and plants produce more prominent flowers. The difference between these two types is important. Some herbicides affect only one or the other. Grass lawns are narrowleaf; dichondra is broadleaf.

Life cycle—Most common weeds are either summer annuals, winter annuals or perennials. Annuals are continually renewed by seed. Therefore, they can be eliminated by herbicides that prevent seeds from germinating. Perennial weeds such as bermudagrass and oxalis that spread by both rooting stems and seeds are the most difficult to eradicate. They usually require a combination of herbicides for control.

Herbicides—*Selective herbicides* kill target weeds without injuring the surrounding grass lawn. There are many kinds and degrees of selectivity. Selection varies with the specific material, formulation, application rate and prevailing temperatures. Selective herbicides are available combined with fertilizers for easy dropspreader application.

Nonselective herbicides kill both weeds and grass, and make no distinction between broadleaf and narrowleaf. These are normally used for spot weeding or for complete renovation.

Translocated or *systemic herbicides* are absorbed by the weed and move within it. These are necessary for control of most perennial weeds. They may be either selective or nonselective.

Contact herbicides do not move within the plant and affect only those parts touched by the spray. Contact sprays are most useful for annual weeds.

Pre-emergent herbicides prevent germination of weed seeds. Most often applied in combination with a fertilizer, they control annual weeds such as crabgrass and annual bluegrass. All other herbicides that are applied to growing plants are *post-emergent*. Herbicides recommended for home gardeners are listed on page 57.

INSECT PESTS

Damage caused by insects is often difficult to distinguish from damage caused by disease, dry soil, dog urine or spilled gasoline. Check to be sure insects are actually causing the problem. This means a close examination of the damaged section and surrounding lawn area. You should find insect pests in sufficient quantity before using an insecticide.

Detecting lawn pests—The *pyrethrum test* is one of the best detection methods. Most nurseries stock or can order pyrethrum, an organic insecticide. Mix 1 tablespoon of commercial 1 or 2 percent pyrethrum in 1 gallon of water. Using a sprinkling can, apply this mix as evenly as possible over 1 square yard of lawn. If sod webworms, cutworms and other caterpillars are present, they will come to the surface within 10 minutes. It is normal for a few to emerge, but if you find more than 5 cutworms or 15 sod webworms per square yard, you need to apply insecticide. If pyrethrum is not available, use 1/2 cup laundry detergent dissolved in 1 gallon of water.

Grubs do not come to the surface with the pyrethrum test. Look for them by examining the soil around roots. If grubs are numerous, roots will be eaten away and the grass can be rolled back like a carpet. More than three grubs per square foot is enough to warrant insecticide treatment.

Check for chinch bugs by pressing a bottomless coffee can into the soil at the edge of the suspected area—where the bugs are most active. Add water with a garden hose. If present, chinch bugs will float to the surface within 10 to 15 minutes. More than 20 per square foot indicates that treatment is necessary.

The photos on pages 62 and 63 will help you identify common lawn pests.

Applying lawn insecticides—For above-ground pests such as chinch bug and sod webworm, water thoroughly and allow the grass to dry before spraying. Then withhold water as long as possible after spraying. For grubs and below-ground feeders, water thoroughly 1 or 2 days before spraying. Then water after spraying to the point of runoff to carry insecticide into the root zone where pests feed.

Wetting agents used in conjunction with sprays *might* help control lawn pests. If a wetting agent is used and not watered in, it acts to hold spray on the grass, which aids control of above-ground pests. For grub control, it is essential to water thoroughly and immediately following application of a wetting agent.

DISEASE

Lawn disease is easier to prevent than cure. Adapted grasses and good cultural practices make lawns resistant to most diseases. If a disease does appear, the healthy lawn is able to quickly recover.

The factor that contributes most to disease is too much or too little nitrogen fertilizer. Excessive fertilizer produces soft, lush growth that is susceptible to

Rhizoctonia and *Fusarium* patch. Nitrogen starvation favors development of *Sclerotinia* dollar spot, red thread and rust.

Diseases are the most difficult of all lawn problems to accurately diagnose and control. Several good fungicides are available. If applied at the right time in the right amount, they help control lawn diseases. But most often a change in maintenance practices is a better cure. If you plant well-adapted, disease-resistant grass, provide adequate water and fertilizer at the best times, and mow at the proper height, diseases rarely become significant problems.

GALLERY OF WEEDS, INSECTS AND DISEASE

The following pages show some of the common weeds, insects and diseases you are likely to encounter. If you have problems with a lawn pest that is not described here, check with your county extension agent, nursery personnel or lawn-care consultant in your area.

Products are recommended by common chemical name. A cross-reference of commonly available trade-name products is provided for your convenience. No endorsement of products is intended, nor is criticism of unnamed products implied.

TABLE OF EQUIVALENTS FOR LIQUID MEASURE (VOLUME)

For equivalent amounts, read horizontally in either direction on any given line

Gallons	Quarts	Pints	Fluid Ounces	Cups	Tablespoons	Teaspoons	Milliliters	Liters
1	4	8	128	16	256	768	3785	3.785
	1	2	32	4	64	192	946	.946
		1	16	2	32	96	473	.473
			1	1/8	2	6	29.6	.030
				1	16	48	236	.236
					1	3	15	.015
						1	5	.005
							1	.001

FUNGICIDES

Common Name	Trade Names
anilazine	Dyrene Turf Fungicide, Pro Turf Fungicide III, Best Turf Fungicide
benomyl	Tersan 1991, Pro Turf DSB Fungicide
captan	Orthocide, Captan
chlorothalonil	Daconil 2787, Best Turf Disease Control
cycloheximide	Acti-dione TGF
ethazol	Koban, Terrazole
fenaminosulf	Lesan
iprodione	Chipco 26019
mancozeb	Fore, Dithane M-45, Best Multipurpose Disease Control
maneb	Tersan LSR, Dithane M-22
oxycarboxin	Plantvax
PCNB	Fungiclor, Terraclor, Pro Turf Fungicide II, Turfcide
thiophanate	Cleary's-3336, Pro Turf Systemic Fungicide
thiophanate-methyl	Fungo 50, Topsin-M, Chipco Spot Kleen
thiram	Tersan 75

INSECTICIDES

Common Name	Trade Names	Pests
Bacillus popilliae	Doom, Milky spore disease	Japanese beetle
Bacillus thuringiensis	Biotrol K, Dipel, Thuricide	Sod webworm, armyworm, cutworm
carbaryl	Sevin	Sod webworm, fall armyworm
chlorpyrifos	Dursban	Many lawn pests — see label
diazinon	Spectracide	Many lawn pests — see label
isofenphos	Oftanol*	Grubs, hyperodes weevil, bill bug, chinch bug, sod webworm
popoxur	Baygon	Mole cricket
propyl thiopyro-phosphate	Aspon, Ortho Chinch Bug Spray	Chinch bug, sod webworm
trichlorfon	Dylox, Proxol	Grubs, sod webworm, chinch bug

*Commercial applicators only

HERBICIDES FOR LAWNS AND GROUND COVERS

Common Name	Trade Name(s)	Remarks*
Selective against broadleaf weeds in grass lawns		
Bromoxynil	Nu-Lawn Weeder	Kills broadleaf weed seedlings on contact. Use on new lawns 10 days after germination and until weed seedlings have 3 to 5 leaves.
Dicamba + 2,4-D	Super D Weedone, Scotts Lawn Weed Control, Scotts Spot Dandelion Control, Super Pax Weed 'N Feed, Provel Lawn and Turf Herbicide	For English daisy and other difficult-to-control broadleaf weeds when dandelion, plantain and other 2,4-D-susceptible weeds are present.
Dicamba + 2,4-D + MCPP	Miller's Lawn & Turf Weed Bomb, Best Lawn Weed Killer, Acme Super Weed-No-More, Miller's Lawn & Turf Weedkiller	Controls many lawn weeds when applied at low rates. Bentgrass and hybrid bermudagrass lawns are sensitive. See label.
MCPP (mecoprop)	Chipco Turf Herbicide MCPP	Particularly effective against common chickweed, mouse-ear chickweed, clover, plantain, knotweed, pigweed, ragweed, lambsquarters and ground ivy.
Selective against narrowleaf weeds in grass lawns		
DSMA/MSMA	Chacon Crabgrass Control, Weedone Crabgrass Killer, Scotts Summer Crabgrass Control, Acme Crabgrass & Nutgrass Killer	Controls crabgrass, dallisgrass and nutsedge. Temperature, soil moisture and grass type determine degree of selectivity. See label.
Selective against narrowleaf weeds in dichondra lawns		
Dalapon	Dowpon M Grass Killer	Water thoroughly 1 or 2 days before application. Apply uniformly, barely wetting leaves. Excessive spray will reduce selectivity.
Nonselective herbicides effective against narrow or broadleaf weeds		
Cacodylic acid	Scotts Spot Grass & Weed Control, Germain's Fresh Start Grass & Weed Killer, Acme Weed-N-Grass Killer	Top-kills weeds and grasses on contact. Use to control unwanted growth around trees, shrubs, buildings, in walkways and along fences. Controls annual weeds before seeding lawn. Controls winter weeds in dormant bermudagrass lawns.
Nonselective against narrow or broadleaf perennial or annual weeds		
Glyphosate	Roundup, Kleenup Systemic Grass and Weed Killer	Effectively controls tough perennial weeds such as bermudagrass, kikuyugrass, tall fescue and oxalis, among many others. Apply to vigorously growing, mature weeds. No soil activity or residue.
Pre-emergent for lawns and/or ground covers:		
Benefin	Balan	**Lawns**—Apply 2 to 3 weeks before crabgrass germinates in spring. For established lawns only. **Ground covers**—Not recommended.
Bensulide	Betasan, Scotts Halts Crabgrass Preventer, Super Pax Crabgrass Control with Betasan	**Lawns**—Apply 2 to 3 weeks before germination of crabgrass in spring or annual bluegrass in fall. **Ground covers**—Use in fall for winter grasses, late winter for summer grasses. For: Ajuga, dichondra, Fragaria, Gazania, Hedera, Hypericum, Juniperus, Pachysandra terminalis, Sedum, Trachelospermum, Vinca.
DCPA	Dacthal, Ortho Garden Weed Preventer, Acme Garden Weed Preventer Granules, Lilly/Miller Weeder	**Lawns**—For crabgrass, apply 2 to 3 weeks before initial germination. Do not use on bentgrass or dichondra. **Ground covers**—Can be sprayed over plant tops. Does not leach; good in sandy soil. For: Maleophora luteola, Eunoymus, Hedera, Juniperus, Lonicera japonica, Pachysandra terminalis, Potentilla.
Dichlobenil	Casoron	**Lawns**—Not recommended. **Ground covers**—Controls many weeds and some shallow-rooted, established weeds. Cultivate 2 to 3 inches into soil, especially in warm soil. For: Arctostaphylos uva-ursi, Euonymus, Hedera helix, Juniperus, Lonicera japonica.
Diphenamid	Enide, Scotts Super Bonus for Dichondra, Tuco Enide Dichondra and Ornamental Weed Control	**Lawns**—For dichondra lawns only. Pre-emergent and early postemergent control for grassy weeds. Apply fall and spring for annual bluegrass; late winter for crabgrass. **Ground covers**—Apply before or after planting. Apply with light raking, then water. For: Mesembryanthemum crocea, Ajuga reptans, Baccharis pilularis, Ceanothus, Gazania, Hedera canariensis, Juniperus, Potentilla, Sedum, Soleirolia soleirolii, Trachelospermum, Vinca.
EPTC	Eptam, Black Leaf Eptam Weed Control, Greenlight Eptam Weed & Grass Granules, Science Eptam Garden Weed Control	**Lawns**—Not recommended. **Ground covers**—Work immediately into top 2 or 3 inches. Water in if soil dry, or apply with irrigation water. For: Iceplants, Ajuga reptans, Euonymus, Fragaria, Gazania, Hedera, Hypericum, Juniperus, Pachysandra terminalis, Sedum, Vinca.
Oryzalin	Surflan	**Lawns**—Not recommended. **Ground covers**—Does not require soil cultivation. Can be sprayed over plants. Controls many summer annual weeds. For: Ice plants, Baccharis pilularis, Euonymus, Gazania, Hedera canariensis, Juniperus, Osteospermum fruticosum, Sedum, Trachelospermum jasminoides, Vinca minor.
Trifluralin	Treflan, Pro-Gard Pre-Seeder Weeder, Pre-Seeder Weeder Liquid	**Lawns**—Not recommended. **Ground covers**—Cultivate or water into soil within 24 hours of application. Apply to dry soil. For: Ice plants, Euonymus, Gazania, Hedera, Hypericum, Juniperus, Lonicera japonica, Osteospermum fruticosum, Potentilla, Sedum, Vinca.
Siduron	Tupersan	**Lawns**—Selectively controls certain germinating annual weed grasses such as crabgrass and bermudagrass. Do not use on newly seeded bentgrass or bermudagrass lawns. Apply to bare soil as final operation following seeding. **Ground covers**—Not recommended.
Simazine	Princep	**Lawns**—Not recommended. **Ground covers**—Many. See labels.
Soil fumigants		
Calcium cyanamide	Tag Line Cyanamid	Use 50 pounds per 1,000 square feet. Apply after soil is prepared. Cultivate 25 pounds into top 2 to 3 inches, remaining half on surface. Keep soil moist for 3 weeks, wait 4 to 6 weeks before seeding.
Metham	Vapam, Best Vapam Soil Fumigant	Dilute in water and apply to well-cultivated soil. Water after application to seal soil surface, or cover with plastic tarp. Wait 3 to 6 weeks before seeding.

*Read the label of the specific product you use. Active ingredients may be formulated differently by different manufacturers for different purposes.

Weeds

Annual Bluegrass

Winter-growing narrowleaf annual. Perennial in some climates or situations. Prefers cool, infertile, compacted, moist soils. Germinates in fall; sets seed in spring. Often dies in summer, leaving brown patches.

Use bensulide, benefin or oxadiazon. Apply in early fall to dry lawn and lightly water into grass.

Bermudagrass

Perennial narrowleaf. Popular, low-maintenance lawn grass. Common weed of cool-season lawns in warm-season and transition climates. Wiry stems root at joints. Seedheads are similar to crabgrass.

Pre-emergent control with siduron. Selective control in dichondra lawns with dalapon carefully applied at correct rates. Nonselective control with glyphosate or dalapon.

Buckhorn Plantain

Perennial broadleaf. Leaves are long and narrow. Flower stalks grow to 12 inches high. Rosette growth habit. Broadleaf plantain, a close relative, has shorter, wider leaves and shorter flower stalks. Roots are fibrous and shallow.

Selective control with 2,4-D + MCPP + dicamba.

Burclover

Annual broadleaf. Spring and fall annual known for its spiny, twisted, seed pod or *bur*. See photo. Leaflets are whitish and have red spots when young. Colonizes in dry, infertile soils where grass is thin. Appearance and control similar to the closely related weed, *black medic*.

Selective control with early spring sprays of 2,4-D + dicamba or 2,4-D + MCPP.

Crabgrass

Summer-growing narrowleaf annual. Often found in thin, overwatered lawns. Most vigorous with midsummer heat, humidity and intense light when cool-season grasses are semidormant:

Use siduron for spring-seeded lawns. Apply DCPA, bensulide or benefin in established lawns 2 to 3 weeks before crabgrass seeds germinate in spring, approximately the time forsythia or crocus bloom. Also check with your nursery or cooperative extension agent for germination dates in your area.

Curly Dock

Perennial broadleaf. Develops a large taproot and usually appears as a dandelionlike rosette in lawns. Flower stalks become 2 to 3 feet tall. Many closely related species: fiddle dock, bitter dock, green dock, golden dock, willow dock.

Selective control with 2,4-D + MCPP + dicamba.

Dallisgrass

Perennial narrowleaf. Produces clumps that regrow fast after mowing. Clumping grass, spreads by seeds. Prefers low, wet areas. Common in southeast and southwest United States.

Nonselective control with glyphosate or dalapon. Selective control with DSMA or MSMA.

Dandelion

Perennial broadleaf. Common, variable and adaptable weed. Not competitive or aggressive. Often colonizes in thin lawns. Rosette growth above ground, taproot below.

Use 2,4-D or 2,4-D + MCPP, spring or fall.

English Daisy

Perennial broadleaf. Tough but charming weed—some people plant it in lawns. Grows spring and fall in most areas. Thrives all year along Pacific Coast, Newfoundland, England and similar mild-summer areas. Leaves appear in rosettes and daisylike flowers are showy. Tolerates low soil fertility.

Selective control with 2,4-D + dicamba or 2,4-D + MCPP.

Kikuyugrass

Perennial narrowleaf. Sometimes grown as a lawn. Very fast-growing, competitive weed in warm-season lawns. Increasingly common in southwestern United States. Deep roots, thick rhizomes and stolons. Looks similar to St. Augustinegrass except leaves have sharp points—unlike the blunt tips of St. Augustine. Silky seedheads are inconspicuous. Seed production is stimulated by mowing. No selective control.

Pre-emergent control with siduron. Spot treat established stands with glyphosate or dalapon.

Mallow

Annual broadleaf. Tough weed but most common in new lawns or lawns that receive irregular and high mowing. Leaves are irregularly round with red spots at base.

If vigorous lawn growth does not discourage it, spray weeds in spring with combination 2,4-D + MCPP + dicamba.

Oxalis

Perennial broadleaf. One of the most persistent of all weeds. Spreads with creeping, rooting stems and seed. Likes shade or full sun. Cloverlike leaves are water repellent. Flowers are small and yellow. Grows fastest in spring and fall.

Spot treat with nonselective glyphosate. Selective control with 2,4-D + MCPP + dicamba. Pre-emergent control with oxadiazon or siduron.

Prostrate Pigweed

Annual broadleaf. Common weed that invades many lawns. Leaf edges are rough and leaf tip is notched. Stems are 1/2 to 2 feet long. Flowers are densely clustered at stem ends, appearing spring to fall.

Pre-emergent control with EPTC. Selective control with 2,4-D + dicamba.

Spotted Spurge

Summer-growing annual broadleaf. Forms a prostrate, fast-growing, circular mat in lawn. Each leaflet has a red spot. Milky sap runs from broken stems and taproot. Very short life cycle—10 to 14 days in southern areas.

Pre-emergent control with DCPA. Selective control in grass lawns with 2,4-D + MCPP + dicamba.

Tall Fescue

Perennial narrowleaf. Attractive, tough lawn grass when planted alone. Acts as a weedy, clumping grass if it invades cool-season lawns. Upright, wide, coarse-textured leaves have rasplike edges.

No selective control. Spray clumps with glyphosate or dalapon.

Whitestem Filaree

Annual broadleaf. Usually a low, clumping weed. Stems are whitish. Plant is usually 6 to 8 inches in diameter and 4 inches high. Leaflets are toothed; flowers are small and purple. Seed pods are shaped like a stork's bill.

Pre-emergent control in dichondra lawns with napropamid. Selective control in grass lawns with 2,4-D + MCPP + dicamba.

Armyworm pupa

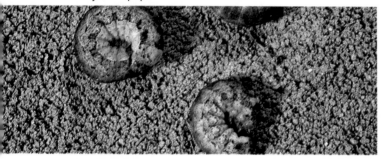

Variegated cutworm

Billbug larva

Billbug adult

Chinch bugs. At top, immature stages of growth. At bottom, adult chinch bugs.

Pests

Armyworm and Cutworm

These two pests are closely related. Both cause above-ground damage to lawns. There are many forms of both. Armyworms have three stripes and an inverted Y on their heads. Cutworms are fat and usually curled. Both are about 1-1/2 inches long and feed primarily at night. Detect cutworm with pyrethrum test. See page 55. Armyworms often feed above ground during daytime so special detection methods are not necessary. Treat if you find more than five armyworms or cutworms per square yard.

Damage usually occurs first in spring. Both pests are susceptible to natural fungus diseases in humid areas and to attack from several parasitic insects.

Use *Bacillus thuringiensis*, carbaryl, chlorpyrifos, diazinon or trichlorfon.

Billbug

Both larvae and adults are damaging to lawns. Adults are 1/5 to 3/4 inch long and distinguished by their prominent snout. They burrow into grass stems near soil surface, cutting off stems. Adults create yellow-to-brown circular dead spots that look similar to fertilizer or gasoline burn. The grass, with stems severed, is easily pulled up. Larvae feed on roots and cause irregular dead areas. Grass can also be pulled up easily.

Use carbaryl, chlorpyrifos, diazinon or isophenphos.

Chinch Bug

The chinch bug is a black and white insect that grows to 1/5 inch long. It feeds on grass leaves and stems, causing sections of lawn to yellow and eventually brown. Young chinch bugs—nymphs—are red and white. They do most of their damage in hot, dry weather. Detect by close examination, raking, flooding or by bottomless can test. See page 55. Most serious in southern United States where St. Augustinegrass is a favored host. In eastern United States, bentgrass and bluegrass are attacked. Active all year in Florida.

Use Aspon, chlorpyrifos, diazinon or trichlorfon spray. Water lawn thoroughly before spraying. In New York, treat in early June, then again 2 to 3 weeks later.

Greenbug

Greenbug is an aphid that feeds on Kentucky bluegrass lawns. Colonies develop on leaves. They suck juices from grass, causing a burnt-orange color. Damage often occurs under trees. Normally, populations are kept low by a variety of natural predators such as lady bugs. Infestations are sometimes severe on Kentucky bluegrass lawns in the north central United States.

Use sprays of chlorpyrifos or diazinon.

Grubs

A grub is the immature stage of several kinds of beetles. Most infamous is the Japanese beetle grub. Others are June and May beetles, masked chafer, Asiatic garden beetle, Oriental beetle, European chafer and *Phyllophaga crinita*. Most are 1 to 1-1/2 inches long, white or grayish, curled into a C- or U-shape. They are normally discovered 1 to 3 inches below soil surface.

Symptoms are irregular brown spots and rootless sod. Birds, raccoons or armadillos tear up sod to feed on grubs. All grasses are susceptible. Most damage usually occurs late summer and early fall. Annual treatments July through August are usually best. Treat whenever you discover more than three grubs per square foot.

Grubs are controlled with insecticides. Treatment requires three steps. First, water thoroughly. Apply 1 cup of concentrated wetting agent such as Aqua-Gro L per 1,000 square feet if soil does not absorb water easily. Second, apply recommended amounts of diazinon or trichlorfon. Third, water thoroughly immediately after application. Insecticide should flow through thatch into soil. Do not allow runoff.

Grubs of Japanese beetle can be controlled biologically with milky spore disease, available in regions wherever this pest is common. Use insecticides to reduce high grub populations, then begin milky spore program and cease insecticide use.

Sod Webworm

The sod webworm is one of the most common and damaging lawn insect pests. Adult is known as lawn moth. Small, buff-white moths fly zig-zag pattern inches above grass in evening hours, laying eggs. Damage is apparent about 2 weeks later when larvae or caterpillars begin to feed. Larvae hide in web-lined tunnels at soil surface. They emerge in morning and night to feed. Birds feed on them in the early morning hours. First damage can be identified as irregular brown patches. Combination of sod webworm damage and summer heat can kill large sections of lawn.

Detect sod webworm with pyrethrum test. See page 55. Treat if you find 15 or more sod webworms in a square yard.

Mow and water well the day before treatment. Use chlorpyrifos, *Bacillus thuringiensis*, diazinon or trichlorfon. Apply spray to dry grass. Withhold water several days after spraying.

Greenbug

White grub eggs   White grub larvae

White grub pupa   White grub adult

Sod webworm larvae   Sod webworm adult

63

Diseases

Brown Patch

Symptoms are irregular brown areas several inches or several feet in diameter. Leaves and stems turn olive-green, wilt and die. Centers of infected areas may recover, resulting in a ring of dead grass.

All grasses are susceptible. The disease is favored by excessive thatch and excessive nitrogen. High temperatures and humidity also promote the disease.

Control disease by reducing shade and improving aeration and drainage. Water deeply and infrequently. Fungicides are best as preventatives and will only retard existing disease.

Use anilazine, benomyl, chlorothalonil, iprodione, PCNB, thiram, thiophanate or thiophanate-methyl.

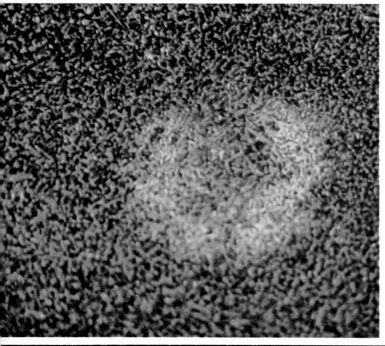

Fusarium Blight

This is a common and often serious disease in bluegrass lawns. Occurs during heat of late summer and early fall. Begins as small circular area. Crown of dead plants appears brown or black and tissue becomes hard. Dead leaves look bleached. Disease is encouraged by hot, dry, windy weather. Attacks lawns that are water stressed, and lawns that have been given excess nitrogen fertilizer.

Control by watering thoroughly. Use a wetting agent to ensure deep and complete soaking of root zone. Remove thatch and avoid applications of nitrogen in summer. Use Kentucky bluegrasses that are resistant to this disease: 'Adelphi', 'Columbia', 'Enmundi', 'Parade', 'Sydsport' and 'Vantage'. Add 20 percent improved perennial ryegrass by weight to Kentucky bluegrass seed to make lawn more resistant to this disease.

Control with fungicides is difficult. Benomyl, thiophanate and thiophanate-methyl are recommended.

Fairy Ring

Fairy ring is caused by one of many natural decay fungi. This is why fairy ring is most common in lawns with thick thatch, or in soil where dead tree roots or wood construction material is buried.

Symptoms are circles or semicircles of dark green grass. Mushrooms are frequently present. Grass often dies just beyond the band of dark green due to lack of water. The fungus does not parasitize the grass.

Maintain adequate fertility and dethatch if necessary. Aerate to improve water penetration. Wetting agents may help water penetrate infected area.

Melting Out, Helminthosporium

Watch for purple or brown leaf spots with brown- or straw-colored centers in Kentucky bluegrass lawns. In bentgrass, fescue, ryegrass and bermudagrass, look for brown leaf spots with purple borders.

High temperatures and humidity promote the disease, which first appears on water-stressed plants. Most damage occurs on close-cropped lawns. Cool, moist conditions favor the disease strain that attacks Kentucky bluegrass.

Mow at recommended height. Avoid giving lawns excess spring nitrogen. Reduce shade, improve aeration and moisture drainage.

Use fungicides when disease first appears. Recommended are anilazine, captan, chlorothalonil, cycloheximide, iprodione, mancozeb and maneb.

Red Thread

The name of this disease is very descriptive—obvious red or pink threadlike strands of fungi emerge from the grass blade. Gradually, infected area assumes a water-soaked appearance just before drying to a tan color.

Red thread is a disease that is found in slow-growing, nitrogen-deficient lawns. It is most prevalent in the cool, humid climates of the Pacific Northwest and Atlantic Northeast, but occurs elsewhere. It is particularly active during spring and fall. Temperatures between 60F and 75F (16C and 24C) and foggy, moist air are ideal conditions for this disease.

Grasses most susceptible are the fine-leafed fescues and some improved perennial ryegrasses.

Control by raising fertility level. If that does not stop the spread of the disease, check soil pH and adjust until within the recommended 6 to 7 pH range. Low pH, acidic soils encourage disease. The chart on page 35 shows how much ground limestone to use to adjust soil pH. If cultural measures are ineffective, use chlorothalonil or mancozeb fungicides.

Rust

This disease is easily identified by rust-colored spores on leaves and stems. Affects Kentucky bluegrass and ryegrass when weather is cool to moderately warm and moist. Spores need 10 to 12 hours of continuous moisture to infect grasses. Maintain adequate fertility because slow-growing lawns are most seriously affected. Most infected portions of leaves are removed by weekly mowing. Spores inside mowed leaves die rapidly.

Control by removing clippings. Spray with oxycarboxin.

Winter Overseeding and Renovation

Overseeding, sowing seed of a fast-growing grass such as annual ryegrass *over* an existing dormant lawn, is a common practice in many areas. Winter overseeding of dormant bermudagrass or zoysiagrass is a fall ritual practiced by many lawn owners in the Sunbelt states. These warm-season grasses accept high summer temperatures in stride; but turn an unappealing straw-brown in winter. Overseeding makes an attractive winter lawn and also prevents invasion of aggressive winter weeds.

Renovation is a similar but more extreme version of overseeding. The important difference is that the existing lawn is killed and regrowth is prevented. Overseeding creates a temporary lawn while the permanent lawn is dormant.

WINTER OVERSEEDING

Timing of winter overseeding varies with your location. In Canada and the northern regions of the United States, the best time is mid-September. In southern regions it ranges from late October to mid-December.

All of the cool-season grasses are potentially useful for winter overseeding. Annual ryegrass is by far most common for home lawns because of its low cost and fast establishment. Improved, turf-type, perennial ryegrasses have superior color, texture and disease resistance, but cost significantly more. The ryegrass known as Oregon Intermediate is an excellent alternative, offering advantages of both annual and turf-type perennial ryegrass.

When lawns are overseeded, they are sown double the rate compared to the seeding of a new lawn. For example, use 12 to 16 pounds of ryegrass per 1,000 square feet of lawn.

An organic dressing over the newly seeded lawn is necessary to keep the top soil layer and germinating seedlings moist. Make topdressing layer 1/4 to 1/8 inch thick. You'll need 15 to 20 cubic feet—7 to 10, 2-cubic-foot bags—per 1,000 square feet. Enough fertilizer to supply 1 to 2 pounds of *actual* nitrogen is also recommended. See page 52.

Seedbed preparation—This is the most important, and most laborious phase of winter overseeding. There are many methods and sequences of installation, but most important is seed-to-soil contact. Seed lying on top of thatch above the soil is not likely to germinate and grow. Remove top growth as much as possible so that seed is firmly pressed into the soil. The series of photographs at right shows a step-by-step renovation procedure.

RENOVATION

In the past, renovation simply meant invigorating an established lawn by raking with a hand or power *dethatching* rake. Later, the idea of *aerating*—providing air passages in the soil—was added to the concept. Today, renovation means something a little different. The word is now used to describe the process of converting an existing weedy lawn or lawn of undesirable grasses into a lawn of desirable grasses.

Tools of renovation—Dethatching and soil-coring machines are the basic tools required for lawn renovation. There are several variations. Some heavy, front-throw reel mowers can be adjusted to *scalp* a lawn—cut it low enough to slice through thatch to the soil level. A sod cutter is perhaps the fastest way to get rid of an old lawn. These machines and other heavy equipment are available at local rental agencies.

You will also need a herbicide sprayer—either a pressurized pump or a hose-end type, a roller, seed spreader and topdressing applicator. These, too, are available at some nurseries and rental agencies.

How to renovate a lawn—There are as many ways to renovate a lawn as kinds of grasses and specific situations. If the weeds are annuals or the present lawn grass is compatible with the new grass you intend to plant, scalp mowing or severe dethatching might be sufficient preparation before reseeding. If these are not sufficient, an existing lawn can be stripped with a sod cutter. With old sod removed, a new sod or seed lawn is easy to install.

The renovation process becomes more complicated if perennial weeds such as bermudagrass, bentgrass, kikuyugrass or dallisgrass are present. Without some kind of chemical control, these weeds will appear in the new lawn as they did in the old lawn.

Complete renovation of a lawn infested with perennial weeds will require an application of the herbicide glyphosate. Before you apply the glyphosate, fertilize and water the present lawn so that it is growing vigorously. Don't mow for about 2 weeks, allowing it to grow taller than normal. When you spray the herbicide, be especially careful to adequately cover edges around sidewalks, curbs and driveways. The best time to kill bermudagrass with glyphosate is fall.

After spraying, wait 7 days, and then rototill, scalp mow or strip sod. Allow area to dry before replanting.

Replace the old lawn with new sod or sow seed. If you choose sod, refer to page 45. If you choose to reseed and bermudagrass, kikuyugrass or oxalis were prevalent weeds in the old lawn, use the pre-emergent herbicide siduron. See page 57. Glyphosate will kill existing weeds but has no effect upon their seeds. If seedlings of these weeds establish in the new lawn, your renovation gains can be lost in a short time.

Renovation

These photos show the steps to take in upgrading an existing lawn. Follow these same steps to overseed a winter-dormant lawn such as bermudagrass.

1. Mow existing lawn as low as possible. A heavy reel mower makes the lowest cut.

2. Use vertical mower to cut into old lawn and loosen soil surface. Thatch is brought to surface, and lawn is opened for good seed-to-soil contact.

3. Use aerator to lift plugs of soil from lawn. Air and water penetration is facilitated and soil compaction is relieved. Fertilizers and organic materials can be raked into holes to benefit soil directly around roots.

4. Sow seed at twice the rate recommended for a new lawn. Centrifugal spreader, shown above, covers large area fast. Drop spreader is more controllable. Apply half the seed walking one direction, the remaining half walking in a crisscross direction.

5. Apply fertilizer in quantity recommended for new lawns—1 to 2 pounds actual nitrogen per 1,000 square feet. Use organic topdressing to help maintain moisture around germinating seed. Spread by hand, as shown, or borrow or rent special applicator. See page 44.

6. Water frequently to maintain moist seedbed until seeds germinate. Depending on weather, brief waterings several times daily might be necessary.

Lawn Care Schedule
Warm-Season Grasses

Warm-season grasses dominate in southern regions and summer rainfall areas of the high plains. They grow vigorously in midsummer with temperatures between 80F and 95F (27C and 35C). Compared to cool-season grasses, they are more drought, heat and wear tolerant. Many have a low, creeping growth habit, usually with above-ground runners. Most tolerate low mowing and brown during winter dormancy.

Illustrations below show basic timing of most important lawn chores utilizing simple hand tools.

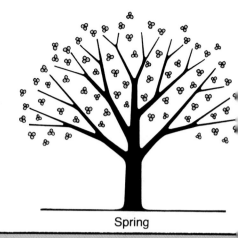

Spring

PLANTING—Sow seed of bermudagrass, bahiagrass or centipedegrass after soil has warmed thoroughly in spring. Late spring is also best time to plant sprigs or stolons of improved bermudagrass and St. Augustinegrass. Lay sod of warm-season grasses in late spring through summer.

Seed

Sod

WATERING—The rule of 1 inch of water per week holds true for warm-season grasses. Growing season and distribution of rainfall are important variables. Best time to water is just before dawn. Check to be sure water soaks into soil.

MOWING—Mow frequently to maintain proper height. Try to reduce grass height by one-third or less with each mowing. Mowing frequency is determined by growth rate. Increase mowing frequency during late spring and summer—periods when the lawn grows fastest.

FERTILIZING—Bahiagrass and centipedegrass can be fed with one spring and one fall application. Heavy feeders such as bermudagrass and St. Augustinegrass need regular applications every 30 to 60 days. Make last fall application 1 month before lawn goes dormant.

DETHATCHING—Best time to dethatch warm-season grasses is 2 to 3 weeks after spring green-up. This timing favors fast recovery of lawn. Bermudagrass and zoysiagrass accept heavy dethatching. Dethatch centipedegrass, bahiagrass and St. Augustinegrass lightly.

AERATING—Aerate any time to reduce soil compaction and improve penetration of air, water, fertilizer and insecticide. Aerate prior to over-seeding to improve germination of winter lawn. Aeration will also reduce water runoff and increase water penetration.

WEEDS—Control summer annual weeds with early spring pre-emergent herbicide. Control winter annual weeds with fall application of a similar product. Spray winter weeds in dormant lawns with post-emergent herbicide.

Crabgrass

Annual bluegrass

Clover

INSECTS—Chinch bugs favor St. Augustinegrass. Spray early summer and again 2 to 3 weeks later to limit damage. Check for grubs spring and summer. Combat with insecticides midsummer and fall.

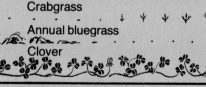

Chinch bugs

Grubs

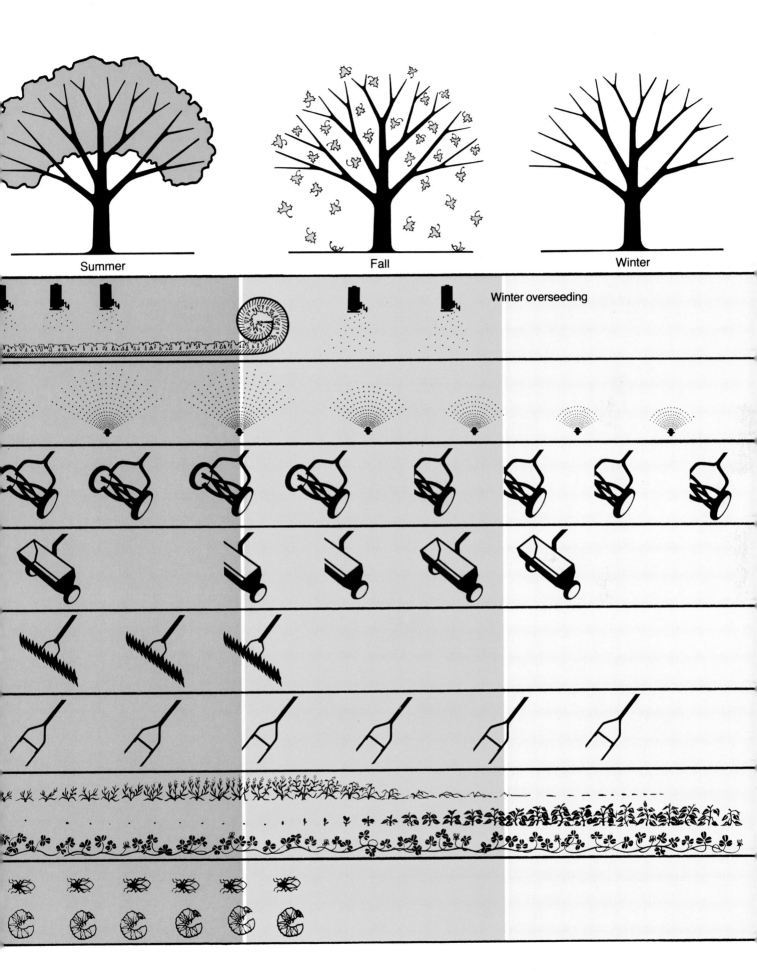

Summer

Fall

Winter

Winter overseeding

Lawn Care Schedule
Cool-Season Grasses

Cool-season grasses are the most important lawn grasses. They thrive throughout northern regions. They prefer brisk spring and fall temperatures between 60F and 75F (16C and 24C). Their growth habit is more upright, so they are cut higher than warm-season grasses. Essentially dormant through midsummer, they remain green if irrigated.

Illustrations below show basic timing of most important lawn chores utilizing simple hand tools.

Spring

PLANTING—Sow seed of Kentucky bluegrass, fescue and ryegrass in fall, while soil is still warm from summer but air is cool. Early spring is second-best planting time. Lay sod anytime or when available. Plant bentgrass sprigs in fall.

Seed

Sod

WATERING—Lawns need approximately 1 inch of water per week. In a few locations, annual rainfall is adequate, but most lawns need additional water from sprinklers. Water during early morning, before dawn if possible. Always water thoroughly.

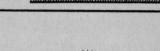

MOWING—Healthy and vigorous lawns need frequent mowings spring and fall. Reduce height of tall lawn gradually. Never cut more than one-third at once unless renovating. Raise cutting height and reduce frequency during summer to improve heat and drought tolerance.

FERTILIZING—Apply 75 percent of the lawn's yearly allotment of fertilizer in fall months, the remainder in spring. Limit single applications of fast-release fertilizers to 1 pound and slow-release fertilizers to 2 pounds actual nitrogen per 1,000 square feet.

DETHATCHING—Dethatch in early spring or early fall, just before peak growth periods. Kentucky bluegrass requires regular thatch removal. Of the cool-season grasses, turf-type ryegrasses and tall fescues are least prone to development of thatch.

AERATING—Aerate to reduce soil compaction and improve penetration of air, water, fertilizer and insecticide. Aerate sloping lawn to reduce water runoff and increase water penetration rate.

WEEDS—Use a pre-emergent herbicide in spring for crabgrass and similar summer annual weeds. Use pre-emergent herbicide in fall for annual bluegrass and similar winter annual weeds. Combine pre-emergent and post-emergent herbicides to eliminate perennial weeds such as oxalis.

Crabgrass

Annual bluegrass

Clover

INSECTS—Sod webworm infests just about every type of lawn. Check for these night feeders with pyrethrum test. See page 55. Manage Japanese beetle grubs with milky spore disease. Midsummer and fall insecticide treatments are necessary to control all other kinds of grubs.

Sod webworm larva and adult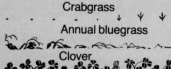

Grubs

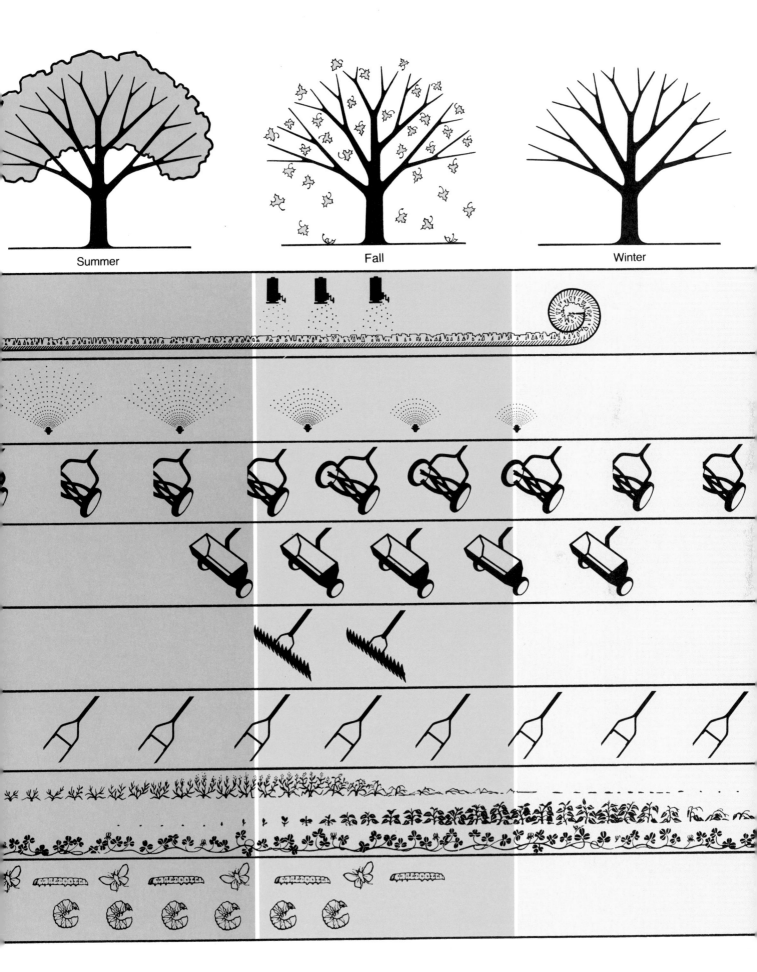

Summer

Fall

Winter

Ground Covers

What classifies a plant as a *ground cover* is often a matter of opinion. Plants that are *perennial, evergreen, trailing* or *clumping,* and *grow to one foot high or less* are potentially useful as ground covers. But this book has less rigid definitions. The following pages include some low shrubs, many perennial border "renegades," some flowering annuals and some herbs. The reason: If you choose a plant you like and it covers the ground, then it is a ground cover!

Ground covers are automatically associated with low maintenance—even neglect. Most require less time and upkeep than many plants, and certainly less than a lawn—*after they are established.* But until then, ground covers require considerable time, effort and expense—often equal to or greater than a lawn.

Few low-maintenance covers will become established and thrive on their own. Keep the following in mind to help ensure success with your ground cover plantings.

• Choose a plant that is adapted to your area. It should have a reasonable chance of thriving in the particular situation. For example, don't plant a sun-loving plant in the shade, or vice versa.

• Learn the plant's cultural requirements and meet them. The individual descriptions on pages 84 to 171 will tell you each plant's particular soil, sun, water and maintenance needs.

• Improve the soil to help plants become established faster and grow better. Adding amendments to the soil is one of the best investments you can make to ease future maintenance.

• Water newly planted ground covers regularly. This is especially important the first weeks after planting. Even the most drought-tolerant native plants require supplemental water the first one or two seasons.

• Weeds ruin more ground cover plantings than anything else. Don't let them get a foothold. Rid the soil of weed seeds as much as possible before planting, use a mulch and utilize herbicides if necessary.

Words frequently used to describe ground cover functions apply here. This planting of *Pachysandra terminalis* **fills** the lower spaces, creating a **balanced, layered** effect. It **links** path to shrubs and **blends** different plantings together. It **cools,** serving as **living mulch,** and **controls,** keeping weeds to a minimum.

Ground Cover Basics

SOIL

As with a lawn, the majority of ground covers prefer a fertile soil high in organic matter. Generally, soil preparation for lawns and ground covers is the same. The goal is to improve the soil in the root-zone area—the top 6 to 8 inches. The best way to do this is by adding organic matter. Add enough so that this top layer is one-third organic matter by volume. This means adding a 2- to 3-inch layer of an organic material such as sawdust, peat moss, ground bark, decomposed manure or compost over the soil, and working it in. "Raw," uncomposted organic material such as sawdust uses up nitrogen fertilizer when it decomposes. Add 1 to 2 pounds actual nitrogen per cubic yard of raw amendment.

Before you plant is the time to adjust the soil pH, which is determined by a soil test. Raise pH by adding ground or dolomitic limestone. Lower pH by adding sulfur. Charts that show amounts of organic matter, limestone or sulfur to use are on page 35.

If you do not test the soil, or a soil-test facility is unavailable, the general guide for preplant fertilizer calls for 1-1/2 to 2 pounds of 10-10-10 fertilizer per 100 square feet. See page 53 for a description of fertilizers and fertilizer formulas.

Sometimes improving the total soil area is neither necessary nor practical. If the area is exceedingly large or steep, complete soil amendment is not wise. Digging up and amending the soil could aggravate erosion problems. And, some native plants prefer unimproved, sandy soil instead of fertile soil high in organic matter.

When you plant wide-spreading shrubs such as *Ceanothus* or *Juniperus* species, amend the soil immediately surrounding the rootball, but do not add amendments to the entire area. Unless your soil is very sandy or heavy clay, it is best to fill the planting hole with the same soil that you took out. If you have a heavy clay or light, sandy soil, blend two parts native backfill soil with one part organic material such as compost, peat moss or shredded bark. If you are planting from containers, this 2:1 mix provides a transition between the usually lightweight container soil mix and native soil.

WEED CONTROL IN GROUND COVERS

Ground covers are not low-maintenance plants until they develop a dense, weed-choking cover of foliage. Until that time, it is possible to spend more time weeding your new ground cover planting than caring for a new lawn of comparable size. Depending on plant spacing and growth rate, this weed-battling period can last from a few weeks to a few years. After the planting establishes a cover, soil is shaded where weed seeds sprout and their growth is blocked. But even then, perennial weeds such as bermudagrass, field bindweed and nutsedge might invade. That's why it is very good advice to assume that some kind of weed control will be necessary, both before and after planting.

You'll find a chart listing the best herbicides for both lawns and ground covers on page 57.

Before planting—Where tough perennial weeds are not a problem, the best method of preplant weed control is repeated cultivations. Turn soil and existing weeds under with shovel or power tiller. Water to germinate weed seeds brought to the surface by the cultivation, then turn soil under again. Repeat this cycle until few weeds appear after watering.

A *nonselective herbicide* such as cacodylic acid can help with this process. Instead of repeat cultivations, spray new weed growth. This will save work and time because buried weed seeds are introduced to the surface with each cultivation.

Nonselective herbicides effective against both annual and perennial weeds are necessary if the planting area includes perennial weeds such as bermudagrass, dallisgrass or Johnsongrass. Two applications of an herbicide such as glyphosate are necessary to rid an area of such weeds.

Soil fumigants might be necessary where the weed problem is severe. Fumigants kill perennial and annual weeds, germinating seeds and most dormant weed seeds. Two of the best fumigants for home gardeners to use are calcium cyanamide and metham. Both require a waiting period of 3 to 6 weeks before soil can be planted. Other fumigants are available, such as the highly toxic methyl bromide. Only professional weed control operators use it.

After planting—Remember that a soil-shading ground cover is the best weed defense. Providing adequate water and nutrients for optimum growth will enable the ground cover to spread over the soil faster.

A thick layer of mulch aids growth of the ground cover and is one of the best methods of preventing weed invasion. A weed-free mulch shades the soil surface, preventing germination of weed seed waiting there. Weeds that do manage to grow through a mulch layer are easily pulled compared to weeds pulled from hard-packed soil.

Pre-emergent herbicides are great aids for control of summer and winter annual weeds. Apply pre-emergent herbicides just after planting and before weed seed germinate and begin growth. Remove sprouted or mature weeds in established plantings before applying the herbicide.

If you plan to use a pre-emergent herbicide after planting, set each plant deep enough to completely cover the root mass with soil. After planting and before applying the herbicide, water the planting area to settle the soil around the plants. Be certain to read the product label carefully to be sure it is safe to use around the ground cover you intend to plant.

Rainfall or a light watering is necessary to activate the pre-emergent herbicide chemical in the soil area where weed seeds germinate. On a newly planted slope, be careful that soil carrying herbicide does not run off onto lawn or other landscape plants.

PLANTING

Ground cover plants are available at the nursery in individual containers, in flats or in separate cells of plastic "6-paks." Containers are usually plastic or metal. Metal containers require cutting before you can plant them. They are awkward to cut at home, so let nursery personnel do it for you. But do not have containers cut unless you can plant that day. After cans are cut, plant roots dry quickly.

Arrange plants on the site in approximate planting positions. Make adjustments in spacing and position. Refer to the chart on page 76 for proper spacing between rows and the number of plants necessary.

Set large, woody plants at the same soil level as they were in their containers. If soil is loose from tilling, set plants slightly higher to allow for some settling.

When to plant—In general, early fall is the best time to plant ground covers. Temperatures are moderate, rainfall is plentiful and weed competition is less severe than in summer. Soil temperature cools more gradually than the air, so root growth continues further into fall than you might expect. By spring, plants are partially established and can grow with maximum vigor.

If you live where the soil freezes, plant in fall or spring. If you choose fall, plant soon after summer heat has passed to allow maximum time for establishment before freezing weather arrives. Use a mulch to insulate soil. This will keep the soil warmer long into fall. A mulch will also prevent premature thawing of frozen soil in spring, which can damage plants.

Planting on a slope—The degree of slope and threat of erosion determines the method of planting. In many cases, planting in a triangular or staggered fashion, firming small basins around each plant, will be adequate. A mulch of straw or shredded bark further protects soil. If planting on a steep slope or wherever erosion threatens, refer to Erosion Control on page 78.

Planting from Containers

1. Before planting, position plants in their containers to determine proper spacing. See chart, page 76.

2. Remove plant by lightly tapping, pressing or turning the pot upside down until rootball is free.

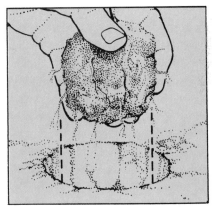

3. Amend the soil with organic matter if required. Make a hole large enough to accommodate rootball without bending roots.

4. Set plant at or slightly above soil line to allow for some settling.

5. Firm soil around plant just enough for it to remain upright. Too much pressing compacts top few inches of soil.

6. Water plant to settle the soil. Protect from sun and wind until roots are firmly established.

SPACING GROUND COVERS

Close spacing of plants will normally cover an area faster than wider spacing. The expense and mature size of plants are limiting factors. Don't space plants too closely. Keep the plant's growth habit and spread in mind as you plan spacing. *Hedera, Hypericum, Vinca* and *Pachysandra* species are usually planted on 1-foot centers. Fast-spreaders such as *Arctotheca* and *Baccharis* species are spaced on 18- to 36-inch centers. Shrubby, spreading plants such as *Abelia, Carissa, Juniperus, Rosa* and others need at least 36 inches between plants. Some require even more. For example, some *Ceanothus* species grow best with 5 feet of space between plants.

Positioning plants in a triangular pattern rather than rectangular pattern is most efficient for covering the ground. Triangular-spaced plants are all one distance on-center, and a shorter distance between rows. The chart on this page shows distances between rows for various spacing and the number of plants required for 100, 500 and 1,000 square feet of coverage.

WATERING

All newly planted ground covers deserve attentive watering. New plants have limited root systems, and are stressed when transplanted. No matter where you live, regular supplemental water is usually necessary for at least the first two seasons. Many shallow-rooted ground covers need attention during periods of drought. Even some native plants require occasional watering during summer months.

Just as for lawns, water ground covers *thoroughly* and *efficiently*. Soil should be moistened to the depth roots are expected to grow. The best watering method is one that adequately meets the needs of the ground cover. It should also ignore the needs of nearby weeds, and prevent water from running into the gutter.

Hand watering with a hose works fine for small areas and plants with shallow roots. But even in small areas you should check for adequate water penetration. Sprinkler watering is sufficient for somewhat larger areas. Adequate irrigation of a very large area requires some kind of permanent sprinkler system.

An underground sprinkler system for ground covers is basically the same as for lawns. The main difference is in the height of the riser or pop-up. You need to account for the ultimate height of the mature ground cover.

If you are considering an underground system, seek the advice of an irrigation consultant. It is money well spent. This is especially true if you are planting on a slope. A slope adds complex variables requiring experience to understand.

Drip watering—This important watering method is not practical for lawns or closely spaced ground covers such as *Hedera, Hypericum* or *Vinca*, but is ideal for larger, widely spaced plants. Drip systems apply water slowly and over a small area. Many types are available, and most are relatively simple to install. Drip systems can also be automated just as any lawn sprinkler system.

If you live in an arid climate or where water is in short supply, seriously consider installing a drip watering system. You'll save water due to reduced evaporation and reduced runoff. Drip watering systems can save up to 25 percent of the normal water cost.

Number of Plants You Will Need

On-center spacing*	Distance between rows	Plants/square foot	Plants/100 square feet	Plants/500 square feet	Plants/1,000 square feet
6 inches	5 inches	5	461	2,080	4,610
8	7	3	260	1,300	2,600
10	9	2	166	830	1,660
12	10	1	115	575	1,150
15	13	1	74	369	738
18	15	1	52	256	512
24	21	—	29	145	290
30	26	—	19	93	185
36	30	—	13	64	128
4 feet	3½ feet	—	7	36	73
5	4	—	5	23	46
6	5	—	3	16	32
8	7	—	2	9	18
10	8	—	1	6	12
12	10	—	1	4	8

*Distance from center of one plant to center of adjacent plants.

Drip watering systems are ideal for establishing native, drought-resistant ground covers on slopes. Most sprinklers apply water faster than the soil on a slope can absorb it, causing runoff and erosion. Watering by drip eliminates such problems.

It is most practical to install a simple, inexpensive system for watering native ground covers. After plants are able to live on natural rainfall and adjust to periods without water, remove or disconnect the system.

FERTILIZING

Ground cover plants have such varied nutrient needs that giving exact specifications is impossible. In general, ground covers need less fertilizer than lawns. But to maintain an attractive cover, regular applications of fertilizer are necessary. As a general guide, apply between 2 and 4 pounds of actual nitrogen per 1,000 square feet per year. Use a complete fertilizer such as a 10-10-10. The best time to fertilize is in the early fall. Spring applications are also helpful with some plants. One or two summer applications of fertilizer may also be required, depending on soil fertility and plants used. You can find more information in the individual ground cover descriptions beginning on page 84. Also refer to page 52 for more about fertilizers.

PROPAGATION

If you have a large area to cover with ground cover, or would like to use relatively expensive plants, propagating your own makes good sense. Or the planted area can gradually expand as the supply of plants increases.

Cuttings—This is the best way to propagate ground covers such as English ivy and euonymus. A cutting is a 3- to 6-inch long section of healthy growth. The best time to take cuttings varies with the plant. As a general rule, take cuttings after new growth is finished and before it has hardened. Determine this stage of growth by bending the stem or twig. If it can be bent 180 degrees without breaking, it is too soft. If it cannot be bent at all without breaking, it is either too hard or too thick.

Set cuttings in a flat filled with rooting medium composed of fast-draining potting soil. A mix with equal proportions of sand, peat moss and vermiculite works well. Maintain high humidity with a transparent cover of glass or plastic and be sure leaves receive adequate sunlight. It is a good practice to check the cuttings frequently, but allow 4 to 6 weeks for the first sign of root development.

Layering—This is the propagation method many ground cover plants use naturally. A stem grows over the top of the soil, and where moisture is adequate, roots develop. You can speed up this process by mounding soil over trailing stems. Rooted stems can be removed from parent plant and transplanted.

Division—This is a common method of increasing the number of ground cover plants. To divide plants, remove and replant side shoots or small plants from a large, established clump. Spring is typically the best time to divide ground covers. Liriope, star jasmine, periwinkle, daylily, ajuga and many others are commonly propagated this way.

Once you establish an area with ground cover, there is generally an ample supply of small plants available for division. It is simple to remove them to extend the planting or bolster thin areas without harming the main planting bed.

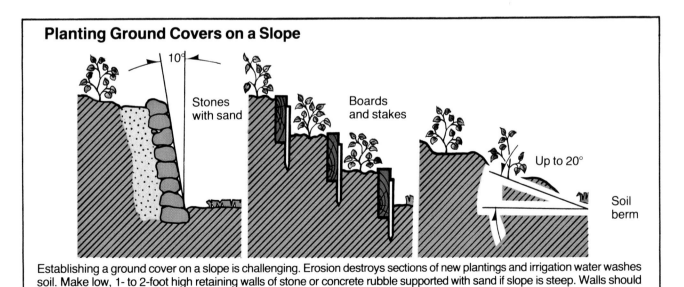

Planting Ground Covers on a Slope

Stones with sand

Boards and stakes

Up to 20°

Soil berm

Establishing a ground cover on a slope is challenging. Erosion destroys sections of new plantings and irrigation water washes soil. Make low, 1- to 2-foot high retaining walls of stone or concrete rubble supported with sand if slope is steep. Walls should span width of slope or position them in front of plants. Simple terraces strengthened by boards and stakes protect less-steep slope plantings. Plantings on slopes of 20 degrees and less are adequately served by soil berms that catch and hold water.

Jute netting was applied first, secured with heavy wire staples. Knife-cut holes permitted planting rooted cuttings of English ivy.

The slope at left 3 years later. Established ivy is attractive, supresses weeds and protects slope.

Erosion Control

Bare slopes are certain to erode. The impact of falling rain and water runoff soon creates gullies in the soil surface and washes topsoil away. Wind also erodes soil.

A complete cover of vigorously growing plants is one of the best ways to prevent erosion. But it is a challenge to establish a slope planting—bare slopes usually have little or no topsoil. In addition, subsoil is infertile and either rocky or heavy clay—subject to severe soil loss during periods of heavy rainfall. Protecting slopes from erosion involves three phases:

1. Diverting water away from slope with ditches and drain pipe.
2. Protecting soil with organic mulch or netting.
3. Planting and maintaining a ground cover.

Divert water—Build a small ditch or dike at the top of the bare slope to channel runoff to a suitable safe point such as a storm drain or heavily vegetated area. Try to keep the runoff path nearly level. If it must be steep, line path with concrete or rock or use corrugated pipe to carry water down steep slopes to a safe outlet.

Prevent water from flowing along one route on the slope. If soil is loose, cover potential gully area with plastic sheets overlapped like shingles. Overlapping is important: It prevents water from getting beneath and creating more severe problems. Anchor sheets with wire staples made of coathangers or with rocks. To plant, cut holes in plastic. Drip irrigation lines may be installed either below or on top of the plastic.

If slopes are steep, cut terraces to disperse the flow of water and trap the eroding soil. This will also make a better planting site. Terraces should be largest at the bottom of the slope where flow of water is greatest. A rough-graded surface is more erosion resistant than a smooth one.

There are "slope-stabilizing" chemicals available, but investigate them carefully before relying upon them. Some are of minimal value and may inhibit plant growth.

Apply a mulch—Mulches are beneficial used alone or in combination with seed or small plants. A well-secured mulch shields bare soil from the force of sprinkler drops or raindrops, as well as protecting it from running water. It also protects grass seed and young plants. Common mulches for slopes include straw, hay, bark or coarse wood chips, jute netting, excelsior padding, large rocks and gravel.

Commercial landscaping firms can "plant" a slope with a spray of wood fiber and seeds—a process called *hydromulching*. A hydromulch of wood fiber alone without quickly germinating seed is better than nothing, but less effective on a steep slope than other mulches.

You can use weed-free alfalfa hay as a mulch to protect soil until plants are well established. Spread evenly over the surface in a layer about 2 inches deep. About 100 pounds is required to cover 1,000 square feet. Firm it into the soil by punching every few inches with a spade, or cover with staked-down netting of jute, plastic or wire.

Bark, shredded fir bark, pine needles or coarse wood chips are useful as mulches, especially if partially mixed into the soil surface. They can discourage weed growth if layered more than 1 inch thick. Because bark mulch is usually lightweight and larger than wood chips, it is more likely to blow or wash off the slope. Generally, both wood chips and bark mulch are less effective for erosion control than an equal weight of straw.

Fill small gullies that develop after a rain with additional mulch, or protect with overlapped plastic sheets or jute netting.

Rock mulches are not commonly used on slopes, but do make a rough, protective seedbed and reduce both wind and water erosion. Pea gravel is likely to wash away. Use 1-1/2- to 2-inch diameter rock or larger.

Netting—Jute or excelsior mats of netting are effective if properly anchored. These are sold in rolls by horticultural supply outlets. Secure them to the slope with wire staples. It is important that the mat maintains close contact with the soil surface. On rough surfaces where soil contact is lost, erosion can occur under the mat. Mats are more expensive than straw or hay but are convenient to install, longer lasting and more effective.

Plant a cover—If desirable plants are not encouraged, weeds will probably take up residence. In some cases you may be able to take advantage of natural weed growth to control erosion. You can mow weeds or kill them with contact herbicides without disturbing the soil.

Grasses are the No. 1 choice where a fast cover is needed. Annual grasses and unirrigated perennial grasses become dry in warm-summer areas and can create a fire hazard. However, even dead grass protects the slope from erosion.

Plant grasses in fall before the rainy season. Spread seed by hand or use a mechanical spreader. Use a 20-20-20 starter fertilizer to provide at least 2 pounds of actual nitrogen per 1,000 square feet.

In general, annual grasses become established faster than perennial grasses. In either case, watering before the rainy season will speed establishment. Also consider adding a legume such as rose clover or birdsfoot trefoil to grass plantings. Legumes supply nitrogen, which helps the grasses to grow, and provide a habitat for quail and other wildlife.

Refer to the list on page 80 for other erosion-controlling slope covers. Check further with local nurseries and your county extension agent.

Preventing Erosion

Specific needs of individual sites in potential erosion areas vary, but usually include at least one of these illustrated techniques. Temporary aids such as mulches, burlap and overlapping sheets of plastic normally last until a vegetative cover is complete. For more elaborate solutions such as diversion ditches and stone terraces, consult a qualified engineer or landscape architect.

Ground covers **79**

Ground Cover Selection Guide

EROSION CONTROL

Plants that root as they spread and cover the ground completely are used to control erosion on banks and slopes. Roots of the plants listed below grow deeply and strongly. Some measure of drought tolerance is necessary because water is difficult to apply to slopes. Plant in fall to allow time for establishment before summer heat. Mulch to control weeds and to further protect soil. Grasses provide the fastest cover for slope stabilization. See page 78.

Abelia	Grasses: Brome
Arctostaphylos	Fescue
Arctotheca	Orchardgrass
Artemisia	Rye
Arundinaria	Grevillea
Atriplex	Heaths and heathers
Baccharis	Hedera
Ceanothus 'Point Reyes'	Hemerocallis
Centranthus	Hypericum
Cistus	Juniperus
Comptonia	Lantana—trailing types
Convolvulus	Lonicera
Coprosma	Lotus
Coronilla	Mahonia
Cotoneaster	Myoporum
Drosanthemum	Oenothera
Eschscholzia	Rosa
Euonymus	Rosmarinus
	Vinca

Sedum dasyphyllum

SHADE TOLERANT

These plants are some of the most reliable for the different degrees of shade. Those marked with an asterisk tolerate a combination of shade and dry soil.

Aegopodium*	Liriope
Anemone	Lysimachia
Asarum	Mentha
Asparagus*	Moss
Astilbe	Omphalodes
Campanula	Ophiopogon
Cymbalaria	Pachysandra
Euonymus	Paxistima
Ferns	Ranunculus
Galium*	Ribes*
Hedera	Sarcococca
Hosta*	Soleirolia
Hypericum	Taxus
Iris	Vancouveria
Lamiastrum	Vinca
Lamium	Waldsteinia
Laurentia	

DROUGHT TOLERANT

Drought tolerance is related to climate adaptation and healthy growth. Keep in mind that no plant is drought tolerant until established. Water deeply and infrequently after plants are established to promote drought tolerance. Plant roots are then forced to go deeply into the soil. If watering is shallow, roots stay near the surface and are more susceptible to water shortages.

Acacia	Grevillea
Achillea	Hypericum
African daisies	Iberis
Arctostaphylos	Ice plants
Artemisia	Juniperus
Baccharis	Lantana
Bamboo	Myoporum
Brooms	Oenothera
Ceanothus	Phyla
Centranthus	Polygonum
Cistus	Ribes
Convolvulus	Rosmarinus
Coprosma	Sedum
Coronilla	Teucrium
Cotoneaster	Thymus
Dalea	Verbena
Eschscholzia	

POPULAR AND RELIABLE

Here are the most commonly planted ground covers. They are proven to be adaptable to most climates and are widely available.

Ajuga	Juniperus
Arctostaphylos	Mahonia
Cotoneaster	Pachysandra
Euonymus	Potentilla
Hedera	Rosa
Hemerocallis	Sedum
Hosta	Thymus
Hypericum	Vinca
Iberis	

FIRE RETARDANT

Shape and growth habit are important when selecting a fire-retardant ground cover. For example, upright rosemary is not fire retardant but trailing rosemary is. Ground-hugging plants ignite less readily. Succulent plants that rapidly develop a cover several inches thick are ideal. Plants with high moisture or high salt content tend to be fire retardant.

Artemisia
Atriplex
Baccharis
Cephalophyllum 'Red Spike'
Cistus
Convolvulus
Delosperma 'Alba'
Gazania
Maleophora crocea
Myoporum
Phyla
Rosmarinus
Santolina
Sedum
Teucrium

BETWEEN STEPPINGSTONES

These are low creepers that will withstand footsteps now and then.

Armeria	Lobularia
Aubrieta	Mazus
Cerastium	Mentha
Chamaemelum	Phyla
Cotula	Sagina
Erodium	Soleirolia
Galium	Thymus
Hernaria	Veronica
Laurentia	

SHOWY FLOWERS

Many ground cover plants produce colorful flowers. By growing plants with different bloom periods for each season, you can have color the year-round.

African daisies	Hemerocallis
Agapanthus	Hosta
Astilbe	Iberis
Bougainvillea	Lantana
Campanula	Lobelia
Catharanthus	Lobularia
Centranthus	Lysimachia
Chrysanthemum	Myosotis
Convallaria	Oenothera
Convolvulus	Omphalodes
Dianthus	Phlox
Dyssodia	Rosa
Eschscholzia	Rosmarinus
Felicia	Spirea
Heaths and heathers	Trachelospermum
Helianthemum	Verbena

DRAPE AND TRAIL

Many of the best ground covers grow flat along the ground because they are pulled by gravity. The habit is accentuated if they grow over a wall or edge of a bank.

Arabis	Lamium
Arctostaphylos	Lantana
Asparagus	Lobelia
Baccharis	Lobularia
Bougainvillea	Lysimachia
Ceanothus	Myoporum
Cerastium	Osteospermum
Cotoneaster	Picea
Euonymus	Pinus
Felicia	Rosa
Gazania	Rosmarinus
Helianthemum	Santolina
Juniperus	Thymus

Vinca minor

LARGE AREAS

Two kinds of plants are listed here. Some, identified with an asterisk, will not stay confined to small areas. Give them a large area, or they will take it on their own. Others are manageable, but most effective in large-scale, mass plantings. Check the individual descriptions.

Acacia	Lantana
African daisies	Lonicera*
Baccharis	Lotus
Ceanothus	Myoporum
Comptonia*	Oenothera
Coronilla*	Pachysandra
Cotoneaster	Plumbago*
Euonymus*	Polygonum*
Forsythia	Prunus
Hedera	Rosa
Hemerocallis	Sedum
Hypericum*	Vinca
Juniperus	

Two species of *Thymus: T. praecox arcticus* flowers over layer of *T. pseudolanuginosus.*

POTENTIAL WEEDS

These plants are aggressive spreaders—perfect in some situations. But be aware of what you are planting. These plants have a reputation of being pests if they get out of control or if they grow too fast.

Aegopodium	Phalaris
Atriplex	Phyla
Aurundinaria	Polygonum
Coronilla	Ranunculus
Hypericum	Sagina
Lonicera	Veronica
Lysimachia	Vinca
Oenothera	

GROUND COVERS YOU NEED TO MOW

Many ground covers are best if mowed occasionally. The leafy carpet is more even and vigorous with young growth, and flower display is more dramatic. To mow these plants, use a rotary mower you can adjust to cut very high, or rent a weed mower. See plant descriptions for more details.

Achillea	Fragaria
Aegpodium	Hedera
African daisies	Hypericum
Arundinaria	Liriope
Aurinia	Lonicera
Baccharis	Phlox
Dianthus	Vinca
Euonymus	

BENEATH TREES AND SHRUBS

Plants that can grow in soil dominated by tree or shrub roots are among the most useful. Evergreen ground covers that grow several inches high such as *Vinca major* allow falling leaves to sift through, hiding the leaves.

Duchesnea	Ophiopogon
Epimedium	Pachysandra
Euonymus	Paxistima
Hedera	Polygonum
Hemerocallis	Ribes
Hypericum	Sarococca
Liriope	Vancouveria
Nandina	Vinca

SELF-SOWERS

Here are the carefree, easy-come, easy-go ground covers. Not for tidy perfectionists, they disappear with heat or cold. But they come back each season, sometimes in unexpected places. These plants might be considered weeds but for their appealing flowers or growth habit.

Aurinia	Felicia
Brooms	Geranium
Catharanthus	Lobelia
Centranthus	Lobularia
Chrysanthemum	Moss
Dimorphotheca	Myosotis
Dyssodia	Polygonum
Eschscholzia	Portulaca

BULB COVERS

These plants complement flowers or are simply used as a living mulch over the ground where bulbs are planted. Ground covers eliminate the mess of splashed soil when bulbs are watered, and cover the drying leaves of bulbs as they go dormant. Taller bulbs are usually combined with higher-growing ground covers. As a rule, ground cover should be half the height of flowering bulbs.

Arabis	Laurentia
Arenaria	Lobelia
Aubrieta	Lobularia
Aurinia	Lysimachia
Campanula	Mazus
Cerastium	Mentha
Chamaemelum	Myosotis
Cotula	Omphalodes
Cymbalaria	Phyla
Erodium	Potentilla
Galium	Sedum
Geranium	Soleirolia
Hedera	Thymus
Herniaria	Vancouveria
Iberis	Veronica
Juniperus	Vinca
Lamiastrum	Waldsteinia
Lamium	

REGIONAL FAVORITES

Some ground covers are popular and reliable in distinct regions of the United States. England is much like the Northwest, and Australia can be compared to the West.

North, Northeast and Eastern Canada

Arctostaphylos	Moss
Comptonia	Pachysandra
Coronilla	Paxistima
Euonymus	Picea
Forsythia	Pinus
Heaths and heathers	Potentilla
Hedera	Sedum
Juniperus	Vinca

Northwest and British Columbia

Arctostaphylos	Mahonia
Aubrieta	Moss
Aurinia	Oxalis
Broom	Paxistima
Gaultheria	Pernettya
Heaths and heathers	Picea
Hypericum	Pinus
Lysimachia	Prunus

Coastal Regions

Arctostaphylos	Heaths and heathers
Atriplex	Helianthemum
Baccharis	Hypericum
Carissa	Ice plants
Ceanothus	Juniperus
Cistus	Myoporum
Coprosma	Pittosporum
Fragaria	Ribes

Desert

Acacia	Lantana
African daisies	Oenothera
Atriplex	Phyla
Baccharis	Rosmarinus
Catharanthus	Santolina
Dalea	Verbena
Euonymus	Vinca
Grevillea	

West

Acacia	Eschscholzia
African daisies	Grevillea
Agapanthus	Myoporum
Arctostaphylos	Ribes
Baccharis	Rosmarinus
Ceanothus	Santolina
Convolvulus	Trachelospermum
Coprosma	

Mountain States

Arabis	Mahonia
Arctostaphylos	Phlox
Artemisia	Picea
Aubrieta	Rosa
Baccharis	Sedum
Cerastium	Thymus
Juniperus	Waldsteinia
Lysimachia	

South

Asarum	Ilex
Convallaria	Lamium
Euonymus	Liriope and Ophiopogon
Ferns	Pachysandra
Gardenia	Phlox
Hedera	Trachelospermum
Hosta	

Arctostaphylos hookeri 'Wayside'

LAWN ALTERNATIVES TO WALK ON

No cover is as perfect for play as a grass lawn. But the ground covers listed here can be mowed and will tolerate considerable foot traffic.

Achillea	Mazus
Arenaria	Moss
Chamaemelum	Phyla
Cotula	Thymus
Laurentia	Veronica
Lotus	

Phlox subulata

Achillea tomentosa is a delicate-looking plant with bright flowers—perfect for small areas.

Encyclopedia of Ground Covers

This encyclopedia includes approximately 200 of the top-rated ground cover plants. The basic criteria for inclusion was suitability for a particular geographical region or purpose, and availability. Many, such as *Juniperus, Hedera* and *Vinca* species are commonly available from local nurseries coast to coast. Others are common to one region and rare to others. The lists of ground covers on pages 80 to 83 reflect these and other distinctions uncovered by our catalog search.

A few ground cover plants included here are for the gardener seeking something different. Frequently, such plants are available only from speciality nurseries or by mail order. For your convenience, a listing of mail order nurseries appears on page 174.

All plants are listed alphabetically by their botanical name. Though perhaps unfamiliar at first, botanical names are by far the best way to avoid confusion. Occasionally, botanists differ regarding a plant's proper name. That's why this encyclopedia is cross-referenced throughout with both common names and botanical synomyms.

Planting and care information represents the combined knowledge of the author, numerous consultants and ground cover nurseries. Basics such as distance between plants, notable pest problems and treatments, and low-temperature hardiness are also found here.

Welcome to the world of ground covers!

Aaron's beard. See *Hypericum*

ABELIA GRANDIFLORA 'PROSTRATA'
Prostrate abelia

Prostrate abelia is a dwarf form of a well-known and deservedly popular shrub. Tough yet decorative, use it like 'Wheeler's Dwarf' pittosporum—massed for a solid cover on banks or in small groupings blended with other low ground covers. It has been used with much success on freeway banks and slopes.

Height is 1-1/2 to 2 feet and spread is to 4 feet. *A. g.* 'Sherwoodii' grows slightly taller and wider. New leaves are glossy red then become bright green when mature. Flowers are bell shaped and small, but abundant throughout summer.

Planting and care—Plant from containers 3-1/2 feet apart for solid cover. Give full sun, regular water and fertilizer. Drought tolerant once established.

Hardy to 0F (−18C). Partially deciduous when exposed to cold temperatures.

ACACIA REDOLENS

This is a low, spreading member of the fast-growing, evergreen, heat- and drought-tolerant *Acacia* family. It is a fine choice for erosion control on dry banks.

Height usually remains below 2 feet, but spread is wide—to 15 feet. Long, narrow, golden green leaves form a dense carpet. Yellow flowers, which cause some people allergy problems, appear in early spring.

Planting and care—Full sun is most important requirement. Any well-drained soil is okay. Plant in fall, usually from 1-gallon containers. Water frequently first season. Drought tolerant once established. Although excellent for most Southwest gardens, it is not completely

Aegopodium podagraria 'Variegatum' is a vigorous ground cover when grown in full sun. Clusters of white flowers produce large quantities of viable seed.

hardy. This prevents its use in colder areas of the high desert, such as Globe, Arizona and Albuquerque, New Mexico.

Hardy to about 20F (−7C).

ACHILLEA TOMENTOSA
Woolly yarrow

Woolly yarrow is an evergreen, hardy, sun-loving, easy-to-grow plant. Native to northern temperate areas. It is adapted to dry, exposed locations. It is not fussy about soil and is fire retardant.

This low-growing yarrow reaches 6 to 9 inches high, spreading about as wide. Fernlike leaves are light olive-green. Canary-yellow flowers are borne in flattish clusters. They completely cover foliage in spring.

Planting and care—Plants are available in a variety of sizes—1-gallon containers, flats or plastic packs. Space fast-spreading clumps 6 to 12 inches apart. Mow faded flowers with a rotary mower for repeat bloom. Divide clumps to propagate.

Hardy to −40F (−40C).

Adiantum pedatum. See *Ferns*

AEGOPODIUM PODAGRARIA 'VARIEGATUM'
Goutweed

Goutweed is an easy-to-grow plant for difficult situations. It is one of the few plants that thrive in dry, shaded soil.

Goutweed was popular with Victorian gardeners. They used it to edge flower borders, but usually discovered—as you might too—that it is not always a polite garden citizen. Because it spreads by both seeds and creeping roots, goutweed will eventually dominate any area where it is planted.

Plant is deciduous, grows 6 to 12 inches high and spreads indefinitely. Leaves are gray-green and have white edges. Parsleylike flowers appear in spring. Mow or clip them off before they mature to prevent or slow invasions of seedlings.

Planting and care—Some nurseries offer plants, usually in 1-gallon containers. More often, it is passed from neighbor-to-neighbor in shovel-dug clumps. Space clumps about 2 feet apart in full sun or part shade. Mow two or three times a season with a rotary mower set to cut as high as possible.

Plants die to the ground with first hard frost but roots are hardy to about −40F (−40C).

AGAPANTHUS
Lily-of-the-Nile

Agapanthus species are favorites of professional landscapers, but rarely considered ground covers. Plants can be used in many ways—as accents or border—and they excel in containers. They are complementary in color and texture when planted *en masse*, such as around a lawn.

Lilylike leaves are long and narrow. Flowers appear in ball-shaped clusters on straight stems that grow from base of plant. Peak flower display occurs in late spring and lasts as long as two months.

There are three species and five named forms of *Agapanthus*. Plants are usually blue or white, large or dwarf.

A. africanus produces blue flowers in spring and early summer on top of 1-1/2-foot stalks.

A. inapertus has deciduous leaves and deep blue flowers that hang from the top of large, 4-1/2-foot stalks.

(Continued on page 90)

Osteospermum fruticosum

AFRICAN DAISIES

As a group, African daisies include five different but closely related plants. They are *Arctotheca, Arctotis, Dimorphotheca, Gazania* and *Osteospermum* species.

ARCTOTHECA CALENDULA
Cape weed

Plants grow fast to make a thick, gray-green carpet over any kind of soil. They have been used extensively on slopes and banks along California's freeways. Foliage texture is a bit coarse close up, but cape weed is excellent for covering large areas. Interplanting cape weed with gazanias or ivy softens that coarse look and produces an attractive cover.

Cape weed is an evergreen perennial, growing 1 foot high or less and spreading as much as 18 inches in one season. Leaves are gray-green, thick and have deeply indented edges. Bright yellow, 2-inch wide flowers cover foliage in late spring and occur intermittently through summer.

Planting and care—You will typically find plants in flats. Space

African daisies blend to create a colorful, striking effect. Yellow *Arctotheca calendula* is in foreground, with purple and white *Osteospermum fruticosum.*

clumps 15 inches apart for a fast cover. More distant spacing is acceptable. If possible, mow or trim cape weed once a year to rejuvenate plants and improve their appearance. Excellent heat and drought tolerant once established.

Temperatures of about 24F (−4C) will damage leaves, but recovery is fast in spring.

ARCTOTIS HYBRIDS
African daisy

These are annual African daisies, primarily valued for their early spring flowers. Height may reach 18 inches but is usually less. Leaves are hairy, fairly coarse in appearance with deep indentations. Flowers are about 3 inches in diameter.

They may be orange, purple, cream, red, pink or yellow. Flowers always have a dark ring around an almost-black center.

Several strains of *Arctotis* are available. Normally you will find those known as Giant Mixed or T.M. Hybrids in seed packets or in the bedding plant section of nurseries. A new group of hybrids—resulting from a cross of *Venidium fastuosum* and *Arctotis*—are perennials with larger flowers and plants. Inquire at your local nursery. Also see Sources, page 174.

Planting and care—In mild climates plant *Arctotis* in fall—they will live through the winter, behaving like a perennial. Plant in early spring elsewhere. Flowers look best the first spring. Plants will seed themselves, but following generations will produce only orange flowers. Take cuttings if you want to maintain flower color.

Hardy to about 24F (−4C).

DIMORPHOTHECA
Cape marigold

Cape marigold is a colorful annual that blooms in winter and spring. It is perhaps the best and most colorful ground cover for Southwest desert gardens. Simply give them full sun and a modest amount of water. They will grow well in almost any soil.

There are two important species. *D. pluvialis* is less common and noted for its single variety, 'Glistening White'. It grows 8 inches high with 4-inch, white flowers that have blue centers. Leaves are deeply toothed.

Hybrids of *D. sinuata* are more common. Leaves are slightly wider and shorter and lack the deep, regular indentations or teeth of *D. pluvialis*. Flowers are 1-1/2 inches wide and usually have orange petals. Hybrids may be white, yellow, salmon, apricot or orange. Flower centers are dark brown.

Planting and care—Plant in fall, if you live where winter gardening is possible. Broadcast seeds and press them into the soil. Water regularly to germinate and establish plants if rains are infrequent. Plants will reseed themselves, although the range of flower colors will gradually diminish.

Hardy to about 20F (−7C).

GAZANIA
Gazania

Gazanias are perennial, evergreen African daisies. They provide a tremendous display of color that peaks in spring but continues until frost. There are many hybrids of gazanias but only two basic types—*clumping* and *trailing*.

Arctotheca calendula makes a carpet of color under and around crape myrtle.

Osteospermum ecklonis is a taller, mounding species of trailing African daisy.

Orange and yellow varieties of clumping gazania are interplanted to make this stunning display. All-at-once flowering can be promoted by mowing plants in early spring.

Clumping gazanias—These are mounding plants, normally classified as *Gazania rigens*. Leaves are toothed, dark green on top and gray-green underneath. Daisylike flowers are 3 inches wide. Plant them 1 foot apart to make a solid cover, or use in containers or rock gardens.

Three strains of clumping gazanias are available as seed, rarely as plants. Several named varieties are available only as plants. Colorama strain flowers are white, gold, yellow orange, cream, red, yellow and pink. Fire Emerald strain flowers are lavender-pink, pink-rose, orange, yellow, cream and bronzy red. All have a green center ring. Sunshine strain has very large, 5-inch flowers of mixed colors.

Named hybrids of *G. rigens* include:

'Aztec Queen'—Yellow flowers with bronze stars.

'Burgundy'—Wine-red flowers.

'Copper King'—Immense flowers produced in great profusion. Very colorful, bright orange petals with brown center stripes. More cold hardy than most other gazanias.

'Fiesta Red'—Dark red flowers.

'Gold Rush'—Large, clear orange flowers ringed black in the center.

'Moonglow'—Double, golden yellow, 2-1/2-inch flowers. Very free-flowering.

'Orange'—Brilliant orange with small, black center.

'Pink Hybrid'—Rosy pink with reddish purple undertones.

'Rainbow'—Orange-gold flowers similar to 'Copper King' but double instead of single flowers.

'Royal Gold'—Bright yellow, double flowers.

Trailing gazanias—These are usually considered a subspecies of clumping gazania, *Gazania rigens leucolaena*. Flowers are smaller and entirely yellow. Leaves are silvery and not toothed. Wide-spreading stems allow plants to be spaced 5 feet apart for a solid cover within two seasons at most. Use on banks or let plants drape over low walls.

Hybridizers have crossed trailing and clumping gazanias to obtain larger flowers on spreading, but less gangly plants. Notable varieties are:

'Sun Burst'—Deep orange, 2-inch flowers become light orange at the petal tips. Silvery gray leaves.

'Sun Gold'—Very compact habit. Deep buttery yellow flowers bloom the year-round.

'Sunrise Yellow'—Compact spreader with bright green leaves and large, 2- to 3-inch, clear yellow flowers.

Planting and care—Both clumping and trailing types have similar daisy flowers. Either can be used as summer annuals in cold-winter areas. Both are heat tolerant and not particular as to soil. They grow best if given moderate water and fertilizer. Rejuvenate planting beds by mowing once a year.

Hardy to 20F (−7C).

OSTEOSPERMUM
Trailing African daisy, Freeway daisy

A large bank planting of *Osteospermum* species in full flower is a stunning sight. Leaves are completely covered by a layer of white flowers that bounces light back like a giant reflector.

Osteospermum species are excellent slope covers. They are evergreen and somewhat fire retardant if well watered.

There are two important species and three popular named forms of *Osteospermum: O. ecklonis* is the larger version. It grows 3 or 4 feet high and spreads 1 to 2 feet per year. White, 3-inch flowers have dark centers and are light purple on back. Bloom is most profuse in spring.

O. fruticosum is the more common species. It grows fast, covering as much as a 4-foot circle in one season. Height is usually less than 1 foot. It is more easily mowed and cut back. Flowers reach peak bloom in spring but also produce abundant bloom in the fall. Popular named forms of *O. fruticosum* are:

'African Queen'—Large, purple flowers fade to white by the second day.

'Burgundy Mound'—Low growing to 10 inches. Spreads in a more mounding, restrained fashion than other African daisies.

'Hybrid White'—More upright growth habit. Blooms profusely fall and spring.

Planting and care—These spreading perennials are tolerant of many soil types and require full sun. In fact, flowers will open only in full sun. Plant from containers or flats, preferably in early fall. Drought tolerant once established, plants survive on one or two waterings a season, depending on soil type and exposure—west and south are hottest. Avoid overwatering in heavy clay soils, which promotes root rot.

In time, plants become stiff and shrubby. Some varieties develop a thick mat of stems and dead leaves, similar to Algerian ivy. Because of this, it is best to mow or cut them back once every year or two in spring, just before the period of greatest growth.

Like other African daisies, *Osteospermum* species are hardy to 20F (−7C).

Deep orange 'Sun Burst' and yellow 'Sun Gold' trailing gazanias spread around junipers.

Dimorphotheca, cape marigold, is suitable as a border plant.

Agapanthus species planted *en masse* produce a dramatic color display.

Ajuga reptans 'Variegata' makes inches-high carpet under *Rhododendrons*.

(*Agapanthus*, continued from page 85)

A. *orientalis* is the most common species. Many nurseries catalog them as *A. africanus*. Keep in mind that if you buy "white" or "blue" Lily-of-the-Nile, you will get *A. orientalis*. Foliage clumps are 2-1/2 to 3 feet high. Flower stalks may be 5 feet tall. Flowers are white or blue and may be double or giant.

'Mooreanus' is offered by Wayside Gardens as a cold-hardy selection. Their catalog says: "It will winter over with little or no protection where temperatures do not go much below zero." It features blue flowers on top of 18-inch stalks. A white version, 'Mooreanus Snowball', is also available.

'Peter Pan' is a dwarf form. It is common and widely available in mild-climate regions, or by mail order. Leaves make a mounding clump 10 inches high. Flowers are blue and appear on stalks that are usually less than 18 inches tall. Plant 8 inches apart for a solid cover.

'Queen Anne'—Clumps spread 12 to 16 inches wide. Flowers are blue and appear over a long season on stalks that reach 2 feet high. Plant 10 inches apart for solid cover.

'Rancho White'—Essentially a white form of 'Peter Pan'. Sometimes sold as 'Peter Pan Albus'.

Planting and care—Lily-of-the-Nile are easy to grow. Full sun is best but some shade is okay. Any well-drained soil is fine. Plant from 1- or 5-gallon containers in fall if possible, but plant any time in mild-winter regions. Pests are not a problem, and plants survive on little water and fertilizer once established. Maintenance consists of removing dead flowers stalks and dividing plant clumps every few years, in spring. For a solid ground cover, plant 2 feet apart.

Hardy to about 20F (−7C).

AJUGA REPTANS
Carpet bugle

Ajuga reptans is an excellent, showy cover for moist, slightly shaded locations. Plants are very dramatic in flower but their primary virtue is colorful, shiny leaves. Dark green leaves grow 2 to 4 inches wide but are usually larger in heavy shade. Blue flowers are produced on 6-inch spikes. Carpet bugle does not make a permanent plant-and-forget ground cover. Plants require occasional grooming.

Ajuga genevensis and *A. pyramidalis* are related species. They do not produce runners so are more rock garden plants than ground covers. Both have been crossed with *A. reptans*—naturally, and by hybridizers—to produce many varieties. Catalogs list the following popular varieties:

'Alba'—Leaves are dark green. White flowers are produced on 6-inch spikes.

'Burgundy Lace'—Leaves are burgundy-wine in color with variegations of white and pink.

'Gaiety'—Leaves are a striking bronzy purple; flowers are blue.

'Giant Bronze'—Metallic, crisp-textured leaves are larger than other ajugas. Plants may grow to 9 inches tall in shade. Also known as 'Giant Ajuga'. Hardy to −5F (−21C).

'Giant Green'—Bright green leaves.

'Jungle Bronze'—Small, rounded leaves are wavy with slightly serrated margins. Exhibits mounding-type growth. Hardy to −5F (−21C).

'Jungle Green'—Not as mounding as 'Jungle Bronze'. Green leaves are large and rounded with crisp edges. Hardy to −5F (−21C).

'Pink Beauty'—Lustrous green leaves on 4- to 5-inch plants. Pink flowers appear May through June.

Ajuga reptans 'Variegata' creeps around a stone walkway.

Akebia quinata is an old-fashioned, deciduous vine, useful as a mounding, spreading ground cover.

'Purpurea'—Very similar to common ajuga except leaves are darker bronze. Also sold as 'Atropurpurea'. 'Silver Beauty'—Leaves are colored light cream, dark green and white. 'Variegata'—Leaves edged with creamy yellow.

Planting and care—Plants spread by runners to form a dense mat. Plant in spring or fall from flats or plastic packs, 6 to 12 inches apart. Rich, moist soil is ideal.

Ajuga should be watered and fertilized regularly. Remove dead flowers by clipping or mowing. Plants or sections occasionally die out from leaf or root diseases. Divide healthy plants to fill in bare spots.

Ajuga generally prefer shade, although varieties with variegated leaves are better with full or nearly full sun. Keep ajuga confined—they are known to creep from a flower border into lawn to become a pest.

Hardy to −40F (−40C) except as noted for certain varieties. Protect from cold winter winds.

AKEBIA QUINATA
Five-leaf akebia

Akebia is a *utility plant:* it has a variety of landscape uses. Trained and frequently pruned along a trellis or fence, it will assume a delicate, refined look. If you allow it to climb up and over fences and buildings, it will have a wild, woodsy appearance. Basically, it is a vine, but like many vines does an admirable job of covering the ground. Height is about 2 feet when allowed to sprawl over ground. Plants will climb up and into nearby trees and shrubs. Keep that in mind when you choose a planting site.

Medium green leaves are borne on stalks and divided into 2- to 3-inch leaflets. Wine-red flowers appear in spring but are not very decorative. Edible but tasteless fruit appear after flowers.

Planting and care—Plant in sun or shade. Akebia grows in almost any soil. Allow approximately 5 feet between plants. Hard, to-the-ground pruning will not destroy the plant and serves to rejuvenate and contain it.

Hardy to −20F (−30C).

Algerian ivy. See *Hedera*

Allegheny pachysandra. See *Pachysandra*

American barrenwort. See *Vancouveria*

ANEMONE HYBRIDA
Japanese anemone, Windflower

Japanese anemone is a well-known, fall-blooming perennial that is hardy, deciduous and long-lived. It can also be appreciated for its virtues as a ground cover.

Plants are a bit slow to establish but begin to spread fast after two or three seasons. Eventually they form a dense, summer-long cover. Plants grow about 1 foot high and form 3- to 4-foot wide clumps within a few seasons. Leaves are dark green, soft and have 3 to 5 lobes. They develop directly from a ground-level crown.

Many varieties are available. They differ mainly by their flowers. Most flowers are 1 to 3 inches wide borne on top graceful, 2- to 4-foot stems. They may be single or semi-double, or double in white, pink or rose. Their graceful waving in a slight breeze inspired the name *windflower.*

Popular varieties are:

'Alba'—Single. White, 2- to 3-inch wide flowers.

'Margarette'—Double. Pink and very free-flowering.

'Profusion'—Semidouble. Deep rose-pink and free-flowering.

Arctostaphylos uva-ursi stays low and spreads wide among *Pinus mugo* and *Juniperus* species. Bark mulch helps control weeds.

'September Charm'—Single. Delicate, silvery pink subtly shaded with rose.

'Whirlwind'—Semidouble. White flowers.

Anemone vitifolia 'Robustissima' is very similar in appearance to *Anemone hybrida*, but is more cold hardy and more tolerant of wet soil. Plants are robust and develop many silver-pink flowers on 2-1/2- to 3-foot stems. Specimens have survived in the Low-Maintenance Test Garden of the Arnold Arboretum with minimum winter protection, and where the soil was too wet for other varieties.

Planting and care—Look for anemones in spring in the "Perennials" section of the nursery. Shady areas with moist, well-drained soil are ideal. Wet, clay soils encourage winter root rot. In summer, be generous with water if soil tends to dry rapidly. Propagate by division.

Hardy to −20F (−29C). Apply a mulch around plant roots after soil freezes in fall to prevent premature thawing and resulting heaving.

Annuals. See African daisy, *Catharanthus, Eschscholzia, Lobelia, Lobularia, Myosotis, Pelargonium, Portulaca* and *Verbena*.

ARABIS CAUCASICA
Wall rockcress

Wall rockcress is an old-fashioned, low, spreading, evergreen plant. Although generally considered a rock garden or edging plant, it is in every way a ground cover. Try it as a cover over bulbs, tucked into corners or let it spill over tops of walls. Plants grow 6 to 10 inches high and spread 12 or more inches. Leaves are silver-gray, smooth and relatively thick. In early spring, 1/2-inch white flowers completely cover plant. *Arabis caucasia variegata* leaves have creamy-yellow margins.

Varieties of *A. c. variegata* include:
'Floreplena'—Early flowering with double white flowers on 6- to 8-inch stems.
'Spring Cream'—Bright, clear pink and large flowered.

Related species include:
Arabis alpina has more textured leaves and is available in both pink and white-flowered forms.
A. procurrens normally grows only a few inches high, with dark green leaves and abundant white flowers. It spreads by underground runners.

Planting and care—Mail order nurseries will send you plants in small plastic pots. Your local nursery likely keeps them in 1-gallon containers, perhaps in flats.

Plant 8 inches apart to make a solid cover. Gritty, sandy, fast-draining soil is best. Some drought is okay but it should have afternoon shade in hot areas. Shear spent flowers after bloom. Wall rockcress seems to need a good winter chill—in warm-winter areas it is often short-lived.

Hardy to about −40F (−40C).

ARCTOSTAPHYLOS
Kinnikinnick, Manzanita

Kinnikinnick is a very hardy, low, wide-spreading, evergreen ground cover of the manzanita clan. Unlike most of its relatives, it prefers a cool and moist environment with well-drained soil. In the Pacific Northwest it is grown to perfection. Mountain area gardeners endorse it. Eastern forms of kinnikinnick are favored in New England and the Maritime Provinces of Canada, especially along the Atlantic coast. It is excellent on steep slopes, under deciduous oaks, around rocks and spilling over walls.

Arctostaphylos uva-ursi works well as a large-area slope cover.

Don't let the labels of "eastern" and "western" forms trouble you. Botanists detect no basic difference, although some argue that the many forms of kinnikinnick are actually dozens of subspecies. The best advice is to obtain plants from a local source.

Plant is low growing, rarely more than 10 inches high. It spreads slowly, to 15 feet wide and more. Branches root as they creep. By the time a plant becomes a 15-foot mat you can't tell where one plant begins or ends.

Leaves are bright, glossy green, leathery and about 1 inch in diameter. They completely cover stems, making a dense cover. Cold weather gives them a reddish cast.

Urn-shaped flowers are only 1/3 inch long, white, but sometimes pinkish. They appear in spring. Bright red fruit that follow are loved by birds.

Two common selections of kinnikinnick are 'Radiant' and 'Point Reyes'. 'Radiant' has relatively light green leaves that are widely spaced. It sets a heavy fruit crop. 'Point Reyes' has darker green, closely set leaves. It is more heat and drought tolerant than 'Radiant'.

Four other manzanitas are available that perform very well as ground covers in western gardens:

Arctostaphylos edmundsii 'Carmel Sur'—Very highly rated ground cover. Fast growing to 6 feet wide and 1 foot high. Creeping stems produce short, erect branches that feature neat, gray-green leaves. Tolerant of garden conditions but does require good soil drainage. Rarely produces flowers.

A. 'Emerald Carpet'—Makes a dense, uniform 1- to 2-foot high carpet. Spreads to 6 feet. Leaves are fine textured, almost round and about 1/2 inch long. They remain a bright, emerald-green even through prolonged drought. But inland plantings will need deep, bimonthly waterings and good drainage. The plant is excellent for hillsides.

A. hookeri 'Monterey Carpet'— Becomes a dense, 1-foot high, 10-foot wide ground cover. Branches are dark red; leaves are glossy green. Likes some shade and requires good soil drainage. Produces white flowers.

A. h. 'Wayside'—Relatively fast growing to 3 feet high and about 8 feet wide. Spreading, rooting branches develop into fairly open

ground cover. Supply plants with light shade and good soil drainage. Excellent with native oaks.

All *Arctostaphylos* are propagated by cuttings. Only named varieties are or should be available in nurseries.

Planting and care—Fall is the best planting time. Plant kinnikinnick approximately 3 feet apart if purchased in gallon containers. Space closer if using cuttings. Plants are fairly exacting in soil requirements. Well-drained, sandy, acid soil is required for success. Plants need water in summer, especially the first season or two. Kinnikinnick is not recommended for south or west-facing slopes in inland areas. Leaf tips will brown if there is too little water.

Kinnikinnick is slow to start. Keeping weeds out of planting beds is the major problem. Use a mulch to retard weed growth and to preserve soil moisture for the rooting branches.

One of the most hardy ground covers. Survives temperatures as low as −50F (−45C).

Arctotheca calendula. See African Daisies

Armeria maritima is colorful yet surprisingly drought tolerant.

Arctotis hybrids. See African Daisies

Arenaria. See Moss

ARMERIA MARITIMA
Common thrift

Common thrift is a neat and tidy evergreen plant, long favored for use in rock gardens. It also works well in front of borders, in containers and between steppingstones.

Plant grows 3 to 6 inches high, forming a clump up to 18 inches wide. Gray-green leaves are narrow and grasslike but stiff. Dense, globular, 3/4-inch flowers are borne in profusion on top of 10-inch stems. They are typically pink but selected forms may be white, rose or red. Flowers are in bloom throughout spring, summer and fall in coastal areas. In other regions flowers are most abundant spring and fall.

The many *Armeria* species hybridize freely, resulting in many cultivated forms. Some of the more common are:

'Alba'—A small, choice form with pure white flowers.
'Brilliant'—Bright pink flowers.
'Laucheana'—Densely tufted, 6-inch plants. Flowers are intense rose-pink.

'Royal Rose'—Abundance of bright pink flowers on top of 15-inch stems.
'Vindictive'—Deep rose-red flowers.

Planting and care—Plants are available in flats, plastic packs or gallon containers. Fall is best planting time. Space plants 8 to 10 inches apart. Relatively poor, dry but well-drained soil is best. Rich, moist soil encourages root rot and generally causes plants to be short-lived. Full sun is necessary at the coast, but afternoon shade is fine, perhaps beneficial, elsewhere. To maintain plantings, remove faded flowers with a mower or clippers. Apply a balanced fertilizer such as 10-10-10 in the fall. Propagate by dividing plants in spring.

Hardy to −50F (−45C).

ARTEMISIA
Silver spreader, Angel's hair

Artemisia is a large and varied genus that includes many drought-tolerant, silvery gray plants. Two that serve particularly well as ground covers are *Artemisia caucasica*, commonly called silver spreader, and *A. schmidtiana*, angel's hair. They

both make striking border or accent plants.

Silver spreader grows from 3 to 6 inches high and eventually forms a clump 2 feet wide. It came to nurseries and gardens via the University of California at Riverside and their Forest Fire Laboratory. It is fire resistant and a good choice for a bank cover around Southwest homes surrounded by flammable hillside growth.

Angel's hair grows 2 feet high and spreads 1 foot wide. Look for 'Silver Mound'. It is lower—6 to 12 inches high—and makes an interesting low border. Silver-white leaves are fernlike with a woolly texture, and are fragrant when crushed.

Planting and care—Plants are normally available in 1-gallon containers. Plant in fall in any well-drained soil. Space plants about 18 inches apart. Both species tolerate extremes of heat and drought. Once established, little or no water is needed in summer. Feel free to cut plants back severely in early spring if necessary to rejuvenate. New growth will cover plant by fall.

Silver spreader is hardy to −20F (−29C). Angel's hair is hardy to −10F (−24C).

Asarum caudatum grows best in shade and moist soil.

Asparagus densiflorus 'Sprengeri' drapes gracefully over a wall.

Arundinaria. See Bamboo

ASARUM
Wild ginger

Given the right conditions—heavy shade and moist, humus-rich soil—the gingers make beautiful, fast-spreading ground covers. Many species are available. Most are native to North America; one is native to Europe. Roots have a pungent quality, vaguely reminiscent of tropical, culinary ginger. In no other way are the plants related.

Plants form a mat 6 to 10 inches high with a similar spread. Green leaves are heart shaped, 2 to 7 inches across. Cold weather gives them a purple tint. Bell-shaped flowers are an unusual purple-brown color. They appear in spring but are hidden by leaves.

Commonly available species are:

Asarum canadense, Canadian wild ginger. Deciduous. Native to much of northeastern United States and Canada. Hardy to −34F (−40C).

A. caudatum, British Columbian wild ginger. Evergreen. Native to western Canada and south to California's Santa Cruz Mountains. Excellent under redwoods. Glossy green leaves. Attractive, high-quality ground cover. Hardy to 0F (−18C).

A. europaeum, European wild ginger. Evergreen. Spreads by underground runners. Hardy to −20F (−29C).

A. shuttleworthii 'Callaway'. Evergreen. Spreads by underground runners. Selected form of a southeastern native originating at Callaway Gardens, Pine Mountain, Georgia. Leaves are mottled, smaller than the species. Hardy to 0F (−18C).

Planting and care—Plant in spring from divisions or containers 8 to 15 inches apart. Water regularly through summer. Protect from slugs and snails.

Refer to descriptions of species for hardiness.

ASPARAGUS DENSIFLORUS 'SPRENGERI'
Sprenger asparagus, Asparagus fern

Sprenger asparagus is a popular house plant. It also serves as an excellent, outdoor container plant and evergreen ground cover in mild-winter areas. It is especially suited to raised planters. Cut foliage is attractive in arrangements.

Growth habit is open and mounding to 2 feet high. Bright green leaves are needlelike and reach 3 to 5 feet long. New leaves project from a ground-level clump. Older plants produce small, white, 3/8-inch flowers in spring, followed by round, shiny, bright red berries in fall.

'Sprengeri Compacta' is lower growing, to 1-1/2 feet, and has more closely set leaves.

Planting and care—Plants are available in various sizes of containers. Fall is normally the best planting time, but anytime is okay. Space plants 1 to 2 feet apart, in full sun or some shade. No soil preference; plants also tolerate salty soil. Excellent drought tolerance after they are established. Plants do look more attractive with regular water and fertilizer.

Hardy to 25F (−4C).

ASTILBE JAPONICA
False spiraea

False spiraea is a reliable perennial with brightly colored flowers.

Astilbe japonica at peak flower. Cut back after flowering and divide clump every 3 to 5 years.

Massed or arranged in slowly expanding drifts, they also make a good ground cover for shaded areas with moist soil. False spiraea is especially beautiful planted near streams or ponds.

Height, flower color and bloom period vary with the particular variety, of which there are many. Most are 18 to 30 inches high and have leaves divided into tooth-edged leaflets. Bright white, pink or red flowers appear in late spring.

The related *Astilbe chinensis* 'Pumila' is much lower, reaching about 4 inches high, and spreads more. Pink flowers appear in summer.

Planting and care—Plants are normally available in 1-gallon containers. Shop for plants in late spring so you can chose a flower color you like. Partially shaded, rich soil is best. Roots are shallow, so don't cultivate near plant. Mulch with oak leaf mold, if available, or with other organic mulch. Requires regular watering. Cut back faded flowers. Propagate by division.

Hardy to −20F (−29C).

Athyrium. See Ferns

ATRIPLEX SEMIBACCATA

Australian saltbush, Creeping saltbush

All *Atriplex* species are deep-rooted plants and extremely tolerant of heat, drought and poor, salty soil. Australian saltbush tolerates these poor conditions and is fire retardant. It is an excellent, fast-growing, low-maintenance ground or bank cover around southwestern hillside homes.

Plant grows about 1 foot high and quickly spreads several feet to make a rangy but dense mat. Leaves are about 1/2 to 1-1/2 inches long, gray and closely set.

'Corto' is a superior variety with the most uniform growth habit. Leaves have a gray-green cast. It reaches up to 10 inches high and spreads to 6 feet wide.

Planting and care—Container-grown plants are available. Plant in spring on 3-foot centers to make solid cover within one season. Tolerant of soil quality, but does need good drainage. Give regular water the first season. Propagate by seed.

Hardy to 15F (−9C).

AUBRIETA DELTOIDEA
Common aubrieta

An evergreen rock garden plant, common aubrieta is very popular in Northwestern and mountain gardens. Its colorful bloom appears in early spring. Plants are often combined with other spring bloomers such as *Arabis*, *Aurinia*, *Iberis* and *Phlox* species. Try growing aubrieta in or on top of stone walls, between steppingstones and as a bulb cover.

Plants grow as a mat 2 to 6 inches high and 1 foot or more wide. Tiny leaves are gray-green. Many named varieties are available in shades of rose, red and purple.

Planting and care—Propagate named varieties by fall cuttings. Sow seed of common kinds in spring. Plant in full sun. Well-drained soil is important, especially in winter. Aubrieta is relatively drought tolerant in summer but requires water before and during flowering if rains are light. Remove faded flowers before seed set.

Hardy to −20F (−29C).

AURINIA SAXATILIS
Basket-of-gold

Basket-of-gold is a mat-forming perennial of the mustard family. It

Baccharis pilularis 'Twin Peaks #2' needs little watering after it is established. Occasional misting washes away dust and improves plant appearance.

'Twin Peaks #2' replaced a grass lawn that formerly carpeted this front yard. Maintenance is negligible by comparison.

is hardy and persistent in most gardens, and one of the first to bloom in spring. Use as a border accent, draping over or on top of stone walls and in rock gardens.

Plants grow 8 to 12 inches high, spreading 12 inches wide. Leaves are gray-green and 2 to 5 inches long. Bright yellow flowers are small and arranged in tight clusters.

Varieties are:

'Citrina'—Abundant, lemon-yellow flowers.

'Compacta'—Bright yellow flowers, compact plants.

'Plena'—Bright yellow double flowers.

'Silver Queen'—Compact plants and attractive lemon-yellow flowers.

Planting and care—Plants are commonly available in 1-gallon containers. Plant in spring, in full sun in almost any kind of well-drained soil. Give moderate water. Cut back plants halfway to ground after flowering to rejuvenate. Plants will seed themselves, but named varieties are propagated by cuttings. Tap roots make plants difficult to transplant.

Hardy to −30F (−34C).

Australian saltbush. See *Atriplex*

Baby's-tears. See *Soleirolia*

BACCHARIS PILULARIS
Dwarf coyote brush

Baccharis pilularis is a native of coastal California. It is very adaptable and has become one of the most reliable and most-planted ground covers in the West and Southwest. Its strong roots hold tenaciously to steep slopes, providing excellent erosion control. Along the coast it grows in sand without additional summer water. It is enthusiastically endorsed by high-desert gardeners.

Plants are propagated by cuttings, so only varieties are available. Look for well-known, named ones. Most common is 'Twin Peaks #2'. It grows 6 to 12 inches high and spreads to 6 feet or more. Leaves are 1/2 to 1 inch long and bright green. Flowers are yellowish or white and not showy. They appear October to November.

Another variety is 'Pigeon Point'. It is faster growing, greener and more mounding. One plant will form a 10-foot wide clump.

Planting and care—Plant from cuttings in flats or from 1-gallon containers. Space cuttings 30 to 36 inches apart. Plants in 1-gallon containers can be spaced farther apart. If soil is moderately rich and watered regularly, plantings will form a solid cover in one year. If soil is poor, growth is slower and closer spacing is recommended. A mulch will help speed growth by cooling soil, preserving soil moisture and supressing weeds.

Plants are fast growing. Prune once a year in spring just before the period of fastest growth. Prune with a rotary mower if it can be set high enough. Hedge shears, loppers or hand clippers are also used. Fertilize after trimming with 1 pound of 10-10-10 or similar fertilizer per 100 square feet. Be sure to water fertilizer into soil.

Hardy to 0F (−18C).

Baja primrose. See *Oenothera*

BAMBOO
Arundinaria

Low-growing, spreading bamboos are useful ground covers in some gardens. Most common is *Arundinaria pygmaea*. It is a strong, fast spreader. Grows 1/2 to 1-1/2 feet high depending upon soil quality and amount of water and fertilizer

Bamboo is a useful plant but can be invasive. Confining *Arundinaria pygmaea* to a raised planter eliminates the problem.

Berberis verruculosa grew to this mature, natural height after several years.

received. Works well as a bank cover—its spreading roots hold the soil. Leaf texture and appearance is interesting. Keep confined by planting in a restricted area. Mow to reduce height.

Hardy to about 0F (−18C).

Arundinaria disticha grows 1 to 3 feet high and is more refined in appearance. Cut back to the ground every year or two or the plant will begin to look thin and weedy.

Hardy to 10F (−12C).

A. humilis grows 1 to 4 feet high. It is an aggressive spreader with more arching stems. Hardy to 0F (−18C).

A. variegata has white, variegated leaves, thicker stems. It will tolerate light shade. Hardy to 0F (−18C).

A. viridistriata has green and gold variegated leaves. Grows 1 to 2-1/2 feet high. Hardy to 0F (−18C).

Planting and care—Plants are normally available in 1-gallon containers. Plant any time. It is important to keep these plants confined. In raised planters, parkways, and similar areas surrounded by concrete, bamboos are an attractive, durable ground cover. Drought tolerance is very good, but regular water and fertilizer will improve appearance.

Barberry. See *Berberis*

Barren strawberry. See *Waldsteinia*

Barrenwort. See *Epimedium*

Basket-of-gold. See *Aurinia*

Bellflowers. See *Campanula*

BERBERIS
Barberry

Dwarf barberry is a dependable and attractive ground cover or low shrub. Because plants have spiny stems, they make a formidable low barrier. All barberries are deciduous, although they may keep some leaves through mild winters. Most are varieties of *Berberis thunbergii*, the Japanese barberry. Another is *B. verruculosa*, warty barberry.

Probably the most popular barberry is *B. thunbergii* 'Crimson Pygmy'. It rarely grows higher than 18 inches and spreads to about 30 inches. Leaves are nearly round and about 3/4 inch long. In full sun their color is deep purple-red; in shade they are green. Yellow flowers appear in spring. 'Dobold' is similar in every respect except leaf color is bright green. 'Rose Glow' is equally dense and compact, but its new leaves have an interesting rosy glow. They become darker red in time.

Warty barberry grows to 24 inches high and wide but is easily held to 18 inches high with occasional clipping. Leaves are about 1 inch long and glossy dark green. This is a very attractive and choice plant for a low border or massed in front of taller shrubs.

Planting and care—Barberries are tough and tolerate poor soil, drought, heat and wind. Plant a double or triple row 15 inches apart to make a solid, 18-inch high cover that no one will cross. Prune selectively with clippers rather than shearing plants. Shape will be more pleasing and interior growth will be less likely to die.

Hardy to −10F (−24C).

BERGENIA
Bergenia

Bergenia species are adaptable, evergreen, spreading perennials that make excellent ground covers in many situations. They accept full sun and dry soil, but flourish in light shade and moist soil. *Bergenia* species spread but don't dominate nearby plants. Mix them with ferns, English ivy or hostas. They are especially suited to rock gardens, near water and in other small areas.

Berberis thunbergii 'Crimson Pygmy' works well as a low hedge.

Bougainvillea 'La Jolla' is colorful and well suited for ground cover use.

Botanists distinguish two species of *Bergenia* that are similar in most practical respects. Spring blooming *B. cordifolia* has wavy, toothed leaves that are heart-shaped at the base. Flowers reach about 15 inches high. *B. crassifolia* blooms midwinter in mild-climate areas. Flower spikes are taller. Leaves are more finely toothed and lack the heart-shaped base.

Leaves of either species are fleshy, leathery and soft looking, but very hardy. Flowers may be pink, rose-pink or white. Plants spread with thick rhizomes over the soil surface.

Planting and care—Plants are normally available in 1-gallon containers. Plant in spring, about 10 inches apart. These are not demanding plants. They persist in most situations with a minimum of attention. Foliage cover is dense and flowers are most abundant when given periodic fertilizer, mulch and regular water. For best appearance, divide every 2 or 3 years by cutting back sprawling rhizomes, leaving about 3 inches of rhizome above the soil. Fertilize spring and fall. Protect from slugs and snails.

Hardy to −35F (−40C).

Birdsfoot trefoil. See *Lotus*

Blue cape plumbago. See *Plumbago*

Blue marguerite. See *Felicia*

Blue star creeper. See *Laurentia*

BOUGAINVILLEA
Bougainvillea

Bougainvillea species are well-known, vigorous, rambling ever-green vines of Hawaii, coastal and southern California, and similar mild-climate areas.

Low and mounding varieties 'Crimson Jewel', 'La Jolla' and 'Hawaii' are excellent as colorful ground covers. Try them on a sunny bank mixed with less colorful plants such as English ivy.

'Crimson Jewel' has very dark green leaves and makes hundreds of brilliant, bright red flowers over a long season.

'La Jolla' has fluorescent red flowers and a compact habit.

'Hawaii' has red flowers and gold-margined leaves. It is also one of the most hardy.

Planting and care—These are easy plants to grow once established, but *plant them carefully*. Roots of bougainvillea do not knit to make a dense rootball as most other plants, so they are easily damaged during planting. If plants are purchased in a metal container, some gardeners recommend planting the whole container and allowing it to slowly rust away. This eliminates the risk of damaging the roots.

The best time to plant is in spring after soil is thoroughly warm. If you live in an area subject to occasional frosts, plant against a warm south wall or under a protective overhang.

Soil should be well drained and mulched in summer. Be generous with water. Occasionally, low-growing bougainvilleas produce upward shoots that should be pruned.

Hardy to 25F (−4C).

BROOMS
Cytisus and Genista

Brooms are among the most reliable, showy and easy-to-grow ground covers. Most are native to Mediterranean climates so are quite tolerant of poor soil, drought and heat. A few prefer cool, moist climates, such as that found in many regions of the Pacific Northwest.

Genista pilosa branches retain small leaves throughout the season, and are covered by masses of flowers in spring.

Leafless branches of *Genista lydia* have unusual texture. In spring they are covered with yellow flowers.

Some brooms are self-sowing weeds. *Cytisus monspessulanus* is the most invasive. It has spread over large areas of northern California. Scotch broom, *C. scoparius,* and Spanish broom, *Spartium junceum,* have also naturalized significantly in the same region.

Cytisus decumbens, prostrate broom, forms a wide, spreading mat about 8 inches high. Bright yellow flowers cover plant in May.

C. kewensis, Kew broom, is perhaps best known. It is a hybrid from England but is a favorite of Pacific Northwest gardeners. It grows into a 6-foot wide and 1-foot high shrub, often used to cascade gracefully down slopes and over walls. In spring it is covered with white, 1/2-inch flowers.

Genista lydia is one of the most adaptable and useful low-growing brooms. Its normal mature height is less than 1 foot, but it spreads about 4 feet. Main branches spread from plant horizontally. Branchlets grow upward from main branches then arch back to the ground. In spring, plant is covered with a solid mat of yellow, pealike flowers.

G. pilosa is similarly spreading and flowering, but grows to 1 foot high.

Planting and care—Brooms are easy to grow. They require little beyond a well-drained, slightly acid soil and full sun. You will find plants in 1-gallon containers. Best time to plant is in fall. If soil pH is high, foliage may turn yellow. Correct with iron sulfate. Prune after flowering to direct growth.

Hardy to −10F (−24C).

Bruckenthalia. See Heaths and Heathers

California lilac. See *Ceanothus*

California poppy.
See *Eschscholzia*

Calluna. See Heaths and Heathers

CAMPANULA
Bellflower

Campanula species is a varied, easy-to-grow group of plants. Many are hardy, low-growing perennials suitable as a small-area ground cover. They are adaptable to many different conditions, but grow best with light shade and well-drained, moist soil. Flowers vary, but most are shaped like small bells—*campanula* is a Latin word meaning *bell shaped.* Of the hundreds of *Campanula* species, four are notable ground covers.

Campanula elatines garganica, Adriatic bellflower, is a delicate, trailing plant, reaching 5 to 6 inches high. It spreads to 18 inches. Grayish leaves are toothed and heart-shaped. Star-shaped flowers are bright blue with white centers. Flowers appear late spring or summer. Cover plants with a mulch after ground is frozen in fall or winter. You may find this plant listed in catalogs or nurseries simply as *C. garganica.*

Hardy to −10F (−24C).

C. portenschlagiana, Dalmation bellflower, is a fine, flowering ground cover when given moist soil and some shade. Maximum height is about 7 inches. Spread is 18 inches. Leaves are deep green, heart shaped and toothed. Flowers are violet-blue and bell shaped. They appear mid to late summer and sometimes in fall. Dalmation bellflower is relatively long-lived and not invasive. Mix with and plant near other low-growing plants.

Hardy to −30F (−35C).

C. poscharskyana, Serbian bellflower, is a larger, more vigorous version of *C. e. garganica.* Flowering stems may reach 1 foot high. Blue flowers come in late spring or early summer. This is a tough bellflower.

Campanula species, the dominant flowering plants here, are good choices for rock gardens.

It will accept some drought but is best with moist soil.

Hardy to −35F (−37C).

C. rapunculoides, Rover bellflower, is very appropriately named—it is a tough and rampant plant. Be aware of the risk if you introduce it in your garden. It will grow over and around just about everything and invades lawns and flower beds without hesitation. To its credit, it will grow where many other plants will not. Green leaves have long stems and a heart-shaped base. Flowers are pale blue, almost white, funnel shaped, and grow on 2- to 3-foot spikes.

Hardy to −40F (−40C).

Planting and care—Culture varies slightly with the species, but the essentials are similar. Plant in fairly good loam soil and partial shade. Full sun is better in cool or coastal areas. Keep plants watered regularly, especially if soil tends to be dry. Clip off dead flowers and divide clumps every three to four years. Watch for slugs and snails.

Candytuft. See *Iberis*

CARISSA
Natal plum

Low, spreading natal plums make excellent evergreen ground covers and low barriers for frost-free gardens. Thorny stems are not as threatening as those of *Berberis* species, but are certainly enough to discourage wayward pedestrians. Natal plum is one of the best choices for coastal landscapes subject to salt spray.

Several named forms of natal plum are in cultivation but only two selections are readily available. Both produce 5-petaled, starlike flowers followed by small, edible fruit.

'Green Carpet' grows 18 inches high and eventually spreads to make a mounding, 4-foot wide clump. Small, dark, glossy leaves are particularly attractive.

'Prostrata' is slightly more vigorous with larger leaves. It grows to 2 feet high and spreads 5 feet wide. Plant sometimes puts forth an occasional upward branch. Attractive as an espalier.

Planting and care—Natal plum is usually available in 1-gallon containers. Plant anytime, but either fall or spring are best. When climate needs are met, the plant is very adaptable. It grows in any kind of soil and in full sun or medium shade. Space plants 15 to 18 inches apart. Along the coast summer watering is not required. Regular watering will be necessary in drier, inland areas.

Hardy to about 30F (−1C) but many plantings thrive in warm, protected microclimates of colder areas.

Carmel creeper. See *Ceanothus*

Carnation. See *Dianthus*

Carolina jessamine. See *Gelsemium*

Carpet bugle. See *Ajuga*

Carpobrotus. See Ice Plants

CATHARANTHUS ROSEUS
Madagascar periwinkle, Vinca

This charming plant offers a very long period of bloom and clean, bright green leaves for very little gardening effort. It is a warm-weather annual in regions that have freezing temperatures, but will persist several years otherwise. It self-sows but is not invasive, and is one of the best sources of summer color for desert gardens. Some nurseries or catalogs may list *Catharanthus roseus* as *Vinca rosea* or periwinkle.

It grows in height to 1 foot or more and about as wide. Leaves are

Catharanthus roseus has a long blooming season. It is a favorite color plant in hot climates.

'Bright Eyes' is the most common variety of *Catharanthus roseus*.

glossy bright green, about 1-1/2 inches long. Flowers are 1-1/2 inches wide and have 5 petals. They are white, red or shades between, depending on variety. 'Bright Eyes' has white flowers with a red center. 'Coquette' is smaller with rose-red flowers.

Planting and care—Nurseries sell *Catharanthus roseus* as bedding plants. Plant in full sun or part shade, 6 to 10 inches apart. You may also start them from seed. Sow outdoors in spring after soil has warmed. Or start indoors in flats, cold frames or greenhouses. In frost-free areas, sow seed in late summer or fall. Seedlings should emerge within 3 weeks. Plants bloom the first season from seed.

Catharanthus is tolerant of most soils but grows most luxuriantly in rich, moist situations.

Hardy to about 25F (−4C).

Catnip. See *Nepeta*

CEANOTHUS
Carmel creeper, California lilac

Ceanothus species are a varied group of California natives. Many are low and spreading ground covers. Some gardeners have had bad luck with them and believe they are generally unreliable or short-lived. To have success, it is important to choose a species or variety suitable for your area and be aware of potential problems. For example, *Ceanothus griseus horizontalis*, Carmel creeper, is tough and long-lived in a coastal climate to which it is accustomed. Inland, it will be short-lived and less successful.

The following are low-growing *Ceanothus* varieties:

C. divergens confusus, Rincon ceanothus—Forms a dense, 3-inch high mat of interlocking leaves. Spreads to 3 feet wide. Flowers are blue to lavender. Native to rocky slopes from Sonoma County to Lake County in California. Small area ground cover.

Hardy to 5F (−15C).

C. gloriosus, Point Reyes ceanothus—Very fast and rampant grower best suited for covering large areas in coastal situations. Rarely survives inland heat and drought. Accepts pruning better than most. Grows 18 inches high and forms a clump to 18 feet wide. Two unnamed forms are common. One is lower, more flat and has dark green leaves. The other is vigorous, taller and has pale green leaves. 'Anchor Bay' is similar to both but much more compact. Leaves are slightly larger and flowers are darker blue.

Hardy to 5F (−15C).

C. g. exaltatus 'Emily Brown'—Grows 18 to 36 inches high and 6 to 10 feet wide. Leaves are deep green. Flowers are beautiful blue-violet. Adaptable, easy to grow and maintain in garden situations, coastal or inland.

Hardy to 10F (−12C).

C. g. porrectus—New to gardeners but promising. Grows 12 to 30 inches high and 7 feet or more wide. Deep green, numerous leaves give it a fine-textured appearance. Very deep blue flowers. Adaptable and attractive bank or ground cover.

Hardy to 5F (−15C).

C. griseus horizontalis, Carmel creeper—This is the most common *Ceanothus* species in the nursery trade today. Unnamed selections vary significantly. Look for named selections. 'Hurricane Point' is vigorous with open growth habit to 4 feet high and as much as 30 feet wide. It thrives along the coast but usually lives less than 5 years inland. 'Yankee Point' is the best variety. It grows 3 feet high and 15 feet wide. A tough plant but needs

Close-up look at flowers of *Ceanothus* species.

Centranthus ruber is colorful, hardy and long-lived.

water during summer in all but cool, coastal areas. Not recommended for hot-summer areas.

Hardy to 5F (−15C).

Ceanothus 'Joyce Coulter'—Fast growing to 3 feet high and 10 to 12 feet wide. Leaves are dark green. Flowers are an attractive blue. Recommended for the interior valleys and southern regions of California and the Pacific Northwest. Excellent for large spaces, either sloping or level. Accepts pruning and heavy soil. Needs water in summer.

Hardy to 20F (−7C).

C. maritimus—Native to a small area of coastal San Luis Obispo County. Grows 2-1/2 feet high and spreads 6 feet wide. Leaves are green on top, whitish or gray below. Flowers are white to pale lavender. Good ground or bank cover. Accepts pruning and is not fussy about soil.

Planting and care—Ceanothus are normally available in 1- or 5-gallon containers, sometimes in flats. Fall planting is best. It allows time for roots to establish before summer heat.

In general, established planting of *Ceanothus* species need no moisture from late spring through summer. They will grow in sandy, infertile soil and most are successful on slopes. In the moist, rich soils of home gardens, some species will grow fast, but some become subject to a variety of root rot diseases. The descriptions below include examples and exceptions.

A destructive disease occurs with winter pruning of older, mature wood. To prevent it, seal pruning wounds immediately and make large pruning cuts only as a last resort.

Stem gall moth is one of the few serious insect pests. Whiteflies and aphids are occasionally troublesome. *C. griseus horzontalis* is highly susceptible.

Do not crowd wide-spreading plants. Although you will have a ground cover sooner, branches begin to pile up and disease is encouraged by overcrowding. Note in the descriptions how wide plants will spread and space accordingly.

CENTRANTHUS RUBER
Jupiter's beard, Red valerian

This is an ideal, low-maintenance plant for mild-winter, Mediterranean-type climates. It is exceptionally drought tolerant and blooms over a long period. It has naturalized in many areas of the West. Use it to stabilize steep, dry slopes. Combine with daylilies, *Vinca* species, wild flowers, creeping buttercup or English ivy for natural, unkempt look at landscape fringes.

Plant grows 3 feet high and spreads indefinitely by roots. It also self-sows. Leaves are bluish green and about 4 inches long. Small, red, pink or white flowers are arranged in dense, terminal clusters.

'Albus' has pure white flowers and produces sterile seed.

Planting and care—These are half-wild plants frequently started from clumps dug from a neighbor's back-forty. Some nurseries do have plants, usually in 1-gallon containers. Plant anytime, anywhere except in damp shade. Space clumps 12 to 18 inches apart for rapid cover.

Hardy to 15F (−9C).

Cephalophyllum 'Red Spike'.
See Ice Plants

CERASTIUM TOMENTOSUM
Snow-in-summer

Snow-in-summer is a carnation relative. It is delicate in appearance but

Cerastium tomentosum, with gray leaves and white flowers, makes a dramatic contrast between lawn areas.

Cerastium tomentosum viewed close-up. Flower is approximately the size of a dime.

hardy and adaptable to most every climate and soil type. Soft, gray leaves form a 4-inch high, 2-foot wide mat. White, 1/2-inch flowers appear late spring to summer. Use it in rock gardens, as edging in front of azaleas or other low shrubs, over a bed of bulbs or on top of low, soil retaining walls. Mountain-area gardeners endorse it. At worst, it will become an invasive but attractive weed.

Planting and care—Plants are available in cans, plastic packs or flats. Plant in spring or fall. Full sun, dry, warm soil and good drainage are the basic requirements. Clip off spent flowers. Divide plants every 1 or 2 years or they tend to become ragged.

Hardy to −40F (−40C).

CERATOSTIGMA PLUMBAGINOIDES
Dwarf plumbago, Leadwort

An ideal ground cover in many respects, dwarf plumbago spreads fast, forming a mat 10 to 12 inches high. Plants will invade nearby shrubs but in an unobtrusive way. Intense blue, 1/2-inch, 5-petaled flowers appear mid to late summer, when blue is a rare color in the garden.

Leaves are dark green with tints of bronze, brown and red. After cold weather the leaves turn almost ruby-red. Most plants die to the ground and come back the following spring.

Planting and care—Plant in sun or partial shade in spring. Any soil is okay. Once established, drought tolerance is fair. Cut all leaves to the ground after first hard frost. Mulch after soil is frozen.

Hardy to −10F (−24C).

CHAMAEMELUM NOBILE
Chamomile, Roman chamomile

Chamomile is an evergreen perennial herb long-favored in England as a lawn substitute. It will bear considerable traffic, though not as much as a grass lawn. It is fragrant underfoot and ideally suited to planting between paving blocks and steppingstones.

Plant produces a grass-green, fine-textured mat 3 to 12 inches high that spreads fast into a 1-foot wide clump. It grows taller with some shade. Flowers are usually golden yellow and buttonlike. Non-flowering forms and selections with white petals are occasionally seen.

Planting and care—Chamomile is usually available in flats, sometimes in plastic packs. Plant in either spring or fall. Space plants 6 to 12 inches apart. Growth is fast with good soil and regular water. Sometimes sections of plantings die out for no apparent reason. Fill in with divisions from another area. Mow with reel or rotary mower to rejuvenate.

Hardy to 0F (−18C).

CHRYSANTHEMUM PARTHENIUM
Feverfew

Feverfew is an old-fashioned plant with old-fashioned charm. It self-sows and can become a weed in some situations. It serves as an excellent border or filler plant.

Feverfew grows 1 to 3 feet high depending on variety. Leaves have a strong odor when crushed. White flowers are 1/4 to 1/2 inch wide and appear throughout summer.

'Aureum' or 'Golden Feather' has chartreuse-green leaves and single flowers. 'Golden Ball' flowers have

Chamaemelum nobile grows over 1 foot high in shade, as long as it is not trimmed or walked upon. With frequent mowing, it makes a tight, low carpet.

Chrysanthemum parthenium 'Golden Feather' flowers profusely all summer.

no petals. 'Silver Ball' flowers are fully double.

Planting and care—Start from seed or nursery plants in spring. Named varieties are propagated by cuttings or division. Space 8 to 12 inches apart. Plant in full sun and provide regular water.

Hardy to −10F (−24C).

Cinquefoil. See *Potentilla*

CISTUS
Rock rose

Rock rose is an excellent, evergreen ground cover or low shrub for Mediterranean climates. In California, these plants are very popular near the coast and along the coast mountain ranges from Santa Barbara to Marin. Near the coast they are totally self-sufficient. Rock rose tolerates considerable summer heat in inland and desert areas, as long as they are irrigated. Plants are fire resistant and provide effective erosion control. Use them in masses or combine with *Ceanothus, Erigonum, Helianthemum* species or African daisies.

Four rock roses have particular value as ground covers:

Cistus crispus is prostrate and rigidly branched. It grows to about 18 inches high and spreads as wide. Leaves are deep green, wavy and fragrant when crushed. Reddish pink flowers are about 1-1/2 inches wide and have a bright yellow center.

'Doris Hibberson' mounds to 3 feet high with an equal spread. Leaves are gray-green and 1 to 2 inches long. Flowers are clear pink and have a texture similar to crepe paper. Los Angeles County Arboretum tests indicate that on exposure to intense heat, plants char instead of bursting into flame. It is therefore recommended for firebreak plantings.

C. hybridus is known as white rock rose. You may find it listed in some catalogs under a formerly used botanical name, *C. corbariensis.* Height is variable between 2 and 5 feet with an equal spread. Leaves are gray-green and about 2 inches long. Flowers are white with yellow centers.

C. salviifolius, sage-leaf rock rose, is the lowest and most spreading of the rock roses. It grows to 2 feet high and spreads to 6 feet. It may be listed in catalogs as *C. villosus* 'Prostratus'. Leaves are gray-green

and about 1 inch long. Flowers are white with yellow centers, and are abundant in spring.

Planting and care—Plants are available in containers. Be particularly aware of circling and matted roots at planting time. Cut and spread them for best results. Fall is ideal planting time. Water and fertilizer needs are minimal. Pests are usually no bother. Occasionally prune out oldest, interior stems and pinch tips to promote bushiness.

Hardy to 15F (−9C).

Common thrift. See *Armeria*

COMPTONIA PEREGRINA
Sweet fern

Sweet fern is a low-maintenance bank cover for Northeast gardeners. Leaves are toothed, narrow and fernlike. Plant looks like a fern but actually is not. Myrtle and bayberry are closely related. Sweet fern spreads by underground, erosion-controlling roots. It is deciduous and cold hardy.

Plant normally grows 1-1/2 to 2 feet high but may reach 5 feet.

Planting and care—Propagate by seed, layering or division of

Convallaria majalis is one of the most reliable ground covers in cold-winter areas.

established clumps. Best growth is in full sun with infertile, acidic, dry or sandy soils.

Hardy to −50F (−45C).

Confederate vine. See *Trachelospermum*

Conifers. See *Juniperus, Picea, Pinus* and *Taxus*

CONVALLARIA MAJALIS
Lily-of-the-valley

This old-fashioned, deciduous perennial is an excellent ground cover. It is particularly favored by northern and northeastern gardeners. *Undemanding, versatile, permanent* and *tolerant* are typical adjectives applied to this plant. Two points should be kept in mind: It does not thrive where winters are mild; and all plant parts—roots, leaves, flowers and fruit—are poisonous. If you have small children, you should avoid planting lily-of-the-valley.

Lily-of-the-valley makes a dense and slow-spreading cover. It is persistent and may even become a difficult lawn weed. Attractive, blue-green leaves grow about 8 inches high and 1 to 3 inches wide. They rise directly from creeping, underground stems. White, waxy, fragrant flowers hang from 6- to 8-inch stems. They appear in late spring and can be used for indoor arrangements. Nurseries offer *Convallaria* species in the fall for winter forcing. Orange-red berries come in fall.

Varieties of the Excellenta strain have much larger flowers. 'Rosea' flowers are pale pink.

Planting and care—Start colonies with parts of the underground stem. These are called *pips*. Plant 1 to 2 feet apart along the eastern and northern sides of your house. Spring is the best time to plant, but any time is okay.

Lily-of-the-valley are not fussy plants, but usually prefer semishade. Soil should be fairly rich. Provide with regular moisture. For best results, fertilize in spring and mulch in fall or winter with manure, peat moss, leaf mold or similar material.

Hardy to −35F (−37C).

CONVOLVULUS CNEORUM
Silver bush morning glory

This evergreen Mediterranean native has proven useful and adaptable in regions with a Mediterranean-type climate. Healthy, thriving plants make good fire-retardant plantings on dry banks and hillsides.

Growth is low and speading, 2 to 4 feet high and as wide. Silver leaves are smooth, oval and 2-1/2 inches long. Flowers look like morning glories and are tinted white and pink.

Planting and care—Plant 1- or 5-gallon container plants in fall. Plant in full sun in fast-draining soil. Avoid planting near heavily watered garden areas. Severe pruning in early spring will renew plants.

Hardy to 15F (−9C).

COPROSMA KIRKII
Creeping coprosma

This is a low, spreading member of a group of popular New Zealand plants. It is drought tolerant once established. It provides erosion control and is one of the best plants for coastal conditions.

Plant grows 2 to 2-1/2 feet high and spreads 3 to 5 feet. Leaves are shiny, glossy light green and 1/2 to 1 inch long. They give the plant a neat, clean look.

Planting and care—Plant from containers in fall. Plant in full sun or

Coprosma kirkii is adapted to coastal conditions.

Coronilla varia flowers viewed close-up.

partial shade. Accepts virtually any soil. Mulch until established to control weeds and preserve moisture. Drought tolerant once established. Prune to keep plants dense.

Hardy to 20F (−7C).

Coral bells. See *Heuchera*

COREOPSIS AURICULATA 'NANA'
Dwarf coreopsis

Use this petite but bright little ground cover as a border edging and to fill in between taller plants. Plant is cold hardy. It is deciduous in cold-winter areas, evergreen where winters are mild.

It is very low growing, forming a mat only 1 or 2 inches high. Dark green leaves are 2 to 3 inches long. Daisylike flowers are bright orange-yellow, about 2 inches wide. They appear on 5- to 6-inch stems spring through summer. In good soil plant will slowly spread into a clump 1 to 1-1/2 feet wide.

Planting and care—Start plants from nursery-bought gallon containers in spring or fall. Space plants 12 inches apart. Rich, moist soil in full sun is best. Remove fading flowers to prolong bloom.

Hardy to −30F (−35C).

CORONILLA VARIA
Crown vetch

Crown vetch is a utility ground cover often used on highway banks and similar large, rough, low-maintenance areas.

It grows to about 2 feet high. Leaves are composed of many small leaflets. Flowers are lavender-pink and bloom continuously in summer. Brown seedpods follow in fall.

Minnesota Agricultural Extension tested the various strains available and found them roughly equivlent. 'Penngift' is widely available.

Planting and care—Plants spread several feet each direction with creeping roots and rhizomes. Divisions are usually planted 1 to 1-1/2 feet apart. Some shade is acceptable but full sun is best. Plants are tolerant of many soil types. May be difficult to eradicate once established. Dries out early in fall and tops die with cold weather. May provide shelter for rodents. Mow, feed and water in spring to rejuvenate.

Hardy to −40F (−40C).

Corsican mint. See *Mentha*

Corsican sandwort. See Moss

COTULA SQUALIDA
New Zealand brass-buttons

This is a very low-growing, interesting, evergreen plant useful as a cover for bulbs, between stepping-stones or as a lawn substitute. *Cotula squalida* is related to and very similar in appearance to *Chamaemelum nobile*.

Plant grows 2 to 3 inches high and spreads a foot or more. Leaves are soft, fernlike and reddish green. They make a texture almost like a shag carpet. Its name comes from the flowers—they resemble tiny brass buttons.

Planting and care—Plant from flats or plastic packs in spring. Locate plants in full sun or light shade 4 to 6 inches apart. Supply with regular water and fertilizer.

Hardy to about 0F (−18C).

Creeping buttercup. See *Ranunculus*

Creeping coprosma. See *Coprosma*

Creeping forget-me-not. See *Omphalodes*

(Alphabetical listing continued on page 111.)

Cotoneaster horizontalis

COTONEASTER
Cotoneaster

Cotoneasters are a large group of shrubs that include many low and spreading forms. Several make excellent ground covers. Most are hardy, tough and easy to grow. Most are natives of northern Asia, the Himalayas and Europe. Most have small, shiny, thick, green leaves, small flowers in spring and red berries in fall. Stems do not have thorns.

Following are brief descriptions of the best ground cover types.

C. adpressus praecox—Fishbone-pattern branches follow ground contours. Grows to about 18 inches high, spreading 5 to 6 feet wide. Leaves are oval, 1 inch long and closely set. They turn brilliant red in fall. Berries are 1/2 inch in diameter, bright red. Deciduous. Hardy to −20F (−29C).

C. apiculatus 'Nana', dwarf cranberry cotoneaster—Large, red, cranberry-size fruit stay on plant all winter. Plant grows to 12 inches high, spreads 4 feet. Branches bend down at the tips. Leaves are round with wavy margins, shiny, bright green on top, turning deep red in fall. Deciduous. Hardy to −25F (−32C).

Cotoneaster microphyllus visually softens a mortarless stone wall.

Cotoneaster horizontalis displays fine, feathery texture and red berries. This one is a little taller than typical.

C. congestus—Grows 3 feet high but hugs the ground. Small, 1/4-inch leaves are round, dark green on top, white below. Berries are bright red, 1/4 inch in diameter. One of the most hardy, evergreen types. Recommended for the desert. Variety 'Likiang' is especially compact, low and attractive.

Hardy to 0F (−18C).

C. dammeri, bearberry cotoneaster—Very low, wide spreading, cascading and evergreen. Often grows no more than 8 inches high. Rooting branches spread rapidly to 10 feet wide. Leaves are oval, 1 inch long. Berries are bright red and showy. Several varieties are available: 'Coral Beauty' has coral-colored berries. 'Lowfast' is 12 inches high and spreads 2 feet per season. It serves as an excellent bank cover. 'Royal Beauty' has deep red berries. 'Skogsholmen' grows 12 to 18 inches high. It has stiff branches and attractive spring flowers.

All are hardy to −10F (−24C).

C. horizontalis, rock cotoneaster—Popular, wide-spreading ground cover. Distinctive characteristic is pattern of secondary branches—all are on the same level and grow in a herringbone pattern. Plant grows 2 to 3 feet high and spreads 15 feet or more wide. Give it room: Don't plant where ends must be clipped. Leaves are 1/2 inch wide, round, glossy green on top, pale below. In fall, leaves turn orange for a brief time, then red before falling. Bright red berries remain on branches long after leaves fall. Subspecies *C. h. perpusillus* is lower and more compact. Deciduous.

Hardy to −20F (−29C).

C. microphyllus, rockspray cotoneaster—Smallest leaves and finest texture of ground cover cotoneasters. Develops into dense, tangled mass of stiff branches. Maximum height is 2 to 3 feet. Spreads to 6 feet wide. Main branches trail and root. Evergreen leaves are small, dark green on top, gray and hairy below.

Cotoneaster dammeri drapes over a low planter wall.

Cotoneaster microphyllus, foreground, covers this steep slope.

Cotoneaster species make excellent low borders, but edges do not take shearing.

Cotoneaster dammeri spreads low, wide and fast.

Berries are rose-red, 1/4 inch in diameter. Three common varieties are: 'Cochleatus', more compact and prostrate than others. It is considered the best variety. 'Emerald Spray' features good fireblight resistance. *C. m. thymifolius* is compact with stiff, upright growth. Berries are smaller, borne in clusters.

Hardy to −10F (−24C).

C. salicifolius, willowleaf cotoneaster—is a tall, shrub cotoneaster with many low, spreading forms. 'Herbstfeuer' grows 6 inches high and spreads up to 8 feet. It is evergreen and becomes maroon-red in winter. Some catalogs list it as 'Autumn Fire'. 'Emerald Carpet' is compact with a dense growth habit and smaller leaves. It is semievergreen. Excellent under taller shrubs and draped over walls. 'Repens', occasionally listed as *C. s. repandens,* also has trailing, rooting branches. Grows 12 inches high and 6 to 8 feet wide. Leaves are dark green and 3 inches long. 'Scarlet Leader' is very low growing, to 6 inches high, and more dense. Good retaining wall and bank cover.

Hardy to −10F (−24C).

Planting and care—Plant cotoneaster in spring or fall. Many kinds are regularly stocked by nurseries, usually in 1-gallon containers.

Full sun and dry, average soil are best, but light shade and moist soil are acceptable. Prune with clippers to remove wayward branches—don't use hedge shears. Scale, red spider mite or lace bug may cause problems. They are easily controlled with soapy sprays, malathion or kelthane sprays.

Fireblight disease occasionally affects cotoneaster. Leaves wilt, look scorched and hang on branches. Prune infected branches, cutting back into at least 4 inches of healthy wood. Dip pruners into bleach to disinfect between cuts. Burn or dispose of diseased wood.

Hardiness varies with species. See descriptions.

Cymbalaria muralis grows best in a moist location.

Dianthus species make a colorful bed in shade of *Callistemon* tree. Cut back after spring flowering for a color display in fall.

Creeping oregano. See *Origanum*

Creeping saltbush. See *Atriplex*

Creeping St. Johnswort. See *Hypericum*

CYCLAMEN HEDERIFOLIUM
Baby cyclamen

Baby cyclamen is cold hardy, vigorous and especially interesting for one unique characteristic—it carpets the ground in winter and is deciduous in summer.

Plant grows to about 3 inches high and spreads into a 1-foot wide clump within two seasons. Leaves are light green with silver-white markings. Flowers are rose-pink or white on 3- to 4-inch stems.

Planting and care—Fall is the best time to plant. Part shade is preferred. Plant 1- to 2-inch long corms smooth-side down just below soil surface. Space 8 inches apart. Any soil is okay as long as it is well drained. Seeds are tiny, but viable, and will self-sow.

Hardy to −10F (−24C).

CYMBALARIA MURALIS
Kenilworth ivy

This is a delicate but persistent—sometimes invasive—ground cover. It is ideal for a shady, moist site. It forms a 1-inch high mat of 1/4- to 1-inch wide lobed, light green leaves. Trailing stems root at joints. Small, blue flowers bloom spring to summer.

Planting and care—Spring or early fall are the best times to plant. Space 6 inches apart. Prefers shade and moist soil. Feeding with dilute liquid fertilizer spring, fall and mid-summer is usually necessary for best growth.

Hardy to 20F (−7C).

Cyrtomium. See Ferns
Cytisus. See Brooms
Daboecia. See Heaths
Dahlberg daisy. See *Dyssodia*

DALEA GREGGI
Trailing indigo bush

Trailing indigo bush is a drought-tolerant, fast-growing, pearl-gray ground cover from Mexico. It has been tested and endorsed by the University of Arizona.

It grows 1 foot high and spreads at least 4 feet wide. Leaves are gray-green and fine textured. Flowers are an attractive, blue-lavender color but are too small to be showy.

Planting and care—Plant in full sun in any soil about 18 inches apart. Water weekly until established, especially if planted in spring or summer. The ideal time to plant is in fall, just before the rainy season. Although notably drought tolerant, supplemental water in summer is necessary for best appearance. It has no known pest problems and is not bothered by rabbits.

Hardy to 15F (−9C).

Davallia. *See Ferns*
Daylily. See *Hemerocallis*
Delosperma 'Alba'. See Ice Plants

DIANTHUS
Pinks

For generations, pinks have been favored plants for edgings and borders. They are hardy, perennial and serve beautifully as ground cover. Most have gray-green leaves and flat, showy flowers in white and red shades. Many flowers have a spicy, clovelike scent.

Epimedium grandiflorum is among the most useful ground covers. It is attractive and easy to maintain.

Two *Dianthus* species are particularly suitable as ground covers:

D. deltoides, maiden pink, grows 6 to 8 inches high, forming an open mat 15 inches wide. Flowers are 3/4 inch wide and have toothed petals. They are commonly a shade of rose but available in white to purple. Start from seed or transplants.

Hardy to −40F (−40C).

D. plumarius, cottage pink, is similar but a little larger. Plants grow 10 inches high. Flowers reach 15 inches high. Flowers have a dark center and are usually fragrant. They bloom midsummer to fall.

Hardy to −10F (−24C).

Many of the new, bedding plant *Dianthus* hybrids can be used as ground covers. 'Snowfire' is technically an annual but lives three or more years in mild-winter areas. 'Lace' hybrids, 'Queen of Hearts', 'China Doll' and 'Magic Charms' series are also highly rated and worth trying.

Planting and care—Pinks are grown in ordinary soil and require no special attention. Nurseries include them with other perennials, or sometimes in the bedding plant section. Plant in early spring, as soon as soil is workable. In mild-winter areas, plant in fall. They prefer full sun, a little lime and rich, moist soil. Cut back after flowering.

See variety descriptions for hardiness ranges.

Dimorphotheca. See African Daisies

Drosanthemum. See Ice Plants

Dryopteris. See Ferns

DUCHESNEA INDICA
Indian mock strawberry

This strawberry look-alike makes a fine, evergreen ground cover in light shade, such as under tall shrubs and trees.

It grows about 6 inches high, sending out trailing, rooting stems just like strawberries. Leaves are bright green and divided into three leaflets. Flowers are yellow, 1/2 inch wide and appear in spring. Birds appreciate the small, red but tasteless fruit that develop well above leaves.

Planting and care—Plant from flats in spring or early fall. Plants grow best in sun or light shade. Space 1 to 1-1/2 feet apart. Rich, moist soil is preferred. Generous water accelerates growth but this may also cause plants to become invasive. Plants are drought tolerant once established.

Hardy to −10F (−24C).

Dwarf coyote brush.
See *Baccharis*

Dwarf plumbago.
See Ceratostigma

DYSSODIA TENUILOBA
Dahlberg daisy, Golden fleece

Dahlberg daisy is a charming, yellow-flowering bedding plant. It is generally considered an annual, but plants will survive mild winters, or self-sow and become naturalized.

Plant grows 8 inches high and as wide. Dark green leaves are finely divided—almost fernlike. Golden yellow flowers are 1/2 inch wide, abundant summer to fall.

Planting and care—Make a beautiful mass display by spacing plants 6 inches apart. Spring is the time to plant. Full sun, rich, well-drained soil and regular water supply are basic requirements. Or sow seed in place—flowers will bloom 4 months later. Excellent companion plant with lobelia.

Eschscholzia californica, shown in a California garden, was easily planted by scattering seed over ground in fall.

Euonymus fortunei 'Minima' is a dwarf, less-spreading version of the *Euonymus* clan.

Normally dies back with first hard frost, but plants often self-sow.

English ivy. See *Hedera*

EPIMEDIUM
Bishop's hat, Barrenwort

Epimedium species are hardy, semi-evergreen to deciduous ground covers, particularly useful around the bases of trees. Unlike many other plants, they tolerate and thrive with the root competion from trees.

Plants grow 8 to 15 inches high, varying with species. They spread unobtrusively with underground runners into 12-inch clumps in 2 seasons. Dark green leaves are leathery and heart shaped, divided into 3-inch leaflets. In spring and fall leaves are tinged red. Tiny, waxy, 1/2-inch flowers are shaped like cups with long spurs. Flowers appear just after new leaves. They may be red, yellow, white, rose or lilac.

Epimedium grandiflorum is the most common species, available with either white or rose flowers. *E. youngianum* 'Niveum' is a delicate,

white-flowering form. Catalogs that specialize in rock garden and perennial plants may list several others.

Planting and care—Plants are long-lived and easy to grow. Plant spring or fall. Space about 12 inches apart. Their ideal location is in light shade, planted in moist, organic soil. Heavy soil restricts their spreading roots. Trim any existing leaves in late winter to clear the way for attractive, fresh, new leaves.

Hardy to −25F (−32C).

Erica. See Heaths and Heathers

ESCHSCHOLZIA CALIFORNICA
California poppy

Probably the best-known annual wild flower of the Western states, California poppy is excellent for naturalizing on banks and rough areas. In the garden, with better care and more water, plants are attractive for a longer time and produce more flowers.

Plants grow 8 to 24 inches high. Leaves are silvery blue-green. Flowers are normally orange and single. Forms with yellow, pink, red, cream and double flowers are well worth investigating.

Planting and care—To plant, scatter 1/2 to 1 pound of seed for every 1,000 to 2,000 square feet. Any soil is okay. Do this in fall just before winter rains. If rains are late or widely spaced, sprinkle planting area regularly. Full exposure to sun is best. The plants you start will make enough seed to establish a permanent colony.

Plants tend to die out with summer heat unless watered.

EUONYMUS FORTUNEI
Winter creeper

Named varieties of *Euonymus fortunei* are among the most hardy evergreens. They are reliable where English ivy and cotoneaster sometimes fail. Essentially, they are vines that spread horizontally as well as vertically.

Winter creeper is excellent for erosion control. It is surprisingly more tolerant of desert sun and heat than *Hedera* species.

Euonymus fortunei

White variegation of *Euonymus fortunei* 'Gracilis' creates highlight in shaded areas. Deciduous azaleas surround planting.

Following are the varieties to look for:

Euonymus fortunei 'Canadian Variegated'—Grows about 18 inches high and about 3 feet wide. Small, waxy, green leaves edged in white. Hardy.

E. f. 'Carrierei'—Lustrous green leaves. Does not climb without support.

E. f. 'Colorata', purple-leaf winter creeper—Deep green leaves become plum color in fall. Most popular and common form. Sprawls wide, climbs high.

E. f. 'Dart's Blanket'—Ground hugging and wide spreading. Deep green leaves have prominent, pale green veins.

E. f. 'Gracilis'—Dense, hardy, bushy, semitrailing habit. More restrained. Leaves are variegated with white or cream. Adapted to small areas and on top of low walls.

E. f. 'Kewensis'—Very low, to 2 inches high. A dwarf form, it makes a dense, fine-textured ground cover. Evergreen.

E. f. 'Longwood'—Dwarf, petite form similar to 'Kewensis'. Relatively fast growing.

E. f. 'Minima'—Dwarf, evergreen. Leaves are slightly larger than 'Kewensis'.

E. f. radicans, common winter creeper—Low-growing, trailing variety from which named varieties derive. Trailing branches root as they go. Leaves are 1 inch long, dark green. Ground or wall cover.

E. f. 'Tustin'—Prominently veined, dark green leaves. Undersides are purplish in winter. Dense growing and hardy.

Planting and care—Winter creeper is very adaptable. Plant in full sun or full shade. Just about any soil is okay. Provide regular water. Best time to plant is spring or early fall. Plants are available in flats, sometimes as rooted cuttings. Space about 1 foot apart for fast cover.

The one drawback is the plant's susceptibility to *euonymus scale*. This insect can be controlled by spraying dormant oil, then Orthene or diazinon during May and June. But scale may persist. Cold winters help control it. If scale gets a foothold in southern gardens, it can wipe out an entire planting.

If possible, set rotary mower high and mow plants to rejuvenate every one or two years. Best time to mow is in spring, before new growth starts.

Hardy to −20F (−29C).

Evergreen current. See *Ribes*

False spiraea. See *Astilbe*

FELICIA AMELLOIDES
Blue marguerite

Blue marguerite is a quality, warm-climate perennial, gaining in popularity. It is not a true marguerite but does have blue, yellow-centered flowers shaped like daisy. Use for borders or color accents.

It grows 1 to 2 feet high and spreads slowly 3 to 5 feet wide. Low branches root in moist soils and seed self-sow. Leaves are 1 inch long, oval, light green, and have a sandpaper texture. Flowers are about 1-1/4 inch in diameter and appear over a long season, primarily in cool weather of spring and fall.

Several named selections are available. One of the best is 'San Gabriel', which has much larger flowers.

Planting and care—Plant is adaptable and easy to grow. Performs best with regular water, improved soil and full sun. Some shade, especially afternoon shade, is recommended for hottest climates. Trim plants with hedge shears every fall or spring, just before new growth appears.

Hardy to 25F (−4C).

Polystichum acrostichoides

FERNS

As you might expect, ferns used as ground covers are a varied lot. Some are hardy and adaptable; others are tender with more exacting requirements. All will lend that exotic fern character to adapted locations of your garden.

Polystichum species prefer bright light with moist soil.

ADIANTUM PEDATUM
Five-finger fern

This is a delicate, particularly graceful fern, reaching 1 to 2 feet high and spreading as wide. Plant spreads by creeping rootstalks. Medium green leaflets rise from shiny, nearly black stalks. Roots are perennial and fronds essentially evergreen. Fronds will die-back during unfavorable growth periods.

Planting and care—Usually available in 1-gallon containers. Plant spring or early fall in loose, highly organic, moist, well-drained soil.

Hardy to −35F (−40C).

ATHYRIUM GOERINGIANUM 'PICTUM'
Japanese painted fern

This is the most colorful of the hardy ferns. Leaflets of the 9-inch long fronds are soft, dull green and have a metallic sheen. Stems and main veins are ruby-red, creating a dramatic contrast.

Plant grows about 15 inches high and makes a dense, weed-choking cover. It is deciduous.

Planting and care—Plant from 1-gallon containers, spring or fall. Grow in full sun or partial shade in moist, mulched soil. Does best in wind-sheltered locations.

Hardy to −35F (−40C).

CYRTOMIUM FALCATUM
Holly fern

Holly fern makes an attractive, evergreen, informal border along entryways or planted under camellias, rhododendrons and similar shrubs.

In some ways plant does not look like a typical fern. Thick, leathery, shiny green leaflets are 3 inches long and toothed, similar to holly leaves. Fronds are 2-1/2 feet or more long.

Planting and care—Plant from 1-gallon containers, 1-1/2 feet apart in light shade. Moist, loose soil is best. Set plants slightly high—planting too deep may cause crown rot. Be generous with water.

Hardy to 25F (−4C).

DAVALLIA TRICHOMANOIDES
Squirrel's-foot fern

This is a cold-tender fern of limited use. But it is interesting and worthwhile in temperate gardens, where it thrives, making an excellent, evergreen ground cover. It is often thought of only as a house plant. Most striking are the brown, fuzzy rhizomes that creep over the soil surface. Dark green fronds are about 12 inches long and 6 inches

Adiantum pedatum grows best with bright light, needing little or no direct sun.

Athyrium goeringianum 'Pictum' has unusual frond coloring.

wide at the widest point. Height is 6 to 8 inches. Plants spread to about 12 inches.

Planting and care—Easy to grow. Plant from containers in spring or fall. Any soil is acceptable. Plant in shaded, protected location. Water generously for best results.

Hardy to 30F (−1C).

DRYOPTERIS ERYTHROSORA
Autumn fern, Wood fern

The large group of *Dryopteris* species includes many, hardy native ferns. Autumn fern is a low-growing, spreading Asian import. It reaches 1-1/2 to 3 feet high and slowly spreads to about as wide with underground rhizomes.

When young fronds emerge, they are delicate looking and reddish. Later they become a rich, deep green.

Planting and care—Plant from containers as early in spring as soil can be worked. Grow in shade and moist, loose soil. Use a mulch and water frequently until established.

Hardy to −20F (−29C).

NEPHROLEPSIS CORDIFOLIA
Sword fern

These ferns often survive in neglected gardens, proof of their resilience. In adapted climates, sword ferns are easy to grow and spread with a vigor approaching invasiveness. Plant them around trees, in narrow beds or in any shaded, confined area.

Bright green fronds are 2 to 3 feet long and very upright. They spread by wiry, hairy rhizomes.

Planting and care—Plant from 1- or 5-gallon containers in shade in about any soil. Regular amounts of water are adequate. Drought tolerance is surprisingly good for a fern.

Hardy to 25F (−4C).

POLYSTICHUM
Christmas fern, Western sword fern

Two species of these hardy, ever-green, North American natives make fine ground covers.

Polystichum acrostichoides, Christmas fern, grows 2 to 3 feet high with an equal spread. It is very similar in appearance to Boston fern and often used as a house plant. Fronds are long lasting in indoor arrangements and are frequently available from florists. It prefers shade but will accept sun in moist soil.

Hardy to −35F (−40C).

P. munitum, western sword fern, is the large fern common to redwood forests of northern California. Shiny, dark green fronds may reach 2 to 5 feet in length. Spread is variable, but usually reaches about 3 feet. Individual plants produce up to 100 fronds. Plant in shade in moist soil high in organic matter.

Planting and care—Start with nursery plants—transplants rarely succeed. Grow in shade. Plants are self-sufficient once established.

Hardy to −25F (−32C).

RUMOHRA ADIANTIFORMIS
Leatherleaf fern

Deep green, finely divided fronds of leatherleaf fern look more delicate than they feel. They are surprisingly smooth and tough. They almost seem artificial. Leatherleaf fern tolerates more light and less water than most ferns. Plant grows 1 to 3 feet high in slow-spreading, evergreen clumps that eventually reach about 18 inches wide. The durable, long-lasting fronds are florist's favorites. Some catalogs list this plant as *Polystichum capense* or *Aspidium capense.*

Planting and care—Plants are available in 1-gallon containers. Plant in shade and moist soil to establish.

Hardy to 25F (−4C).

Dryopteris species are at home in woodland plantings, as shown above. Below, *Dryopteris* combine well with *Trachelospermum* and *Liriope muscari.*

Festuca ovina glauca forms geometric patterns in the garden.

Gray leaves of *Festuca ovina glauca* form a striking contrast to a dark green dichondra lawn.

FESTUCA OVINA GLAUCA
Blue fescue

This plant is hardy and easy to grow. It is a grass closely related to the fine fescues used to make lawns. Unlike a lawn grass, it has a unique growth habit, producing mounding clumps instead of a smooth, even cover. Designers appreciate its contribution to modern, geometric landscapes. Clumps become 4 to 10 inches high. Silver-blue leaves are needlelike, stiff and tough. Seedheads reach another 4 inches high. The silvery color of blue fescue lends a cooling effect to the landscape. Use it for borders, accents or any small spot where you want something different.

Planting and care—Plants are normally available in flats. Plant in full sun, any time of year. Space plants 6 to 12 inches apart. They are completely hardy, adaptable to most soils and drought tolerant. Clip seedheads and divide plants every few years for best appearance. For most intense blue color, occasionally cut tufts to ground level. Mulch between clumps for weed control.

Hardy to −35F (−40C).

Feverfew. See *Chrysanthemum*

Firethorn. See *Pyracantha*

Five-finger fern. See Ferns

Fleeceflower. See *Polygonum*

Forget-me-not. See *Myosotis*

FORSYTHIA INTERMEDIA 'ARNOLD DWARF'

This wide-spreading dwarf *Forsythia* is an excellent, erosion-controlling bank cover.

It is deciduous and grows 2 to 3 feet high in a mounding fashion. Spread is fast to 6 or 7 feet. Stems will root wherever they contact the soil. Unlike its full-size relatives, flowers are not showy and may not come at all the first few springs.

Planting and care—Plant from containers 2 feet apart in full sun. Accepts a little shade. Prefers slightly acid soil.

Hardy to −15F (−26C).

FRAGARIA
Wild strawberry

Strawberries grown for foliage instead of fruit make a beautiful, lush, dark, evergreen mat. They are tolerant, adaptable and will accept a small amount of foot traffic.

Wild strawberry grows 6 to 12 inches high and spreads 12 to 18 inches within a year. Dark green leaves are divided into three leaflets. They are tinged red in winter. White flowers are about 1 inch wide, and appear intermittently. They are followed by 3/4-inch, seedy fruit.

'Hybrid No. 25' is more vigorous and larger than common *Fragaria* species. In addition to producing an attractive, hardy cover, it produces sweet, edible fruit. For maximum fruit production, thin by removing a few plants.

Planting and care—Plant in full sun or partial shade, 6 to 12 inches apart. Plants are available in flats any time or as less-expensive bareroot plants in spring. They are surprisingly drought tolerant but generous water and spring fertilizer produce faster growth and more attractive plants. Mow with a rotary mower just before spring growth appears to promote dense, vigorous

Galium odoratum

Galium odoratum is more tough and resilient than it appears, adapting well to adverse conditions.

growth. Yellowing caused by iron chlorosis may occur in some soils. Apply iron sulfate or chelated iron as a corrective measure.

Hardy to 10F (−12C).

FUCHSIA PROCUMBENS
Trailing fuchsia

This New Zealand native is rare but a gem worth the search.

Trailing fuchsia is an evergreen that grows a few inches high by creeping along the ground. Small, green 1/2- to 3/4-inch leaves are nearly round. Flowers are less than 1 inch long, pale orange to yellow with green sepals. They are followed by bright red fruit that contain viable seed.

Planting and care—Trailing fuschia thrives when given the care and climate required by any fuschia. Plant from 1-gallon containers in cool, but sunny, frost-free areas. Space plants 12 inches apart. Generous water and periodic fertilizer keep plants healthy.

Hardy to 30F (−1C).

Funkia. See *Hosta*

GALIUM ODORATUM
Sweet woodruff

Sweet woodruff is a long-time garden favorite. It is hardy, attractive and useful as a culinary herb. Even though it looks somewhat delicate, it is adaptable to adverse conditions. Sweet woodruff is one of the few ground covers that will grow well in dry shade.

It is evergreen, usually less than 6 inches high but is occasionally higher. Plants spread fast, primarily by roots but also by seed. Sandpapery leaves are arranged in whorls around the stem. Leaves have an unusual, almost vanilla flavor, fresh or dried, that lends the essential character to May wine. Tiny, white flowers appear in clusters at stem tips in spring.

Sweet woodruff is often combined with other ground covers. Try it with *Asarum, Convallaria* or English ivy. It is a fine bulb cover and adapted to growing in crevices.

Planting and care—Roots are strong and grow well in any moist, rich soil. Space plants 6 inches apart for fast cover. Wider spacing, 12 to 18 inches apart, will fill in to make a solid cover but requires more time.

Hardy to −35F (−37C).

GARDENIA AUGUSTA 'RADICANS'
Synonym: G. jasminoides 'Radicans'
Miniature gardenia

If you like gardenias, try this low and spreading form for a small-area cover. It grows only 1 foot or less high and spreads in a mounding fashion 2 or 3 feet wide. Evergreen leaves are smaller but are the same glossy, dark green as full-size gardenias. Some leaves feature white streaks. Flower form and fragrance is the same as regular gardenias but size is a diminutive 1-inch diameter.

Planting and care—Gardenias are vigorous and fast growers when cultural conditions are met. They are native to warm, humid climates of the American Southeast. Soils in this area are usually acidic, rich, moist and fast draining. Without such soil, problems may occur. Add a lot of peat moss, leaf mold or other, acidic organic amendment to the soil. Also use these materials as a mulch. The best time to plant is spring or early fall. Plants are normally available in 1- or 5-gallon containers. Plant in partial shade. Place plants high in the soil when planting

Gaultheria shallon is one of the best ground covers for the Pacific Northwest. It does best with some shade and acid soil.

Gelsemium sempervirens rambles casually over arbor, fence or ground.

to avoid crown rot. Feed monthly and watch for aphids and whiteflies. Spray such pests with soap and water solution or Orthene. Chlorosis may be a problem, but can be corrected with iron chelate.

Hardy to 15F (−9C).

GAULTHERIA
Wintergreen, Salal

Gaultheria species are North American natives. Two of them serve admirably as ground covers in certain situations. *G. procumbens,* wintergreen, is primarily grown in the East. Main stems creep along at soil level. Upright, secondary branches grow to about 6 inches high. Individual plants spread about 18 inches wide. Evergreen leaves are oval, 2 inches long, glossy and grouped at branch tips. Small, white flowers appear in summer. Berries are fire-engine red, and appear in late spring.

This plant is the commercial source of oil of wintergreen, which is extracted from both leaves and fruit.

G. shallon, salal, is a Western species. It makes an outstanding

bank cover in Oregon and Washington. Plant is larger than *G. procumbens,* reaching 1 to 2 feet high and occasionally more. Leaves are bright green, between 2 and 4 inches long. Clusters of white to pink flowers appear in early summer. Black fruit are tasteless.

Planting and care—Either species is available in 1-gallon containers. Spring or fall are the best planting times. Grow *G. procumbens* in a porous, organic, acid soil and some shade. If well adapted, need for additional water or fertilizer is minimal.

Hardy to −30F (−35C).

G. shallon normally grows in full sun and dry soil. It will grow larger given some shade and rich, improved soil.

Hardy to −10F (−20C).

Gazania. See African Daisies

GELSEMIUM SEMPERVIRENS
Carolina jessamine

This is a hardy and vigorous evergreen plant, a favorite of the South. It is the official flower of South

Carolina. Commonly grown as a 20-foot vine, Carolina jessamine is easily kept to a sprawling, 3-foot high ground cover. If you have kids around, be aware that all parts of the plant are poisonous.

Partially deciduous leaves are glossy light green and evergreen. Bright yellow flowers are 1-1/2 inches long, tubular and enticingly fragrant. They come in late winter or early spring, depending on climate.

Planting and care—Plant from 1-gallon containers in spring or early fall. Adapted to almost any soil. Supply plants with regular water, even though drought tolerance is good. If plants are frost damaged or in need of rejuvenation, prune severely in early spring. They will recover quickly.

Hardy to 15F (−9C).

Genista. See Brooms

GERANIUM
Cranesbill

Geranium species are hardy plants with many low-maintenance virtues. They are not particular as to soil, requiring only good drainage. They will grow in full sun or partial

Geranium sanguineum prostratum is a colorful, spreading, easy-to-grow ground cover.

shade and are self-sufficient when established.

Don't confuse true *Geranium* species with the tender *Pelargonium,* which is also known as "geranium." This is an easy mistake because *Pelargonium* is more familiar to most people. See page 156.

Ground cover *Geranium* species are upright, trailing or rambling plants reaching about 1 foot high and usually twice as wide. Leaves are usually divided into many small leaf sections, creating a very fine-textured appearance. Flowers are 1 to 3 inches wide and have 5 petals. They come in rose, blue, purple, pink or white and appear from spring to fall.

Check nurseries and catalogs for the following species and varieties:

Geranium endressii 'Wargraves Pink'—Grows 12 to 18 inches high and spreads as wide with rounded, notched, bright green leaves. Flowers are clear pink and appear summer to fall.

G. himalayense—Grows in clumps 1 foot high and as wide. Leaves are nearly round, 3 to 4 inches wide and have 5 to 7 lobes. Flowers are magenta with dark purple veins, 1-1/2 to 2 inches wide. They are borne on long stalks.

G. incanum—Grows 6 to 10 inches high and spreads several feet wide. Leaves are finely cut. Pink, 1-inch wide flowers bloom spring to fall.

G. macrorrhizum, bigroot geranium—Grows to 1-1/2 feet tall and spreads with thick, underground roots. Leaves have 5 to 7 lobes. Magenta flowers.

G. sanguineum, blood-red geranium—Grows as a clump 1-1/2 feet high and 2 feet wide. Leaves are divided at their base into 5 or 7 toothed lobes. Flowers are usually dark purple but a white form, 'Album', is available. Plants self-sow. *G. s. prostratum* is more compact and has pink flowers.

Planting and care—Plants are normally available in 1-gallon containers. Most nurseries include them in their perennials section. The best time to plant is spring or early fall. Space plants 8 to 12 inches apart. Flowers are most abundant in full sun and loamy, moist soil. Plants are adaptable to other soils. Drought tolerant.

Most are hardy to −35F (−37C). *G. incanum* is hardy to 25F (−4C).

Germander. See *Teucrium*

Golden fleece. See Dyssodia

Goutweed. See *Aegopodium*

Grasses. See *Festuca, Phalaris* and *Zoysia*

GREVILLEA TRIDENTIFERA

This is a very fast-growing, evergreen, drought-resistant, Australian native. It grows close to the ground but occasionally produces erect stems that reach 4 or more feet high. Prune them out as necessary for best appearance. Leaves are light green and needlelike. Creamy white flowers that smell like honey are arranged along branches in clusters.

Planting and care—Nurseries offer plants in 1-gallon containers. Fall is the best planting time—moderate temperatures and winter rains aid establishment. Plant in full sun in any soil. Water frequently to establish roots, then only as needed.

Hardy to 20F (−7C).

Hall's Japanese honeysuckle. See *Lonicera*

Heavenly bamboo. See *Nandina*

Calluna vulgaris

HEATHS and HEATHERS

Heaths and heathers include four species of closely related plants: *Bruckenthalia, Calluna, Daboecia* and *Erica.* Grown in the proper environment—moist, well-drained and acid soil—they are premier low-maintenance plants. They are charming and interesting in their variation. By selecting appropriate species and varieties, you can enjoy bountiful, colorful floral displays in each of the four seasons.

BRUCKENTHALIA SPICUIFOLIA
Spike heath

Very compact and low growing to 1 foot or so high and twice as wide. Leaves are needlelike, have bristly points and are only 3/16 inch long. Pink flowers appear midsummer on 5-inch stems.

Hardy to −10F (−24C).

CALLUNA VULGARIS
Scotch heather

These are true heathers. They grow from a few inches high to 3 or more feet high. They spread 3 to 4 feet

Pastel colors of heaths and heathers blend well.

Calluna vulgaris 'Foxii Nana'

Calluna vulgaris 'Hammondii Aureifolia'

wide. They have naturalized in poor, sandy soils in much of Europe, Asia Minor, British Isles and the American Northeast and Northwest.

Heather leaves are often compared to junipers. They are evergreen, needlelike and overlapping. They are usually pale or deep green but some are yellow, chartreuse, gray or russet. Winter temperatures cause changes in leaf colors with attractive results.

Flowers are small, 1/4 inch long and bell shaped. Colors are white, all shades of pink, lavender and purple. Flowers are arranged along branch tips. They appear any time from midsummer to late fall, depending on climate and variety. Cut flowers are long lasting.

To encourage growth, prune and pinch after flowering but wait until spring to prune the latest bloomers. Check with specialist nurseries in your area for varieties and specific blooming dates.

Hardy to −35F (−37C).

DABOECIA CANTABRICA
Irish heath

This *Erica* species look-alike is distinguished by glossier leaves and larger flowers. It grows 18 inches high with slightly drooping, 1/2-inch long flowers on upright stems. Spread is 2 to 3 feet. A common variety is 'Praegerae'. Deep pink flowers appear midsummer to fall.

Hardy to −10F (−24C).

ERICA
Heath

This is a very large genus that includes many species and hybrids. All are evergreen shrubs with needlelike leaves. Most are bushy, prostrate shrubs and are excellent bank and ground covers. Some tall forms may be suitable as small trees.

Erica carnea, spring heath—A 1-foot high, 2- to 3-foot wide shrub.

Calluna vulgaris 'Gold Haze' produces white flowers on 2-foot-high stems in fall.

Planting combines *Picea*, shrubby *Potentilla* and *Calluna* species.

Evergreens, together with selected varieties of heaths and heathers, create a colorful, low-maintenance entrance.

Mass planting of heather is a strong accent against background of *Juniperus chinensis* 'Pfitzerana'.

Tolerant of alkaline soil. Leaves are 1/4 inch long, similar to *Calluna vulgaris*, arranged in circles along stems. Flowers are also 1/4 inch long, appearing on 1- to 2-inch spikes. They bloom late winter or midwinter in mild-climate areas. Useful varieties include 'Ruby Glow', 'Springwood' and 'Springwood Pink'.

Hardy to −10F (−24C).

E. cinerea, gray or twisted heath— Grows 1 to 1-1/2 feet high with stiff stems. Leaves are glossy green and golden in fall. Summer flowers are red to purple and appear on 3-inch spikes. Wild forms have naturalized along much of the East Coast. Tolerates alkaline soil. Many varieties to choose from. Check with your nurseryman for the best ones.

Hardy to −10F (−24C).

E. darlyensis, darley heath—A vigorous hybrid of *E. carnea* and *E. herbacea*. A dense and creeping plant growing to about 3 feet high. Many varieties available. Flowers are lilac-pink. They appear fall to spring, depending on climate. Tolerant of lime soils.

Hardy to −5F (−21C).

E. tetralix, cross-leaved heath— One of the most cold-hardy heaths. Grows to about 18 inches high and has woolly, evergreen leaves. Rose-red flowers bloom in summer. It has escaped from gardens and has naturalized over much of the eastern United States, particularly along the Massachusetts coast. A native of western Europe.

Hardy to −35F (−37C).

E. vagans, Cornish heath—This plant and *E. carnea* are the most popular heaths. Plant is low and spreading to about 1 foot high. It is not prostrate, but bushy and rounded. Blooms midsummer to fall. Preferred by many for flower color and hardiness. Native to western Europe. Many varieties are available.

Hardy to −15F (−26C).

Planting and care—Plants are typically available in 1-gallon containers. Spring or early fall are best planting times. Most require full sun and regular watering. Acid soil and no lime is the rule for all heaths and heathers. In the Pacific Northwest and Northeast, acid soil is the rule and plants thrive. Elsewhere, plan to amend soil with generous quantities of peat moss, leaf mold or similar organic material. Add enough so that amendment makes up approximately 50% of the soil. If soil is alkaline and heavy, consider the few varieties that tolerate such conditions. Then modify soil to preferred conditions. If drainage is slow, plant in raised mounds or beds.

Roots stay close to soil surface. Keep cultivation around plants to a minimum and use a mulch. Protect from cold temperatures by laying evergreen branches on top of plants. Prune cold-damaged stems and branches in spring.

See individual descriptions for hardiness ratings.

Heather used as an informal border-hedge.

Calluna vulgaris 'Kenneth' grows about 18 inches high. Flowers appear in August and last until mid-September.

Calluna vulgaris 'Mrs. Ronald Gray' is very dwarf—height is a diminutive 2 to 4 inches. Flowers appear in August and last until September.

Hedera helix flower bud cluster.

Versatile *Hedera helix* as ground cover, vine, and, at upper left, a tree.

HEDERA
Ivy

Ivy is probably *the* most commonly planted ground cover, and for many good reasons. It is evergreen, attractive, dependable and predictable. Roots reach deep into the soil to bind and hold banks and slopes. Dwarf kinds of English ivy make excellent bulb covers. Most ivies are adaptable to any type of soil and tolerate sun or shade. Give them shade only in the desert.

Hedera helix, English ivy, is most common and widely grown. Of the hundreds of named varieties available, several are quite hardy. *H. canariensis,* Algerian ivy, is very popular where hardy. It flourishes in most of Florida, southern and coastal California and in similar mild climates. *H. colchica,* Persian ivy, is a hardier, larger-leafed version of Algerian ivy.

Ivy does have some drawbacks. Within a few years, Algerian ivy builds up thick mats of stems that become a haven for rodents and other pests. Ivy is also a favorite habitat and meal of slugs and snails.

Ivy is a prodigious climber. Covering a wire fence may be fine, but clinging, aerial roots can damage wood and painted surfaces.

You may notice some changes if your ivy is allowed to grow vertically, such as up a tree, trellis, fence or house. After several years of growth, it will develop flowering shoots with different shaped leaves. This is *mature* growth—the growth phase that develops flowers and fruit. Technically, common leaf shapes and growth habits are *juvenile.* Any cuttings you make for propagation retain the traits of their source, whether mature or juvenile.

Here are descriptions of popular *Hedera* species and a few selected varieties:

HEDERA CANARIENSIS
Algerian ivy

Fast growing with large, shiny green, 5- to 8-inch wide, lobed leaves. Plant 12 to 18 inches apart to make a solid cover within 2 years. Needs generous water, frequent mowing and control of slugs and snails. Coarse and rather rampant —not for small gardens. *H. c.* 'Variegata' has leaves edged in white. It is more sensitive to heat damage.

Hardy to 15F (−9C).

HEDERA COLCHICA
Persian ivy

Heart-shaped leaves are large— up to 7 inches wide and 10 inches long. 'Dentata', with notched leaves, is the common form. Used often along Atlantic Coast from Philadelphia south.

Hardy to −10F (−24C).

HEDERA HELIX
English ivy

English ivy is the most important and widely grown ivy. It grows more slowly than other *Hedera* species. Planted 12 to 18 inches apart, it makes a solid cover in about four years. Leaves are usually dark green and leathery, less than 5 inches wide and have 3 to 5 lobes.

H. helix has hundreds of varieties. Many mutations occur from it, and new leaf forms or colors occur frequently. All varieties fall into two groups: *coarse and extra-hardy;* or *dwarf, small-leafed and tender.*

Hardy ivies are represented by the well-known 'Baltica' and '238th Street' from the eastern United States. 'Thorndale' and 'Wilson' are similar, hardy ivies that originated in the midwestern United States.

All are hardy to about −20F (−29C).

Dwarf, tender ivies are more numerous. Popular varieties include 'Hahn's Self-branching', 'Needlepoint', 'Glacier' and 'Mapleleaf'. Many make excellent container and topiary plants. Most are quite well suited as ground covers for small and shady areas. They do well among other plants. They are adapted to most of California and the Southwest, and range on the East Coast from Washington D.C. south.

Hardy to −5F (−21C).

Planting and care—Plant ivies in sun or shade. Rich, moist soil is best, but ivies are not particular as to soil quality. Spacing is up to you. Close spacing means a faster cover and fewer weed problems. Wide spacing means fewer plants are required to cover more area. Provide regular water to establish and maintain. In general, ivy needs about as much water as lawn.

Trim the edges of ivy beds two to four times a year, in most situations. Hedge shears—manual, electric or gasoline powered—are used. Trimming edges is much less laborious if done regularly before a thick mat of dry, brittle stems accumulates.

Ivy needs mowing twice a year in long growing-season areas. Mowing fast-growing Algerian ivy is strongly advised. English ivy grows slower, especially in short-season climates. It requires mowing once a year or every other year. Mowing stimulates more uniform, weed-free and attractive growth.

Best times to mow are February and July. If not mowed, Algerian ivy becomes thicker each year. Generally, all ivies are more attractive if mowed.

Ivies are subject to leaf diseases encouraged by watering in the afternoon—the hottest hours of the day. Water in early morning to prevent such diseases.

See species and variety descriptions for hardiness.

Hedera helix with *Juniperus* species creates a low-maintenance, evergreen ground cover.

Hedera canariensis makes a thick, fast-growing slope cover.

Hemerocallis is an excellent choice for color and low maintenance.

Hemerocallis flowers reveal exquisite form and bold color.

HELIANTHEMUM NUMMULARIUM
Sun rose

Sun rose makes an interesting and showy ground cover. It is evergreen, generally hardy and very charming. It admirably conforms to the surface it covers, spilling around and over rocks and down walls. It is adapted to the seacoast, but thrives nearly anywhere in full sun and fast-draining soil.

Describing this plant is difficult. Many varieties and hybrids of *Helianthemum* are commonly sold as "sun rose." Most grow 6 to 12 inches high and spread twice as wide. Leaves are narrow, 1/2 to 1 inch long. They are sometimes shiny green on top or maybe gray on both top and bottom. Flowers are very showy. They may be single or double, 1 to 2 inches wide. They come in variations or combinations of red, pink and yellow. Individually, flowers are short-lived. But the plant is productive enough to provide continuous bloom for two months in late spring to summer.

Planting and care—Plant from 1-gallon containers or flats. Fall is the best time to plant. Space plants 12 to 18 inches apart. Full sun and fast drainage are the important requirements. Avoid overwatering once roots are established. Sun rose prefers alkaline soil. If your soil is acid, amend with ground limestone at about 5 pounds per 100 square feet. Protect plants with a loose mulch in winter if there is no snow cover.

Hardy to −10F (−24C).

HEMEROCALLIS
Daylily

Daylilies are one of the best low-maintenance perennials. They are easy to grow, pest-free and widely adapted. Use them along banks, in light shade under tall trees, as a solid border or combined with other plants. The beauty, variety and quantity of flowers they produce, together with their adaptiveness, make them very attractive and popular.

Plants grow between 3 and 6 feet high. Roots are thick and fleshy. Grasslike leaves have a prominent center vein. Typical lily flowers are clustered on top of long, strong stems. They are between 3 and 8 inches wide. Colors range from pale white to yellow, orange, gold, pink and red. Individual flowers last only one day, but one plant will continue to produce flowers over a 3- to 6-week period. By mixing varieties with different flowering times you can enjoy flowers from spring to fall.

Most older varieties of daylilies are deciduous. Modern hybrids, which are most common today, may be either deciduous or evergreen. *H. fulva*, tawny daylily, is a deciduous, old-fashioned form still frequently planted. It is tall—flowers reach to 6 feet high. Leaves are 2 feet long and 1 inch wide. Flowers are orange-red, 4 inches wide and come in midsummer.

'Kawnso' is a double-flowered type that has naturalized around country homes in Georgia, Alabama and South Carolina.

'Europa' is tolerant of adverse conditions. It is used to cover areas with poor soils and generally grows in inhospitable places.

Daylilies are easy to hybridize and many professionals and amateurs work with them. The result is hundreds of named varieties, many of them outstanding. Among the highest regarded are 'Catherine Woodbury', 'Cherry Cheeks', 'Heavenly Harp', 'Mary Todd' and 'Winning Ways'. Recent American Horticultural Society reports list 'Ed Murray', 'Ruffled Apricot' and

Herniaria glabra grows well in spaces between steppingstones.

Heuchera sanguinea 'Santa Ana Cardinal' shown at peak bloom in late spring.

'Sabie' as most popular. Ask your nurseryman about these, or check with one of the many mail order nurseries that specialize in daylilies. See page 174.

Other varieties more commonly available include 'Chic Gal', 'Cradle Song', 'Frans Hals' and 'Swansdown'.

Many nurseries offer daylilies simply labeled by color. Plant quality is unknown.

You may hear of *tetraploid* daylilies. This means plants have had their chromosome numbers doubled by chemicals. They are usually more vigorous and robust, and have larger flowers. Some are expensive collector's items.

Planting and care—Best planting times are late spring to summer. Most nurseries stock daylilies in 1-gallon containers; mail order nurseries will ship you semidormant crowns or roots. Space plants 12 to 18 inches apart for a weed-smothering ground cover.

Daylilies are adaptable. Loam soil is ideal, but they tolerate heavy, light, dry or wet soils. Full sun is usually best but bright shade is acceptable, sometimes preferred for light-colored flowers. In hottest inland or desert areas, afternoon shade is advised. Spring and fall applications of 10-10-10 or similar fertilizer helps maintain strong growth. Daylilies are drought tolerant but do better with regular water. Be especially attentive to moisture during flowering. Divide plants to propagate or to thin out beds.

Most evergreen kinds are hardy to at least −20F (−29C). Deciduous varieties are hardy between −35F and −50F (−40C and −45C).

Herbs. See *Achillea, Artemisia, Chamaemelum, Galium, Gaultheria, Mentha, Nepeta, Origanum, Rosmarinus, Santolina, Teucrium* and *Thymus*

HERNIARIA GLABRA
Rupturewort

This is an evergreen perennial that is very low and spreading. It accepts occasional foot traffic, and is one of the best plants between brick paving or stepping stones.

Plant grows less than 3 inches high. Trailing stems root as they spread. Leaves are small, 1/4 inch long and shiny green. They become bronze-red in cold weather.

Planting and care—Rupturewort is commonly available in flats from which you cut sections to plant. Plant in full sun or some shade 6 to 8 inches apart. Any soil is acceptable. Maintain regular soil moisture. Fertilize lightly in spring and fall.

Hardy to −5F (−21C).

HEUCHERA
Coral bells

Arranged in rows with other bedding plants in the nursery, coral bells seem common. But their long bloom season, easy care and delicate growth habit are winning over many gardeners.

Plants grow in a clump form 8 to 24 inches high and spread slowly to 3 feet wide. Leaves are evergreen, almost round and have scalloped edges. Bell-shaped flowers are red, pink, rose or white. They grow to about 1/2 inch long. Hummingbirds love them. They are arranged in loose clusters well above leaves. Flowers are long lasting in arrangements. Bloom season varies with climate but late spring to late summer is typical.

Heuchera sanguinea is the best-known coral bells. Leaves are 1 to 2 inches long. Flowers appear on 1- to

(Continued on page 132)

Hosta leaf

Hosta 'Honeybells' produces showy, fragrant flowers.

HOSTA
Hosta, Funkia, Plantain lily

Hostas have always had many admirers. Over the past few years, they have attracted many new ones. Hostas are high-quality, low-maintenance, deciduous perennials. Large, interesting, blue-green leaves are the main attraction. They are always included in lists of the best plants to grow in shade. Plants are hardy and are generally healthier if exposed to some winter cold.

Heights vary between 6 and 36 inches, depending on species and variety. Leaves come in many sizes and shapes, but are generally heart-shaped with large, prominent veins. Flowers of some varieties are very showy—a few are fragrant. All are lilylike and bloom in late summer on graceful stalks.

Varieties of hostas number in the thousands, and their names are confusing. Botanists have not helped much by changing proper names frequently. You will probably find the same plant listed under different names at different nurseries. Synonyms listed here will help avoid some misidentity. For best results, buy from reputable mail order nurseries or purchase nursery plants when they are in leaf.

Of the many species and varieties, the following are most frequently available and recommended as ground covers:

H. decorata—Makes neat mounds 2 feet high. Leaves are oval, 6 inches long, green with white edges. Leaf tips have blunt points. Purple flowers are showy and appear in great profusion mid to late summer. Sometimes listed as 'Thomas Hogg'. Plant 12 to 18 inches apart.

Hardy to −10F (−24C).

'Honeybells'—Grows fast to 2 feet tall with large, shiny, grass-green leaves. Produces the most showy flowers of all hostas. They appear midsummer on 3-1/2-foot stalks. Color is lavender-lilac, marked with blue streaks on a white underbase. Gardenialike fragrance is pleasantly penetrating. Plant 12 to 18 inches apart.

Hardy to −34F (−40C).

H. lancifolia, narrow-leafed plantain lily—Makes 1-1/2- to 2-foot clumps of waxy, dark green, slender, 6-inch leaves that taper into a long stalk. Pale lavender flowers are 2 inches long on 2-foot stems. They appear in late summer. Plant 12 inches apart. May be listed as *H. japonica*.

Hardy to −35F (−40C).

H. plantaginea, fragrant plantain lily—Grows 1 to 1-1/2 feet high and 3 feet wide. Leaves are bright green, rounded, 10 inches long. Trumpet-shaped flowers are white, fragrant and grow 4 to 5 inches long. They appear late summer or fall on 2-foot stems. Frequently listed as *H. grandiflora* or *H. subcordata*.

Hardy to −30F (−35C).

H. sieboldiana, blue-leaved plantain lily—This hosta has the largest and most dramatic leaves. Bluish, gray-green leaves reach up to 15 inches long and are heavily textured, like cardboard corrugations. Plant grows in a clump 15 inches high and 3 feet wide. Flowers are white and appear midsummer but are mostly hidden by leaves. Use to accent shady paths or near pools or streams. Many varieties are available. May be listed as *H. glauca.*

Hardy to −35F (−37C).

H. undulata, wavy-leafed plantain lily—This is one of the most common hostas. It spreads faster and accepts more sun than most hostas. It is excellent for edging or massing. Leaves are green with silver-white variegations and have wavy margins. They reach 6 to 8 inches long. Frequently used in flower arrangements. Flowers are pale lavender and showy. They bloom on 18-inch stalks in midsummer. Often listed as *H. media picta* or *H. variegata.*

Hardy to −35F (−37C).

H. ventricosa, blue plantain lily—A less common hosta but notable on two accounts. Flowers are showy and vivid blue, and seed produce plants true to type, unlike most hostas. Plant quickly grows into a clump 1 to 1-1/2 feet high and 2 feet wide. Deep green leaves are egg shaped and fine textured. Leaves are shiny on undersides and twisted at tips. Flowers bloom mid to late summer on 18-inch stems. Also commonly known as *H. caerulea.*

Hardy to −35F (−40C).

Planting and care—Nurseries keep hostas available in 1-gallon containers. Best planting time is spring, but any time until early fall is okay.

Grow hostas in sun or light to heavy shade. Moist, loam soil is ideal but dry soil is tolerated. Avoid overly wet soil. Supply regular water in summer and fertilize in spring as growth begins. Snails and slugs love hostas. Left alone, they will make a planting ragged by midsummer. Bait two or three times a year or use traps all season long. Remove flower stalks before seed mature. Seed are viable, but not true to type. You may want to experiment with seed. Propagate preferred varieties by division.

Hardiness varies with species and variety. See individual descriptions.

Hosta 'Honeybells' and *Pachysandra terminalis* in foreground.

Hosta decorata in front of *H. plantaginea.*

Hosta surrounded by *Epimedium.*

Hypericum calycinum covers slope.

Iberis sempervirens is drought tolerant and long-lived.

(*Heucheria,* continued from page 129)

2-foot stalks. Plant is hardy to −35F (−37C). 'Santa Ana Cardinal' is larger and more vigorous. Flowers are more profuse and better colored. It is fairly cold sensitive—hardy to about 25F (−4C).

Planting and care—Plant in full sun or partial shade. Almost any soil is acceptable. Drought tolerance is good. Regular watering and rich soil give best results. Remove faded flower stalks. Divide clumps if they become crowded.

Holly. See *Ilex*

Holly fern. See Ferns

Holly grape. See *Mahonia*

HYPERICUM CALYCINUM
Aaron's-beard, Creeping St. John's wort

This is one of the most common ground covers. It is evergreen, adaptable to poor soil and some drought. Roots are strong and knit to hold banks and hillsides, but they also compete with tree roots for water and nutrients. Plants can become invasive. Growth is fast to about 1 foot high, spreading 12 inches in a season to form a fairly dense, uniform carpet. Leaves are 4 inches long and usually medium green. Flowers are an attractive, bright yellow with many gold-tipped stamens in the center. They reach about 3 inches in diameter.

Planting and care—Aaron's beard persists almost anywhere but prefers humid, coastal climates and moist soil. Plant about 18 inches apart in full sun if you live near the coast. In inland areas, plant in partial shade. Weak plantings with silvery leaves are probably infested with spider mites. Mow planting beds, spray with karathane, fertilize and water deeply to control mites. Mow in spring every two or three years to rejuvenate plantings.

Hardy to −20F (−29C).

IBERIS SEMPERVIRENS
Evergreen candytuft, Candytuft

This is a wonderful and deservedly popular plant. Evergreen candytuft fits into the low-maintenance category, although you might not think so judging by its delicate appearance. It is one of the premier edging and border plants and is also an attractive small-area ground cover. The Latin name derives from *Iberia,* an ancient name for Spain, where it is native.

Plants usually grow less than 1 foot high, although some reach 18 inches. Dark green leaves are narrow and about 1-1/2 inches long. Spread is slow and roughly equal to height. White flowers bloom in compact clusters in very early spring and sometimes fall. They completely cover leaves when in full bloom. 'Snowflake', 'Autumn Snow' and 'Little Gem' are recommended, more compact varieties.

Planting and care—Evergreen candytuft is available in a number of forms: 1-gallon containers, individual plastic pots, plastic packs as bedding plants or flats. Spring or fall is best planting time, but exact timing is not critical. Plant in full sun or part shade. Any soil is acceptable. Space plants about 6 to 8 inches apart. Drought tolerance is very good. Cut back after flowering to encourage dense growth, and after severe winters.

Hardy to −35F (−37C).

Drosanthemum floribundum

ICE PLANTS

Ice plants are brightly flowered succulents common to all Mediterranean climates. Outstanding, low-maintenance ground covers near the coast, they grow admirably inland if given a little additional water. Light doses of fertilizer in spring and fall promotes vigorous growth. Small-leafed, low-growing ice plants are excellent on slopes for erosion control. Large-leafed types, namely *Carpobrotus* species, are not recommended for steep slopes.

Planting and care—Ice plants can be planted any time, but either spring or early fall is best. Most kinds are available in flats. *Carpobrotus* species root so easily that fall planting of cuttings from the neighbor's garden often succeeds. All ice plants prefer full sun and well-drained soil.

Hardiness of the different kinds varies, and is included with each individual description.

CARPOBROTUS
Ice plant, Sea fig, Hottentot fig

Excellent coastal ground cover. Grows in shifting sand and helps to

Drosanthemum floribundum provides intense color and protects slope from erosion.

stabilize it. Reaches 12 to 18 inches high and spreads by trailing stems. *Carpobrotus* grows fast, so space 12 to 18 inches apart. Easily propagated by cuttings. Beds occasionally die out in spots, caused by excessive moisture, particularly after prolonged drought. Few pests bother these plants. Two common species are available: *C. chilensis* has 2-inch, straight leaves and rose-purple flowers. *C. edulis* leaves are longer and curved. Flowers are light yellow to pale pink. Fruit is edible but not very tasty.

Hardy to 20F (−7C).

CEPHALOPHYLLUM 'RED SPIKE'

This ice plant is notable for its clawlike, upright leaves and brilliant, abundant, cerise-red flowers. Growth is slow to 3 to 5 inches high

and 15 to 18 inches wide. Reddish leaves point straight up and are moderately fire retardant. Flowers are 2 inches wide and bloom profusely late winter to early spring. Bees like them. Plant in full sun, 6 to 12 inches apart in well-drained soil.

Hardy to 10F (−12C).

DELOSPERMA 'ALBA'
White trailing ice plant

Flowers are not showy but this low-growing ice plant is one of the best for covering steep slopes. Excellent in coastal areas. Slightly fire retardant. Trailing stems grow fast and root as they go. Triangular-shaped leaves are 1 inch long and make a mat 6 to 7 inches high. Small, white flowers are not showy and are favored by bees. Plant in sun 12 inches apart.

Hardy to 20F (−7C).

Drosanthemum floribundum shields barren, rocky soil and adds brilliant color.

DROSANTHEMUM
Rosea ice plant

These are among the most popular ice plants. Two kinds are available. Leaves of both are moderately fire resistant and covered with shiny spots that look like tiny crystals. Both grow in full sun and require little water once established.

D. floribundum, rosea ice plant, is the most important, and is the best ice plant for erosion control. It is very low growing, to 6 inches, and wide spreading. Plant trails attractively and spills over walls. Pale pink flowers are 3/4 inch in diameter and loved by bees. Flowers are abundant and completely cover leaves, beginning in late spring and lasting until early summer.

The other kind is *D. hispidum.* A 2-foot high clumping form with 1-inch purple flowers, it is easily confused with and sold as *D. floribundum.*

Both are hardy to 20F (−7C).

LAMPRANTHUS
Ice plant

These are the large-flowered, brilliant, fluorescent-colored ice plants. Four species and several varieties are available. Growth habit is upright or trailing. Three-sided leaves are long and cylindrical. All *Lampranthus* species have good drought tolerance once established. They are excellent near the warm coastal areas. Cut back after bloom to stimulate bushy growth. Shop for plants by color in spring when they are in flower at the nursery. Flowers attract bees.

L. aurantiacus, bush ice plant, has upright growth to 10 or 15 inches. Leaves are gray-green, 1 inch long and 3-sided. Flowers are 1-1/2 to 2 inches in diameter. Peak bloom is in spring. Space plants 1 to 1-1/2 feet apart. 'Glaucus' has clear, bright yellow flowers. 'Gold Nugget' flowers are bright orange. 'Sunman' flowers are golden yellow.

L. filicaulis, Redondo creeper, is a trailing, slow-growing, small-area ground cover. Plants reach only 3 inches high. Stems are thin. Small, pink flowers appear in early spring.

L. productus, purple ice plant, is excellent for winter color. It has an upright habit to 15 inches high and spreads 24 inches wide. Leaves are gray-green with bronze tips. Purple flowers are 1 inch wide, and appear late winter to spring. Space plants 12 to 18 inches apart.

L. spectabilis, trailing ice plant, is perhaps the most spectacular of all ice plants when in full bloom. Grows 15 inches high and 24 inches wide. Leaves are gray-green. Flowers are 2 inches in diameter and available in pink, rose, red or purple. At peak bloom they make a solid carpet of color. Space plants 12 to 18 inches apart.

Hardy to 20F (−7C).

MALEPHORA

The two following species produce flowers almost all year, but not in the intense, all-at-once fashion of *Lampranthus* species. Both have excellent heat, drought and smog tolerance. They are used extensively along highways. It also may be spelled *Maleophora*.

M. crocea, croceum ice plant, is the most cold-hardy trailing ice plant used for erosion control. It grows 6 inches high and has smooth, gray-green leaves. Reddish yellow flowers are relatively sparse. *M.c. purpureocrocea* has pinkish yellow flowers and blue-green leaves.

Hardy to 10F (−12C).

M. luteola, yellow trailing ice plant, grows about 10 inches high. Leaves are small and light green. It does not produce long runners so is not recommended for erosion control. Flowers are bright yellow and appear almost all year. Space plants about 12 inches apart.

Hardy to 20F (−7C).

OSCULARIA

These ice plants are less common. They grow 1 foot high with upright and trailing branches. Leaves are three-sided and blue-green. Flowers are 1/2 inch in diameter, pink or rose and slightly fragrant. They bloom mostly in late spring.

Hardy to 20F (−7C).

RUSCHIA

Compact grower from 4 to 6 inches high with attractive, 1/2-inch long, blue-gray leaves. Purplish stems are wiry. Lavender flowers are small, and appear in spring. Space plants 12 inches apart.

Hardy to 20F (−7C).

Cephalophyllum 'Red Spike' flowers in early spring.

Delosperma 'Alba' is well adapted to steep slopes and warm coastal areas.

Brilliance of *Lampranthus spectabilis* bloom is muted by gray *Festuca ovina glauca*.

Ilex cornuta 'Dwarf Burford'

Ilex vomitoria 'Nana' is ideal for a low border, hedge or ground cover.

ILEX

Hollies are especially popular in America's Southeast, where some are native. They are some of the most important landscape shrubs available. Hollies bring to mind the image of tall shrubs with shiny, thorny, evergreen leaves and red berries. But some have smooth leaves, yellow, orange or black berries. Several dwarf hollies make excellent shrubby ground covers.

Planting and care—Hollies grow best in rich, slightly acid soil. Supply with regular water from spring to summer through the growing season. Full sun is usually best, but some shade, especially afternoon shade, is recommended for regions with intense, dry heat.

Roots grow close to the surface so cultivate around them carefully. Summer mulches help by keeping roots cool.

Scale, whitefly and mealybug are occasional pests. If they are persistent problems in your garden, use an oil spray in late spring. Leaf-miner is serious in some areas and can be controlled only by *systemic* sprays. These are sprays that are absorbed by the plant to protect itself.

Recommend systemics include Cygon, Meta-systox R and Orthene. Holly bud moth, familiar to Pacifc Northwest gardeners, is best controlled with diazinon. Be sure to read the directions and timing instructions on product labels.

ILEX CORNUTA
Chinese holly

Chinese hollies usually have glossy, leathery, almost rectangular leaves with spines at the corners. Berries are large, bright red and long lasting, although some of the dwarf kinds do not set berries. Best berry production is in long, warm seasons.

Varieties include:

'Carissa'—Extremely dwarf, dense mutation of 'Rotunda'. Leaves are 2 to 3-1/2 inches long and have a single spine at the tip. Produces no berries. Originated in Cairo, Georgia.

'Dwarf Burford'—May eventually reach 5 feet high but remains about 18 inches high for 5 years. Leaves are 1/2 inch long, dark green and spineless. Berries are dark red and small.

'Rotunda', dwarf Chinese holly—May eventually reach 5 feet high but stays as low as 18 inches for up to 6 years. Plant can easily be kept low by pruning. Leaves are long and spiny, 2 to 3-1/2 inches long. Mature plants produce a few berries but they are hidden by leaves.

All are hardy to about 0F (−18C).

ILEX CRENATA
Japanese holly

These are more hardy than Chinese holly. They have black berries and finely toothed, 1/2- to 3/4-inch leaves. Appearance is similar to boxwood rather than typical hollies.

Ilex cornuta 'Carissa'

Ilex vomitoria 'Nana' accepts shearing.

Ilex cornuta 'Carissa' as a low, mounding ground cover.

Ilex vomitoria 'Nana' as natural, unpruned low hedge.

Ilex cornuta 'Rotunda'

Ilex cornuta 'Helleri' as a low hedge and ground cover in front of azaleas.

Varieties are:

'Compacta', dwarf Japanese holly—Very dense with glossy, dark green, 1/2-inch leaves. Densely branched. Berries are black.

'Green Island'—Slow growing to 2 or sometimes 3 feet high. Spreads 4 to 5 feet. Small leaves and open growth habit. Black berries.

'Green Thumb'—Dense and horizontal-branching to 2 or 3 feet high with a wider spread. Leaves are deep green, berries are black.

'Helleri'— Most widely planted Japanese holly. Reaches about 1 foot high with mounding and slightly spreading habit. Leaves are 3/8 inch long. Black berries.

'Mariesii'—Lowest growing of all hollies. Reaches only 8 inches high or less. Small leaves. Black berries.

All are hardy to about −10F (−24C).

ILEX VOMITORIA
Yaupon

Yaupon holly is a native of coastal regions in the American Southeast. Leaves are narrow, usually 1 inch long and dark green. Berries are small and scarlet. Many forms are available. Some can be trained into small trees.

Two excellent dwarfs are:

'Nana'—Grows 18 inches high and 36 inches wide. Leaves are olive-green, about 1/2 inch long. Berries are small, translucent red and appear profusely on previous season's growth.

'Stokes Dwarf'—A more compact version of 'Nana'. Dark green leaves are closely set along branches.

Hardy to about 5F (−15C).

Indian mock strawberry. See *Duchesnea*

Irish moss. See Moss

Isotoma. See *Laurentia*

Ivy geranium. See *Pelargonium*

Japanese anemone. See *Anemone*

Japanese spurge. See *Pachysandra*

Juniperus sabina 'Tamariscifolia'

JUNIPERUS

Needle-leafed, low-growing junipers are the most dependable and practical ground covers. They are evergreen, sometimes with blue, silver or plum-colored tints. When established, junipers are hardy to cold and tolerant of heat and drought.

Junipers comprise a wide and variable group. Height, spread, color and texture vary, as well as landscape use. Many are adapted to covering slopes, banks and large areas. Most drape gracefully over walls and around stones and boulders. Low-growing types produce carpetlike covers, similar to lawns. Taller-growing types are used as dividers and screens, but may shelter rodents and pests. Blue-colored junipers mix effectively with other evergreens and other junipers. A few junipers are particularly well-adapted to coastal conditions.

Planting and care—Junipers are generally predictable and reliable. They are not exacting in their requirements, but do need full sun and well-drained soil. Some shade is tolerated but color fades and foliage drops. They are not fussy as to soil type but good drainage is necessary.

Juniperus sabina 'Tamariscifolia' is one of the most common ground cover junipers. Upward-facing branchlets make it easy to recognize.

Avoid growing junipers in low spots —wherever puddles form naturally during rains. Many are susceptible to root rot in such conditions.

Proper spacing is important to the success of a juniper planting. This usually means spacing junipers more distantly than seems natural. As a rule, most species should be spaced 3 or 4 feet apart. Junipers are slow growing but avoid the temptation to put plants close together. Many spread 6 feet or more in each direction. When they grow into equally spreading neighbors it makes an unattractive ridge. Cares should be taken when planting junipers adjacent to sidewalks or similar borders. If placed too close, you will battle their spreading growth as long as they live. Check the following descriptions for typical spreads and spacing recommendations.

Junipers are generally very tough, pest-resistant plants, but three pest problems are significant: root rot, juniper tip moth and *Phomopsis* tip blight. Heavy, poorly drained soils promote root rot. The junipers most tolerant of root rot, listed in order of preference, are: *J. virginiana* 'Silver Spreader', *J. procumbens* and *J. conferta*.

Tip moth is a common pest, particularly along the California coast and several miles inland. It is not a pest in foggy areas. Only growing tips are attacked. If many are attacked at once, the entire plant looks brown. Most resistant are *J. chinensis sargentii*, *J. horizontalis* 'Youngstown', *J. horizontalis* 'Wiltonii' and *J. procumbens*.

Phomopsis tip blight is a serious pest of many junipers along the Atlantic Coast and in the Midwest. Tips of branches first become brown, then the whole branch and sometimes the entire plant browns. It is encouraged by moist weather, by water splashed onto plants and overhead sprinkling. *J. chinensis sargentii* has good resistance. Species particularly susceptible are *J. horizontalis* and *J. procumbens*. Avoid watering by overhead sprinklers and use a mulch that prevents splashing. Fixed copper and Actidione RZ are effective sprays.

Junipers are occasionally attacked by spider mites. These pests thrive in dry, hot weather and give plants a pale, sickly appearance. Use karathane to control. Wash with a wetting agent or soap and water solution to discourage them.

Bagworms are serious enough in some areas to require control. *J. virginiana* is most favored. Clip off and remove bags if possible. Use *Bacillus thuringiensis* plus a wetting agent to control.

Pine-needle scale and juniper scale are sometimes bothersome to junipers. Use the same oil spray used for spider mites. Mix with diazinon or malathion if the infestation is serious. Read the product label.

Juniper names—All junipers are named, cutting-propagated varieties. Plants grown from seed are quite variable. The great variety of junipers has led to hundreds of forms and considerable confusion over their proper names. For classification, we have relied primarily on *Woody Ornamental Plants*, published by the University of California, and catalogs of major nurseries. Synonyms are included.

JUNIPERUS CHINENSIS
Chinese juniper

The species form of this group is a 60-foot tree. Many varieties, selections and hybrids are included in the following. Several make excellent ground covers.

'Armstrong'—Compact, to 4 feet high and as wide. Leaves are gray-green, similar to 'Pfitzerana'. Growth habit resembles a bird's nest.

'Fruitlandii'—An improved form of *J. chinensis* 'Pfitzerana Compacta'. Growth is vigorous, dense and compact. Leaves are bright green.

'Old Gold', golden Armstrong juniper—Similar but more compact than 'Pfitzerana'. Grows 3 feet high and 4 feet wide. Dependable, bronze-gold color.

'Pfitzerana Aurea Mordigan Compacta'—Same as 'Pfitzerana Compacta' but laced with gold. May be listed as 'Pfitzerana Aureo Compacta' or 'Pfitzerana Mordigan Aureo'.

'Pfitzerana Compacta', compact pfitzer—Dense-growing spreader to 3 feet high and 6 feet wide. Leaves are light blue-green.

'Pfitzerana Glauca', blue pfitzer—Leaves are distinctly blue-silver, becoming purplish silver in winter. Large area, tall-growing ground cover.

'San Jose', San Jose creeping juniper—Less than 2 feet high, creeping to 6 or more feet wide. Leaves are dark grayish green. Slow growing.

Highly recommended but susceptible to *Phomopsis* tip blight.

J. chinensis sargentii, sargent juniper, shimpaku—Grows 1 to 2 feet high and up to 10 feet wide. Good resistance to *Phomopsis* twig blight, and adapted to coastal conditions. Lacy foliage. Popular bonsai plant. 'Glauca' has blue-green leaves. 'Viridis' has bright green leaves.

Juniperus chinensis 'Pfitzerana Aurea Mordigan Compacta'. Flowers of *Potentilla tabernaemontanii* repeat the color of the yellow-gold branch tips of the juniper.

'Sea Green'—Similar to 'Pfitzerana' but more compact and brighter green.

'Sea Spray'—Grows 12 to 15 inches high and spreads to 6 feet. Blue-green foliage is dense and soft. Performs well in hot, arid climates. Widely endorsed.

All are hardy to about −20F (−29C).

JUNIPERUS COMMUNIS
English juniper

One of the most widely adapted junipers. It is very hardy and tolerant of poor conditions. Commonly grown around the world. Fruit of this species are used to flavor gin.

'Hornbrookii'—Grows only 1 foot high and to 4 feet wide. Coarse branching habit.

J. communis montana, mountain juniper—Main branches spread outward to 6 feet wide. Short, upright branches reach 1 foot. Leaves are gray-green. Also known as *J. c. saxatilis*, *J. c. nana*, *J. c. alpina* and *J. c. sibirica*.

Hardy to −50F (−45C).

JUNIPERUS CONFERTA
Shore juniper

Shore juniper is an especially attractive juniper. It can be planted in masses, individually in containers or draped over a low wall. Height is 1 foot or less and spread is 6 to 10 feet.

Some nurserymen list *J. conferta* as *J. litoralis* or *J. conferta litoralis*.

J. conferta tends to brown during summer heat and lose color during winter. It has largely been replaced by the following improved varieties:

'Blue Pacific'—Compact, more dense and slower growing than the species, with attractive, blue-green foliage. Heat tolerance is good. Winter color is superior to species.

Juniperus conferta 'Blue Pacific'. *Hydrangea macrophylla* provides color contrast.

'Emerald Sea'—Even more compact than 'Blue Pacific', often reaching no higher than 6 inches. Attractive green foliage. Grows fast.

J. conferta is native to coastal Japan and has been known to grow right to the tide line. Tolerant of sandy, infertile soil, salt water and salt spray. Accepts inland heat if given plenty of water. Resistant to root rot but needs a well-drained soil.

One of the least cold hardy of all junipers, to −10F (−24C).

JUNIPERUS DAVURICA
Many synonyms. See text.

This species includes three varieties, each known by several names.

'Expansa'—This plant is usually considered a variety of *J. squamata* but its leaves are different from others of that group. It grows in a vase shape, featuring attractive green foliage. The effect is prostrate and mounding, about 2-1/2 feet high, spreading 8 feet or more. Other listed names for this plant are *J. chinensis* 'Expansa', *J. c.* 'Parsonii', *J. squamata* 'Expansa Parsonii' and *J. s.* 'Parsonii'.

Hardy to −30F (−35C).

'Expansa Aureo-spicata'—This is a low-growing and spreading juniper. Height is 2 to 3 feet and spread is 8 to 10 feet. Foliage is gray-green with streaks of gold-yellow. It is an excellent bonsai plant. Other listed names are *J. chinensis* 'Expansa Aureo-spicata', *J. c.* 'Parsonii Aureo-spicata', *J. c. procumbens* 'Variegata', *J. procumbens* 'Variegata' and *J. squamata* 'Parsonii Aureo-spicata'.

Hardy to −10F (−24C).

'Expansa Variegata'—Same plant as above with creamy white

Juniperus horizontalis 'Bar Harbor'

Juniperus horizontalis 'Wiltonii'

variegations on foliage. Other names include *J. chinensis* 'Alba', *J. c.* 'Expansa Variegata', *J. c. procumbens* 'Variegata', *J. procumbens* 'Variegata', *J. squamata* 'Albo-variegata' and *J. s.* 'Parsonii Variegata'.

Also hardy to −10F (−24C).

JUNIPERUS HORIZONTALIS
Creeping juniper

Creeping junipers are the lowest growing of all junipers. They stay below 2 feet high. Some kinds may grow no higher than 2 or 3 inches. Spread is anywhere between 4 and 10 feet. As a guide, space plants 5 to 6 feet apart.

Foliage color is characteristically blue-green or steel-blue. Plants usually take on an attractive, purplish tint in winter.

Plants are adaptable to difficult situations. Native soils for *J. horizontalis* are sandy and rocky, but heavy soils are fine if drainage is adequate. Creeping junipers accept high heat in stride and are endorsed by desert gardeners. Most varieties are susceptible to *Phomopsis* tip blight.

The following varieties are available:

'Bar Harbor'—Grows 1 foot or less in height and spreads 6 to 10 feet. Steel-blue color in summer, plum color in winter. Foliage tends to thin in the center of plant with time, especially in desert areas.

'Blue Chip'—Grows 8 inches high and spreads 6 feet wide. Leaves are dense, soft and slate-blue year-round.

'Douglassii', waukegan juniper—Grows 12 inches high and spreads to 10 feet wide. Silver-blue foliage becomes plum color in fall. New spring growth is bright green.

'Emerald Spreader'—Very compact growth 6 to 8 inches high. Spreads 4 to 6 feet wide. Dense with feathery, emerald-green branches.

'Hughes Silver'—Grows 6 to 12 inches high and 6 to 8 feet wide, with very attractive silver-blue leaves. Sometimes listed as *J. scopulorum* 'Hughes'.

'Plumosa', andorra juniper—Grows 18 to 24 inches high and spreads 10 feet wide. Dense growth with flattened branches and upturned branchlets. Color is gray-green turning plum color in winter.

'Plumosa Compacta'—More compact form of the above, growing 10 to 12 inches high and 4 or 5 feet wide. Bronze-purple in winter.

'Prince of Wales'—Recent Canadian introduction. Grows about 8 inches high and spreads 10 feet wide in a starlike pattern. Foliage is soft apple-green, becoming purple-green in winter.

'Turquoise Spreader'—Wide spreading and dense with dimensions similar to 'Emerald Spreader'. Does not have same tendency to mound in the center. Foliage is turquoise-green.

'Webberi'—Grows 1 foot high and spreads 6 to 8 feet wide. Dense and compact growth habit. Does not thin in the center. Foliage is blue-green, then purplish in winter.

'Wiltonii', wilton carpet juniper—This very popular plant is the lowest and flattest-growing juniper. Reaches 4 inches high and spreads up to 10 feet wide. Similar to 'Bar Harbor' but more dense. Branches are well covered. They are silver-blue, gaining a purple tint in winter. Also known as blue carpet juniper and 'Blue Rug'. Good resistance to juniper tip moth.

'Youngstown', youngstown andorra juniper—The same as 'Plumosa' but with a more dense and compact growth habit. Foliage is bright green. Good resistance to juniper tip moth.

'Yukon Belle'—Outstanding tolerance to cold temperatures. It has been tested to −50F (−45C). Grows 6 to 8 inches high and spreads 4 to 5 feet wide. Silver-blue foliage.

Varieties of *J. horizontalis*, except 'Yukon Belle', are hardy to about −35F (−37C).

JUNIPERUS PROCUMBENS
Creeping juniper, Japanese garden juniper

This low, spreading and attractive juniper is native to the mountains of Japan. Frequently cited as one of the best low evergreens. Grows 8 to 36 inches high and spreads 10 to 20 feet wide. Growth is slow—ultimate spread is reached in about a decade. Branches are stiff and ascending. Leaves are blue or gray-green and prickly to the touch. Susceptible to *Phomopsis* tip blight, but resistant to tip moth and root rot.

Here are descriptions of the two varieties you will find. See *J. davurica* 'Expansa Variegata' for plants listed as *J. procumbens* 'Variegata'.

'Green Mound'—Dense, compact grower. Slightly mounding to 8 inches high and 6 feet wide. Foliage is light green and does not brown out or expose branches.

'Nana'—Grows about 1 foot high and spreads 4 to 6 feet wide in each direction. Blue green foliage. Slower growing than 'Green Mound'. Needs protection from intense sun and heat in desert regions.

Hardy to −10F (−24C).

JUNIPERUS SABINA
Savin juniper

Typical savin juniper grows 4 to 6 feet high and 5 to 10 feet wide. Growth habit is upright and distinguished by secondary branches arranged at 45-degree angles to the ground. Foliage has a strong distinct odor.

The following are low-growing, popular and available varieties:

'Arcadia'—Grows about 1 foot high and spreads to 10 feet wide. Foliage is bright green. More cold tolerant than the species. Good resistance to *Phomopsis* tip blight; medium susceptibility to tip moth.

'Blue Danube'—Grows dense to 1 to 2 feet high and spreads 8 to 10 feet wide. Outstanding blue foliage color.

'Broadmoor'—Grows 12 to 15 inches high. Spreads 4 to 6 feet wide, ultimately to 10 feet. Soft, bright green foliage. Good resistance to *Phomopsis* tip blight.

'Buffalo'—Grows 8 to 12 inches high and spreads to 8 feet wide. Fills in well, forming a dense ground cover.

'Calgary Carpet'—A recent selection of 'Arcadia'. Similar to 'Arcadia' in most respects but has lower, more spreading growth. Foliage is bright green.

'Scandia', frequently spelled 'Skandia'—Also similar to 'Arcadia'. Grows 1 foot high and about 6 to 8 feet wide. Foliage color is more olive-green and changes little through the seasons.

'Tamariscifolia', Spanish, tam or tamarix juniper—Very popular and widely planted. Grows 15 to 30 inches high, ultimately spreading 10 to 15 feet wide but usually much less. Quickly forms a solid, dense cover when planted 3 feet apart. New growth is blue-green becoming dark green. Very susceptible to tip moth in inland California.

'Tamariscifolia New Blue'—Identical to standard tam but with distinctive blue-green color.

'Tamariscifolia No Blight'—A superior strain of popular tam juniper. Color is more blue-green. Highly resistant to tip blight.

Savin junipers are hardy to about −40F (−40C), except for tam varieties, which are hardy to −30F (−35C).

JUNIPERUS VIRGINIANA 'SILVER SPREADER'

This is an unusual, dwarf, spreading form of eastern red cedar tree. It grows 20 inches high and spreads as a 4- to 6-foot wide clump. Valued for its silver-green color and feathery texture. Resistant to *Phomopsis* tip blight and root rot. Occasional problems may occur with cedar apple rust and bagworms.

Hardy to −20F (−29C).

Juniperus horizontalis 'Turquoise Spreader'

Juniperus procumbens 'Nana'

Lamium maculatum grows best in heavy shade.

Lantana montevidensis is a mounding cover, growing over rocks and uneven terrain.

Jupiter's beard. See *Centranthus*

Kenilworth ivy. See *Cymbalaria*

Kinnikinnick. See *Arctostaphylos*

Korean grass. See *Zoysia*

LAMIASTRUM GALEOBDOLON 'VARIEGATUM'
Yellow archangel

Yellow archangel is a vigorous, fast-growing, evergreen perennial. It is one of the best ground covers for shady areas with moist soil. It is often interplanted with hostas and ferns.

It grows 6 to 8 inches high, spreading fast to 1 or 2 feet wide with creeping, rooting shoots. Leaves are deep green, 1-1/2 to 2 inches long and marked with silver variegations. Leaves die to the ground in cold-winter regions but come back early in spring. Yellow flowers are similar to snapdragons and have red tips. They bloom in late spring.

Planting and care—Yellow archangel is easy to grow. Plant any time, although spring is best. Available as flats, plastic packs or in 1-gallon containers. Prefers rich, moist soil in shady locations but is drought tolerant once established. Plants can become invasive but are rarely a serious problem.

Hardy to −20F (−29C).

LAMIUM MACULATUM
Dead nettle

Dead nettle is an excellent, shade-tolerant, deciduous ground cover. It features striking, variegated leaves. "Dead" means that it does not sting when touched, unlike its close relative, wild nettle.

It grows about 7 inches high with heart-shaped, toothed, 2-inch long leaves. They are green with a white or silver marking down the center. Leaves fall when temperatures reach about 15F (−9C). Purple flowers bloom in spring or early summer. 'Album' has white flowers. 'Chequers' has pink flowers and marbled leaves.

Planting and care—Plant in shady areas. Spring is the best time to plant, usually from 1-gallon containers. Full sun is acceptable where soil is moist. Rich soil gives best growth and appearance.

Hardy to −20F (−29C).

Lampranthus. See Ice Plants

LANTANA MONTEVIDENSIS
Trailing lantana

Trailing lantana is one of the most colorful ground covers. It will not tolerate much frost, but is tough and flowers all year where winter climate permits. It is excellent on banks, providing a dependable measure of erosion control. Use it for color accents, in planters or allow it to spill over low walls.

Lantana is essentially a fast-growing, spreading, evergreen vine. Trailing branches make 3- to 6-foot wide mounds 1-1/2 to 5 feet high. Leaves are dark green and about 1 inch long. They have a strong odor when crushed and a slightly rough, sandpaper quality. Plant produces 1-inch clusters of tiny, trumpetlike flowers that develop on branch ends. Many colors are available.

The following variety list includes plants that reach less than 3 feet high.

'Carnival'—Pink, yellow, lavender.

'Confetti'—Pink, yellow, purple.

'Cream Carpet'—Cream-white.

Ophiopogon japonicus lends itself well to a tropical effect.

Liriope 'Gold Band'

Ophiopogon japonicus works well as an edging.

'Dwarf Pink', 'Dwarf White' or 'Dwarf Yellow'.

'Golden Glow'—Yellow-gold.

'Golden Satellite'—Deep gold.

'Kathleen'—Rose-pink with gold centers.

'Spreading Sunset'—Orange-red.

'Sunburst'—Bright yellow.

'Tangerine'—Orange-red.

Planting and care—Lantana is an adaptable plant. In fact, it seems to flower better if placed under a little stress. Any soil is acceptable. Very drought tolerant once established. Full sun is necessary. Plants tend to mildew in shade. Plant about 2 feet apart to make a solid cover. Prune out dead and old wood in spring before growth flush. Whiteflies may be a problem. Use Orthene as the label directs.

Hardy to 20F (−7C).

LAURENTIA FLUVIATILIS
Blue star creeper

Blue star creeper is a charming, creeping, evergreen plant. It is ideal for planting between stepping stones. It will tolerate occasional foot traffic. Plants are particularly striking when grown in containers and allowed to drape over the sides.

Blue star creeper was formerly known and is still listed by some nurseries under the name *Isotoma*.

It grows 2 to 5 inches high and spreads 6 to 10 inches in a year. Grows tallest in heavy shade. Dark green leaves are tiny and pointed. Blue flowers are small and shaped like stars. They appear intermittently but mostly in spring.

Planting and care—Plant clumps 6 to 12 inches apart for a solid cover within one year. Rich, moist soil allows fastest growth. Provide plenty of water and a little shade.

Hardy to 20F (−7C).

Lavender cotton. See *Santolina*

Leadwort. See Ceratostigma

Lily-of-the-Nile. See *Agapanthus*

Lily-of-the-valley. See *Convallaria*

Lily turf. See *Liriope*

Lippia. See *Phyla*

LIRIOPE AND OPHIOPOGON
Lily turf and Mondo grass

Lily turf and mondo grass are so similar we have included them in a single description. Both are tufted, evergreen, grasslike plants of the lily family. Particularly popular in warm climates, either makes an attractive edging for paths, borders for lawns, or they can be used as mass plantings. Locate them in the shade of trees or buildings as you might *Vinca* or *Pachysandra* species. They are not invasive but do compete successfully with tree roots and other plants.

Lily turf is the more common, hardy and vigorous of the two. It is tolerant of poor soil and drought. It adapts to shade and to competition from tree roots. Two species and several varieties are commonly used as ground covers.

Liriope muscari, big blue lily turf, grows the largest. It makes nonspreading clumps up to 2 feet high. Leaves are dark green, 1/2 inch wide and up to 24 inches long. Blue-violet flowers appear mostly in late summer, and are arranged along 4- to 8-inch high spikes. Flowers are showy but usually hidden by leaves.

Garden varieties of *L. muscari* include:

'Gold Band'—Leaves have bright gold borders. Lavender flowers.

'Lilac Beauty'—Lower growing than species. Leaves are dark green.

Lobularia maritima, an annual, is colorful and easy to grow.

Flowers are attractive deep violet.

'Majestic'—Grows 2 feet high and produces numerous, deep violet flowers. Commonly available and frequently recommended.

'Silvery Sunproof'—New leaves are bordered in gold, which turn white later on. Accepts more sun and produces more flowers than the species.

'Variegata'—Grows 12 to 18 inches high. New leaves have yellow edges that become green the second year. Violet flowers are borne on 12-inch high spikes. This plant is nearly identical to *Ophiopogon jaburan* 'Variegata', and is sometimes listed under that name.

Hardy to about 0F (−18C).

L. spicata, creeping lily turf, is more uniform in appearance. It is useful in hot-summer areas where *Pachysandra* species and *Vinca minor* do not thrive. Also used in areas that are too cold for *Ophiopogon japonicus.* It grows 6 to 10 inches high and spreads by underground runners.

It is more hardy than *L. muscari,* to about −20F (−29C).

Ophiopogon species, Mondo grass, is closely related and similar in appearance to lily turf. The largest

is *O. jaburan.* It grows 2 to 3 feet high in clumps with dark green, 1/2-inch wide leaves. A variegated form, *O. j.* 'Vittatos', also called *O. j. aureus* 'Variegata', *L. muscari* 'Variegata' and *L. exiliflora,* has white-striped leaves.

O. japonicus is the most commonly planted mondo grass. It grows 8 to 10 inches high and spreads to about as wide, making a smooth, even carpet. Leaves are dark green and about 1/8 inch wide. Light purple flowers bloom in summer but are mostly hidden by leaves.

Hardy to about 10F (−12C).

Planting and care—Plant *Liriope* or *Ophiopogon* in shade. Spring and fall are best planting times. Plants are usually available in 1-gallon containers, occasionally in flats. Space *Ophiopogon* plants 6 to 8 inches apart; *L. muscari* 12 to 18 inches apart; *L. spicata* 8 to 12 inches apart. Divide established clumps to increase plantings. Light, sandy soil allows fastest growth but nearly any soil is acceptable. Cutting back in spring, before new growth appears, will help maintain health, vigor and best appearance. A rotary mower, set high, is a convenient way to cut back large plantings.

LOBELIA ERINUS
Lobelia

Lobelia is one of the simplest charmers of the garden. Flowers are commonly blue—one of the truest, most brilliant of all garden blues. Lobelia is usually grown as an annual but is a self-sowing perennial in temperate climates.

Plant grows up to 6 inches high, and spreads 6 to 8 inches. Leaves are 1/2 to 1 inch long and roughly elliptical in shape. They are light green or bronze-green. Flowers are light blue or dark blue, although varieties are available that have pink, red-purple and white flowers. Flower center is white or yellow.

Lobelia is available in clumping and trailing forms.

Popular *clumping* forms include: 'Cambridge Blue'—light blue flowers; 'Crystal Palace'—dark blue flowers, bronzy leaves; 'Rosamond'—red-purple flowers; and 'White Lady'—white flowers.

Trailing forms are favorites for draping over planters or the edges of hanging baskets. Varieties include: 'Blue Cascade'—light blue flowers; 'Red Cascade'—plum-red flowers; and 'Sapphire'—dark blue flowers.

Lonicera japonica 'Halliana' effectively covers large areas in a short time.

Planting and care—Lobelia are best grown from nursery-bought transplants. Raising plants from seed to transplant-size seedlings takes about 60 days. Plant in early spring. In mild-winter areas, plant in fall. Space plants 6 to 10 inches apart. Lobelia does best in moist, rich soil receiving afternoon shade. Full sun is fine in cool or coastal areas.

Hardy to about 25F (−4C).

LOBULARIA MARITIMA
Sweet alyssum

Sweet alyssum is a fast-spreading, carefree annual or self-sowing perennial. Easily started from seed, it is sometimes used in erosion control and wild flower seed mixes. It makes an outstanding temporary ground cover between slower-spreading covers such as junipers or ivy. Try using sweet alyssum in containers, over bulbs and as an informal border.

Varieties vary in height from 12 inches to 2 inches. Leaves are narrow and 1/2 to 2 inches long. Flowers are tiny but arranged in 1- to 2-inch long clusters. They are usually white but some are lavender-purple.

The following varieties are superior to common sweet alyssum. If plants self-sow flower color and plant form will eventually revert to common. White kinds include: 'Carpet of Snow'—2 to 4 inches high; 'Little Gem'—4 to 6 inches high; 'Tiny Tim'—3 inches high; and 'Tetra Snowdrift'—12 inches high.

Colored varieties include: 'Rosie O'Day' and 'Pink Heather'—lavender. 'Rosie O'Day' grows 8 to 10 inches high. 'Pink Heather' grows to about 6 inches high. 'Oriental Night' and 'Violet Queen'—dark purple. Each grow 8 to 10 inches high.

Planting and care—Sweet alyssum is one of the easiest plants to grow. Scatter seed over planting area and lightly rake them into the soil. Flowers are sometimes in bloom only 6 weeks after seeding. Transplants are usually available in nurseries. Plant in spring in cold-winter areas; fall in mild-winter areas. Accepts any soil in sun or partial shade. Space 6 to 8 inches apart. Keep moist to establish. Summer heat will kill plants without frequent watering. Shear or mow after bloom.

Hardy to 15F (−9C).

LONICERA JAPONICA 'HALLIANA'
Hall's Japanese honeysuckle

Hall's Japanese honeysuckle is a fine, woody, evergreen ground cover for the right situation, but it should be planted with care. It grows fast, smothering other plants in its path and frequently escapes into places where it does not belong.

Give the plant plenty of room. It quickly covers banks and provides erosion control. As a ground cover it grows 2 or 3 feet high and climbs 15 or more feet. Leaves are soft, dark green and oval. Fragrant flowers are white, changing to yellow. Flowers bloom profusely in spring and sporadically in summer.

Planting and care—Plant in any soil. Early fall is the best time to plant. Nurseries have plants available in 1-gallon containers. Space plants about 2-1/2 feet apart. Prefers full sun and likes heat. Drought tolerant once established. Prune heavily annually in early spring before new flush of growth to keep low and attractive. Without pruning, dry, fire-susceptible undergrowth builds up.

Hardy to −25F (−32C).

Lysimachia nummularia in foreground drapes over a low wall. White flowers are *Iberis amara*. Purple flowers in background are larkspur.

LOTUS
Parrot's beak and Birdsfoot trefoil

Lotus species include two very different but useful ground covers. Parrot's beak, *Lotus berthelotii,* is a silver, trailing perennial for mild climates that does a fine job of covering small areas and draping over walls and planters. It grows 2 feet high and spreads 2 to 3 feet wide. Leaves are silver-gray and very narrow, almost feathery. They die-back in cold winters, returning in spring. Flowers are crimson, 1 inch long and appear midsummer.

Hardy to 25F (−4C).

Birdsfoot trefoil, *L. corniculatus,* is a legume landscape designers have borrowed from farmers. Like its cousins clover and alfalfa, it is a productive forage plant. Around the home it is used as a coarse-textured and hardy lawn substitute. It grows about 5 inches high and spreads fast. Dark green leaves are cloverlike. Flowers are yellow and appear in summer. They make a seed pod shaped vaguely like a bird's foot.

Hardy to about −20F (−29C).

Planting and care—Plant parrot's beak in full sun and well-drained soil. Spring is the best time to plant, usually from 1-gallon containers. Space plants about 2 feet apart. Provide regular amounts of water. Trim tips occasionally to promote bushiness.

Plant birdsfoot trefoil in full sun in dry, well-drained soil. Start with seed sown in spring or fall. Give plenty of water through the hottest months. Mow to keep neat.

LYSIMACHIA NUMMULARIA
Moneywort, Creeping Jennie

Moneywort is a very low, colorful, evergreen, moisture-loving plant. It is at home around rocks, pools, walls and other natural obstacles it can creep over or around. It is generally considered low maintenance, but plants can invade and colonize in lawns.

Plant grows 2 to 6 inches high, forming a dense mat. It spreads 2 feet wide with rooting stems.

Leaves are bright green and about 1 inch in diameter. 'Aurea' has golden leaves. Flowers are golden yellow, 3/4 inch wide. They are most abundant in spring but appear through summer.

Planting and care—Plant in full sun and moist soil. Spring is the best time to plant, usually from flats or individual plastic packs. If plants are in shade, drier soil is acceptable. Plant 'Aurea' only in shade. Space plants 10 to 12 inches apart.

Hardy to −40F (−40C).

Madagascar periwinkle. See *Catharanthus*

MAHONIA REPENS
Creeping mahonia, Creeping barberry

Creeping mahonia is a low and spreading relative of the more common *Mahonia aquifolium,* Oregon grape. A North American native, it grows naturally in the Pacific Northwest, Rocky Mountains and Black Hills of South Dakota. It is hardy and provides good erosion control.

Mahonia repens develops into a dense, irregular ground cover.

Plant grows 2 to 3 feet high and spreads as wide with underground runners. Spiny leaves change colors with the seasons. They are gray-green in spring and summer. In fall they turn bright red, then change to bronzy green through winter. Flowers are yellow and bloom in spring. Plant produces blue-black berries loved by birds.

Planting and care—Early fall is the best time to plant. Look for 1-gallon or 5-gallon containers at the nursery. Plant in full sun except in warm-summer areas, where afternoon shade is necessary. Creeping mahonia will grow in any soil but rich, improved soil allows for fastest spread. Drought tolerant once established. Caterpillars often attack leaves in spring. Use *Bacillus thuringensis* or Orthene to control. Various strains are available that differ in hardiness. Buy from a local supplier.

Hardy to −30F (−35C).

Malephora. See Ice Plants

Manzanita. See *Arctostaphylos*

MAZUS REPTANS

Mazus is an interesting and easy-to-grow plant. Use it between steppingstones or over bulbs. Accepts occasional foot traffic.

It grows to 2 inches high and spreads fast with trailing, rooting stems. Leaves are about 1 inch long and have irregular edges. Flowers are light blue with white and yellow spots. They bloom in clusters in great quantities both spring and summer.

Planting and care—Plant in good, well-drained soil in full sun or a little shade. Spring is the best time to plant, usually from flats. Water regularly. Space plants 6 to 12 inches apart for a cover in 1 season. *Mazus* is an evergreen perennial when grown in above-freezing temperatures, deciduous when grown below freezing.

Hardy to −10F (−24C).

MENTHA REQUIENII
Corsican mint

Corsican mint is perhaps the lowest growing of all ground-covering plants: It reaches only 1/2 inch high or less. Leaves lie right against the soil. Use Corsican mint in small places such as between paving stones. A specialized use is as a bonsai or container ground cover.

Round, bright green, evergreen leaves are about 1/8 inch diameter. They look similar to moss and release a wonderful mint fragrance when touched. Purple flowers are small and bloom in summer.

Planting and care—Space clumps of plants 6 inches apart in moist locations. Spring is the best time to plant. Roots are not deep so frequent watering is necessary, especially if soil tends to be dry. Corsican mint has the look of a shade lover, but does need some sun. Strong morning light, then afternoon shade or partial shade, is ideal. It is not very hardy but persists in cold climates by self-sowing.

Hardy to 0F (−18C).

Mondo grass. See *Liriope*

Moneywort. See *Lysimachia*

Moss pink. See *Phlox*

Moss rose. See *Portulaca*

Scotch moss

MOSS

Mosses include familiar dark green Irish moss, golden green Scotch moss and the more rarely grown native mosses.

ARENARIA AND SAGINA SPECIES
Irish and Scotch moss

These plants differ in small ways. *Arenaria* or *Sagina* species is the Irish and Scotch moss so common in nurseries. Distinguishing between flowers is the best way to tell them apart. *Arenaria verna*, also known as *A. v. caespitosa* and *Minuartia verna*, bears white flowers in clusters. *Sagina subulata* flowers are not borne in clusters. Both are dark green and sold as Irish moss. Both have golden-green forms—*A. v.* 'Aurea' and *S. s.* 'Aurea', commonly known as Scotch moss.

These dense-growing, mosslike plants require cultural conditions quite different from true, native moss. Use them between paving, under ferns or as a mounding cover in a small area.

Planting and care—In cool areas, plant clumps about 6 inches apart in

Scotch moss produces repeating mounds for an interesting, geometric effect.

full sun. They need afternoon shade elsewhere. Prefers moist, rich soil. Golden forms are more tolerant of sun and afternoon heat. Give plenty of water, some fertilizer and expect slugs and snails to invade in force. With optimum growing conditions, these plants self-sow prolifically and can become serious weeds. But normally, mosses themselves must be kept weed-free.

Hardy to −40F (−40C).

Native moss

Native mosses are outstanding, low-maintenance ground covers and lawn substitutes. They are not plants you can buy in the nursery. Rather, you encourage them where they have already started on their own. They require a moist, smooth, acid soil, preferrably with some clay. They like partial shade such as on a north-facing slope and good drainage. These conditions are common throughout the American Northeast and many regions of Canada. Similar conditions exist in parts of the Midwest and mountain areas. For more information on native moss, see page 9.

Planting and care—Soil must be very acid, about pH 5. Use 4 pounds soil sulfur per 100 square feet to shift pH from 6.5 to 5.

Transplant moss clumps in early spring when the weather is cool and the soil moist. Leave no air spaces between soil and moss clumps. Water for the next several weeks until established.

Leaves from deciduous trees must be removed before winter. If leaves are not removed, moss will rot and die. Raking after the first hard freeze prevents loosening of the moss plants, which are then frozen to the ground.

The only maintenance is occasional weeding. Dandelion, thistle, oxalis and veronica are problems. Pull them out by their roots before they go to seed.

Irish moss makes a soft, lush carpet, highlighted by small, white flowers.

Scotch moss complements colors of Japanese maple at left, and blue spruce.

Where adapted, Scotch moss makes a striking lawn.

Myosotis sylvatica in spring. Each flower leaves behind plenty of seed for next year's crop.

Nandina domestica 'Harbour Dwarf' is a dwarf form of heavenly bamboo. It grows 1-1/2 to 2 feet high.

MUEHLENBECKIA AXILLARIS
Creeping wire vine

Creeping wire vine looks delicate, but once established, is a tough, weed-choking, attractive, evergreen ground cover. Use it in and around rocks, draped over walls and for climbing and covering wire fences.

Mature height is a few inches to 1 foot. Plants spread slowly a few feet in each direction by underground runners. Above-ground stems are quite thin and look like stiff wire. Leaves are small, dark, glossy green.

Planting and care—Plant in full sun or some shade in well-drained soil. Plant any time, but either spring or fall is preferred. You will probably find plants in flats, or some nurseries will have them available in 1-gallon containers. Once established, water need is average. Space plants 6 to 12 inches apart. Some leaves drop with freezing temperatures.

Hardy to 20F (−7C).

MYOPORUM PARVIFOLIUM
Prostrate myoporum

Prostrate myoporum is a low and wide-spreading shrub well adapted to warm coastal, temperate and dry-summer climates. It grows fast, provides erosion control on banks. It is also fire retardant.

Plant grows 6 inches or less high and spreads 5 to 10 feet. Roots will form wherever creeping branches connect with moist soil. Evergreen leaves are bright green, 1/2 to 1 inch long. They slightly resemble rosemary leaves. Flowers are white, 1/2 inch in diameter but not showy.

Planting and care—Plant in full sun in any soil that has good drainage. Fall is the best time to plant. Usually available in 1-gallon containers. Space plants 5 feet apart. Drought tolerance is excellent. Salt tolerance is high, an advantage in coastal regions. Additional water is required in summer for inland planting.

Hardy to 20F (−7C).

MYOSOTIS
Forget-me-not

There are annual and perennial types of forget-me-not. Both are useful ground covers. Each has attractive, tiny, usually clear blue flowers. Both prefer cool weather and moist soil, and both are persistent plants in the garden.

Myosotis scorpioides is a perennial. It grows 10 to 18 inches high and as wide, spreading with underground roots. Leaves are oblong and bright green. Flowers are blue with yellow, pink or white centers. Bloom season begins in spring and lasts into summer. Subspecies *M. s. semperflorens* is an 8-inch high dwarf. It flowers in summer and is particularly attractive combined with tulips.

Roots are hardy to −40F (−40C).

M. sylvatica is an annual that dies to the ground with summer heat. It self-sows so abundantly it is essentially a perennial, coming back each year in spring. It grows 6 to 12 inches high. Light green leaves are soft, 1/2 to 2 inches long. Flowers are blue, with yellow, pink or white centers. Varieties with white and pink flowers are available. Plants grow like weeds once established in your garden, but they are usually most welcome.

Planting and care—Start either species as transplants, which should be available from your nursery. *M. sylvatica* can also be started from seed. Plant in early spring or fall in mild climates. Provide improved soil, full or partial sun and regular water.

Nepeta faassenii flower stalks.

Oenothera berlandieri at peak bloom in spring.

NANDINA DOMESTICA
Heavenly bamboo

Heavenly bamboo is not a true bamboo but it does have some bamboo characteristics. It is noted for interesting changes in leaf colors. New leaves emerge pinkish bronze, and soon become pleasing, light green. Cooler fall temperatures bring back the bronze color but add traces of red and sometimes purple. Through winter, leaves are bright red, especially when exposed to plenty of sun and frost.

Heavenly bamboo has good resistance to oak root fungus, a serious problem in western United States. It generally competes well with tree roots.

Most common form is the standard 6- to 8-foot shrub. There are several dwarf, low-growing heavenly bamboos. The best for a ground cover is 'Harbour Dwarf'. It grows 1-1/2 to 2 feet high and spreads with underground runners.

Planting and care—Growing heavenly bamboo is simple. Early fall is the best time to plant, and 1-gallon containers are the best-size plants. Plant in good soil and water frequently until established. Plants will be fairly drought tolerant after the first season. Full exposure to sun is best for brightest leaf color, but some shade is acceptable, even preferred in desert and hot inland areas. Some leaves fall as temperatures reach 10F (−12C). Plant dies to the ground but recovers at 5F (−15C).

Roots are cold hardy to approximately −10F (−24C).

Natal plum. See *Carissa*

NEPETA FAASSENII
Synonym: N. mussinii
Catmint, Catnip

Catmint makes an attractive, widespreading, evergreen ground cover. However, it has one drawback—cats love it! They can ruin a planting by rolling and laying in it.

Maximum height is about 2 feet with a spread to 2 feet wide. Leaves are soft like flannel and dull green. Small lavender flowers appear in summer.

Planting and care—Planting nursery transplants in 2- or 4-inch plastic pots is the best way to get started. Plant in spring in full sun, spacing plants 1 to 1-1/2 feet apart. Any soil is okay. Give regular amounts of water. Shear off spent flowers.

Hardy to about −20F (−29C).

New Zealand brass buttons. See *Cotula*

OENOTHERA
Evening primrose and Baja primrose

Oenothera species are handsome, flowering perennials, native to the harsh conditions of the Southwest desert. Two are particularly valuable as ground covers.

O. berlandieri, Mexican primrose, is planted primarily for its profuse, spring bloom. Use it in outlying areas or for wild or natural landscapes. It grows 6 to 12 inches high and spreads widely with underground roots. Flowers are rose-pink, 1-1/2 inches wide and cup-shaped on upright stems. They open only during daylight. Shear to the ground after bloom. May invade other planting beds. Becomes thin and unattractive as stems die back in winter.

O. drummodii thalassaphila, Baja primrose, is a recent introduction but should soon become popular. The spring flower display of Mexican primrose is more dramatic, but

Oxalis oregano carpets soil and complements lush green ferns.

Oxalis oregano excels in dense shade and moist soil.

Baja primrose has no comparable off season.

It grows about 4 inches high and quickly speads to form a dense mat with above-ground rooting runners. Medium green leaves are 2 to 3 inches long, narrow and pointed. They develop a red tint when drought or cold-stressed. Flowers are soft yellow, 2-1/2 inches wide and held above leaves on 6- to 8-inch stems. They bloom mostly in spring then intermittently through summer. Flowers open in evening and close by noon the following day, hence the common name "evening primrose."

Planting and care—Plant in any soil in full sun. Early fall, before winter rains, is the best time to plant. Nurseries have plants available in 1-gallon cans. Space Mexican primrose 1-1/2 feet apart; Baja primrose 3 feet apart. Once established, plants are drought tolerant, but weekly watering promotes the best and fastest growth. Allow one season to establish and two seasons to form a solid cover. Cuttings root easily. Prolonged drought usually doesn't kill plants, but forces dormancy.

Hardiness has been tested to 20F (−7C) but plant will probably tolerate lower temperatures.

OMPHALODES VERNA
Creeping forget-me-not

Creeping forget-me-not is a European native said to have been favored by Marie Antoinette. It is fast-spreading, with intense blue, white-centered flowers.

Plant grows to 8 inches high and spreads fast and wide with above-ground runners. Leaves are 1 to 3 inches long and create a fine-textured effect. Abundant flowers are 1/2 inch wide and bloom in spring.

Planting and care—Plants thrive in moist soil and shady locations. Spring or early fall are best planting times, but anytime is okay. Creeping forget-me-not is not a standard nursery item. Check with mail order nurseries that specialize in perennials. Space approximately 12 inches apart for a cover in one season.

Hardy to 5F (−15C).

Ophiopogon. See *Liriope*

Oregon boxwood. See *Paxistima*

Oregon grape. See *Mahonia*

ORIGANUM VULGARE 'COMPACTA NANA'
Creeping oregano

This is a form of oregano commonly used as a kitchen herb. Creeping oregano grows only a few inches high, spreads wide and is a useful herb in many recipes.

Maximum height is 2 inches or less. Spread is about 18 inches wide. Leaves are 3/4 inch long, usually wavy and mildly flavored.

Planting and care—There are many forms of oregano. To be sure you are planting a distinct form such as creeping oregano, start with transplants. Nurseries may stock these in their herb section. Check with an herb specialist, either mail order or local, if your garden center cannot find plants. Plant 12 inches apart in full sun. Tolerant of any soil. Provide moderate amounts of water and fertilizer.

Hardy to −25F (−32C).

Osteospermum. See African Daisies

OXALIS OREGANO
Redwood sorrel

Redwood sorrel is one of the most verdant, cool and luxurious-looking

Pachysandra terminalis does well in heavily shaded areas.

Pachysandra terminalis is one of the most reliable and easy-to-grow ground covers.

ground covers. It is native to the Pacific Northwest coastal areas and grows to perfection in the moist, organic soil under redwoods, rhododendrons and around ferns.

Plant grows about 10 inches high and spreads slowly with underground runners. Slightly yellow-green leaves are soft and 2 to 4 inches wide, divided into 3 leaflets. Pink or white flowers are 1 inch wide. They bloom in spring and sometimes in fall.

Planting and care—Plant in partial or heavy shade and moist, highly organic soil. Fall is the best time to plant. Space 12 to 24 inches apart, depending on plant size and anticipated growth rate. Maintain abundant water supply if rains or fog is less than normal.

Hardy to about 5F (−15C).

Pachistima. See *Paxistima*

PACHYSANDRA
Japanese spurge and Allegheny pachysandra

Along with English ivy, *Vinca minor* and wintercreeper, *Pachysandra terminalis* is one of the most common

and widely planted of all evergreen ground covers. It is close to ideal for shady areas in cool, northern temperate climates. It spreads just enough to fill in, without being invasive, to form a dense, uniform, dark green carpet.

Plant grows 6 to 10 inches high and spreads with underground runners. Leaves are 2 to 4 inches long and as wide. They are dark green except when exposed to the sun, which turns them yellow. Fluffy, white, fragrant flower spikes appear in summer.

Varieties of *Pachysandra terminalis,* Japanese pachysandra, are: 'Emerald Carpet'—slightly lower, more dense and with better winter color. 'Variegata' or 'Silver Edge'—leaves feature white margins.

P. procumbens, Allegheny pachysandra, is a North American native. It is resistant to the fungus disease *Volutella pachysandrae,* which can kill entire plantings of Japanese pachysandra. A drawback is that it is only partially evergreen, even completely deciduous in some areas. Also, leaves do not have the lustrous, green quality of the Japanese form.

Height and basic habit is similar to Japanese pachysandra. Leaves are gray to blue-green and slightly

mottled. Purple or pinkish white flowers are attractive and fragrant. They appear on 2- to 4-inch spikes in early spring.

Planting and care—Plant in spring, as soon as soil is workable. Plants are normally available in flats, but inquire about availability of rooted cuttings if planting a large area. You will need to buy a minimum quantity, but cost is much less per plant. Plant in shade, about 6 to 12 inches apart. *Pachysandra* prefers rich, acid soil. Needs plenty of water, especially the first season. Feed twice each growing season.

P. terminalis is hardy to −30F (−35C), and *P. procumbens* is hardy to −20F (−29C).

Parrot's beak. See *Lotus*

PAXISTIMA
Pachistima, Oregon boxwood

Pachistima is a low, slow-spreading, woody, evergreen shrub with many ground-covering possibilities. It is excellent bordering azaleas or rhododendrons because it prefers acid soil and dappled shade. It also does well around the base of trees.

Pelargonium graveolens

Pernettya mucronata, a New Zealand native, is a useful ground cover in the Pacific Northwest.

There are eastern and western forms. *Paxistima canbyi* is native to the mountains of Virginia and North Carolina. It grows 9 to 12 inches high. Leaves are small, leathery, shiny and 1/4 to 1 inch long. They are dark green, becoming bronze in fall and winter.

P. myrsinites, Oregon boxwood, is a Pacific Northwest native. It grows 1-1/2 to 4 feet high and is easily kept low by clipping.

Planting and care—Plant either species in full sun and well-drained, slightly acid soil. Early fall is best planting time. Nurseries stock plants in 1- or 5-gallon containers. Space 12 to 14 inches apart. Where native, natural water supply is adequate. Plants in hot, inland regions require plenty of water. Well-draining soil is necessary.

Hardy to −20F (−29C).

PELARGONIUM PELTATUM
Ivy geranium

Ivy geranium is one of the most colorful ground covers. It is a landscape favorite in no-frost Mediterranean climates. It is the classic, draping container plant for balco-

nies and window boxes. Try mixing it on banks with English ivy.

It is evergreen, grows 1 to 2 feet high and trails 2 to 4 feet long. Bright green, succulent leaves are lobed like English ivy. Flowers may be single or double. They come in clusters of color—lavender, pink, white, rose and red—mostly in late spring and intermittently through summer.

Planting and care—Look for flats of ivy geranium at your local nursery in spring. Fall is second-best time to plant. Summer planting will work but you will have to water frequently. Plant in full sun in any soil. Space about 18 inches apart. Provide with regular water and fertilizer after plants are established.

Hardy to 30F (−1C).

Penngift crown vetch. See *Coronilla*

Periwinkle. See *Vinca* or *Catharanthus*

PERNETTYA MUCRONATA
Pernettya

Pernettya is a low and spreading evergreen shrub particularly noted

for its attractive, long-lasting berries.

It grows 18 to 36 inches high and spreads moderately with underground runners. Leaves are about 1/2 inch long and dark green. They assume a reddish cast in winter. Flowers are small, white and bell shaped. They appear in late spring. Berries come shortly thereafter. They are glossy, fleshy and various colors—black, purple, red, rose, pink or white.

Planting and care—Fall is best planting time. Plant in acid, moist soil and in full sun. Appreciates afternoon shade where summers are dry and hot. Water and fertilizer needs are typical once established. Prune tops to control height and appearance. Prune roots with shovel to control spread.

Hardy to −5F (−20C).

PHALARIS ARUNDINACEA PICTA
Ribbon grass

Ribbon grass is an old-fashioned, hardy and attractive perennial. It is a rampant, sometimes invasive spreader, especially in light, rich soil.

Phalaris arundinacea picta brightens this shady spot.

Phlox subulata forms a solid mass of color.

It grows about 3 feet high in an open, upright manner rather than as a clump like most ornamental grasses. Spread is accomplished with vigorous, underground runners. Leaves are 6 to 12 inches long. They are green with white stripes, sometimes tinged with a touch of pink.

Planting and care—Plant in full sun or some shade. Spring is the best time to plant. Nurseries will have plants in 1-gallon containers. Heavy soil slows spread a little, which is usually an advantage. Given plenty of water and fertilizer, plants grow rampantly, which can be a disadvantage. Planting in a permanent, bottomless, confining container is advised to avoid invasiveness. A short section of concrete storm-drain pipe is excellent for this purpose. Remove ragged leaves in fall.

Hardy to −30F (−35C).

PHLOX SUBULATA
Moss Pink

Moss pink is one of the showiest, hardy, evergreen perennials. Popular in cold-climate areas. Flowers bloom in late spring or summer and make solid waves of brilliant color, similar to some of the ice plants used in mild-climate areas. It is excellent in dry, sunny locations such as on banks and slopes.

Plant spreads to form a mat about 6 inches high and 12 inches wide. Olive-green, needle-shaped leaves are 1/2 inch long and mosslike. They last through winter. Star-shaped flowers are 3/4 inch wide and come in white, blue, rose, lavender or pink.

Planting and care—Grow moss pink in loose but not overly rich or moist soil. Spring is the best time to plant, usually from 1-gallon containers. Space plants 12 to 18 inches apart. Neutral to slightly alkaline soil pH is best. Once established, drought tolerance is fairly good. Cut back or mow plant after flowering.

Hardy to −40F (−40C).

PHYLA NODIFLORA
Lippia

Lippia is one of the great lawn substitutes for desert regions and other areas of the Southwest. It is evergreen, tough and accepts inordinate amounts of heat, sun and foot traffic. If used as a lawn substitute, be aware that lippia's cloverlike flowers attract bees.

Height varies when grown in sun or shade. With full sun it stays 1 inch high or less. In shade it may reach 4 to 6 inches. Spreads wide with above-ground, rooting runners. Lavender flowers are small but clustered into 1/2-inch heads.

Planting and care—Space 1 to 1-1/2 feet apart. Plant any time, spring or fall is preferred. Plants are typically available in flats. Any soil is okay. Water regularly to establish, then give deep, infrequent waterings. If plants wilt, they recover quickly with water. Mow low and often with a reel mower to remove flowers if bees are bothersome.

Hardy to −5F (−21C).

PICEA
Dwarf spruce

Spruces are beautiful, evergreen plants, but full-size species are far too big for most home landscapes. Many dwarf kinds are available for use in gardens. They grow a few feet high and spread as mounds a few feet wide.

Picea pungens 'Glauca Pendula' can spread to 12 feet.

Pinus mugo has been pruned to accentuate natural mounding shape.

Picea pungens 'Glauca Pendula', Colorado blue spruce, is a particularly nice, rather elegant ground cover. Some catalogs and nurseries refer to it as Koster's weeping blue spruce. By either name, it forms a dense mat less than 1 foot high and in time will spread up to 12 feet wide. Foliage color is the same bright blue-green as the upright tree form.

Planting and care—Plant in full sun in any soil. Early fall is the best time to plant. Plants are available as cuttings and in 1- or 5-gallon containers. Growth is slow so larger sizes are better, also more expensive. Check with mail order specialists if you have trouble locating plants. Mulch, fertilize lightly in spring and fall and maintain soil moisture. Spreading and weeping growth habit is natural but give plant some help at the beginning. Remove central leader branches and weigh or stake down the first branches that develop. Doing this will cause it to spread about 8 or 10 inches a year, making a permanent, colorful, weed-choking mat.

Hardy to −50F (−45C).

Pinks. See *Dianthus*

PINUS
Dwarf species

Three dwarf and spreading forms of pine are excellent, small-area ground covers of considerable character.

Pinus densiflora 'Pendula', weeping Japanese pine, is prostrate and handsome, spreading over and around rocks and near pools. Growth is slow, open and graceful, with main branches showing in many areas. Maximum height is about 2 feet with a spread of 6 feet.

Hardy to −30F (−35C).

P. mugo, mugo pine, is a popular, low and mounding pine. Many forms are sold under this name, and some grow quite tall. Look for plants with particularly dense form, or better, buy plants from a grower that specifies ultimate height. Some nurseries label low-growing *P. mugo* as either *P. mugo mugo* or *P. pumila*.

Mugo pine is quite hardy and tolerant of severe weather. Plant in full sun or light shade. Any soil is acceptable.

Hardy to −30F (−35C).

P. strobus 'Prostrata', dwarf white pine, prefers to spread flat on the ground and will drape gracefully over walls. Plants are propagated by grafting the weeping form onto white pine seedlings.

Hardy to −40F (−40C), but protect from cold winds.

Planting and care—Early fall is best planting time. Plants are typically available in 1-gallon containers. Tolerant of poor soil, but supply with good drainage. Use a mulch to moderate soil temperatures and maintain moisture. Fertilize spring and fall with manure—pines are sensitive to nitrogen fertilizers.

PITTOSPORUM TOBIRA 'WHEELER'S DWARF'

'Wheeler's Dwarf' pittosporum is a favorite shrub or ground cover of landscape architects. It requires little maintenance and is reliable and neat in appearance. Evergreen plants blend well with other ground covers and shrubs.

It is easily kept to 12 to 24 inches high with a slightly wider spread. Unpruned height approaches 36 inches. The effect of a mass planting is dense and mounding. Leaves are clean, leathery and shiny dark or light green. They are 2 to 5 inches long with rolled edges and rounded ends. Creamy white flowers are fragrant like orange

Pinus mugo serves as an evergreen background to colorful annuals and fibrous begonias.

Pittosporum tobira 'Wheeler's Dwarf', as purchased from the nursery in a 1-gallon container.

blossoms and appear in early spring.

Planting and care—Fall is the most advantageous time to plant. But these adaptable plants usually succeed no matter when planted. Nurseries keep both 1- and 5-gallon sizes in stock. Plant in full sun or part shade in any soil. Mulch, maintain soil moisture and fertility. Once established, little care is necessary.

Hardy to 20F (−7C).

Plantain lily. See *Hosta*

PLUMBAGO AURICULATA
Synonym: P. capensis
Blue cape plumbago

This is a persistent, vining, mounding shrub. It is often used on banks and as a background filler. Growth is on the rampant side, so allow plenty of room. It produces azure-blue flowers throughout the season. See *Ceratostigma*, page 104, for another plant commonly known as plumbago.

Height is variable. It will climb 10 feet and more on fences. On a bank, height will be about 5 feet. Plant spreads about 10 feet wide. Leaves

are light green and 1 to 2 inches long. Flowers are 1 inch wide, appear in clusters and are very attractive. Colors vary somewhat. Buy blooming plants to obtain the color you want. Spring is peak bloom period but flowers continue throughout the year.

Planting and care—Fall planting is best, usually from 1-gallon containers. Plant in full sun and in any well-drained soil. Water regularly to establish. Drought tolerance is excellent after plants are established.

Hardy to 20F (−7C).

POLYGONUM
Knotweed, Silver lace vine, Fleeceflower

Polygonum species are vigorous, fast-growing, trailing vines and ground covers. Their speciality is a fast, tough cover in poor soil and in difficult climates. Their negative side is invasive, potentially uncontrollable growth.

Polygonum affine, Himalayan fleeceflower, is evergreen, perennial and has showy flowers. It grows 12 to 18 inches high. Leaves are 2 to 5 inches long and turn reddish in winter. Flowers are bright red and bloom in midsummer. Plants are

tolerant of any soil. Plant in full sun or some shade. Give plenty of water for best appearance.

Hardy to 0F (−18C).

P. capitatum is a useful and tough ground cover for temperate climates. If you have a difficult situation where nothing seems to do well, try this plant. It grows 6 inches high and is wide spreading. Leaves are 1 inch long and an attractive bronze-green. Stems and flowers are pinkish and give the plant an overall reddish cast. Moderately invasive roots. If tops are killed by winter cold, plants usually sprout from roots and seed.

Hardy to 30F (−1C).

P. cuspidatum compactum is deciduous but the toughest overall. It mounds to perhaps 2 feet high and spreads widely with underground roots. Leaves are green, 3 to 6 inches long and turn red in fall before falling. Red flowers appear in late summer. Use for erosion control on hot, dry, exposed slopes, generally in the farthest reaches of your landscape. Space plants 2 to 4 feet apart.

Hardy to −30F (−35C).

Planting and care—Early spring planting is best, but plant any time. Plants are normally available in

Portulaca grandiflora is a drought-tolerant, summer-blooming annual.

Potentilla tabernaemontanii hugs the ground.

flats, sometimes in 1-gallon containers. All are tolerant of soil quality. *P. capitatum* is the only species useful in shade, in a tree basin for instance, as well as full sun. Nutrient and moisture needs are minimal once established.

Polystichum. See Ferns

PORTULACA GRANDIFLORA
Rose moss

Rose moss is a self-sowing, brightly colored summer annual. It is easily started from seed or nursery transplants. Once introduced to your garden, plants reseed year after year but never aggressively. Use rose moss to fill in between junipers or other slow-to-cover ground covers.

Plants grow 6 inches high and about 1 foot wide. Leaves are 1 inch long, narrow and fleshy. Flowers are about 1 inch wide and available in many bright colors. Several named strains are available. They may be single or double flower forms. All open only in sun and close in the afternoon.

Planting and care—Plant from seed or transplants in spring.

Tolerant of soil quality and drought tolerant after established. Prefers full sun. Dies with first frost.

POTENTILLA
Cinquefoil

Two cinquefoils are unusually well suited to serve as ground covers. Both have leaves like strawberries, but smaller. They spread with above-ground runners to make a dense, weed-choking mat.

Potentilla tabernaemontanii, spring cinquefoil, is the most frequently planted cinquefoil for a ground cover. Its former botanical name, *Potentilla verna*, is preferred by many nurserymen. It grows 3 to 6 inches high and spreads 12 to 18 inches wide. Dark green leaves are divided into five leaflets and have toothed edges. Flowers are yellow, about 3/8 inch wide and grouped in small clusters. They are most abundant in late spring and appear until fall.

Spring cinqefoil makes a fine lawn substitute if foot traffic is not too frequent. If mowed, it makes a neat, tight mat. Raking leaves from plantings is awkward because tines catch in the runners.

Hardy to about 10F (−24C).

P. tridentata, wineleaf cinquefoil, grows 2 to 12 inches high, and spreads by underground and above-ground runners to 2 feet. It makes a permanent, semiwoody mat. Leaves are medium green and leathery, divided into 3 leaflets. White flowers are about 3/8 inch wide. Use this ground cover in dry, rocky places. Original plants were found growing in rock crevices along the North Shore of Lake Superior. It is ideal under azaleas, rhododendrons and other acid-loving plants.

Hardy to −35F (−37C).

Planting and care—Spring cinquefoil grows fast in full sun, slower in shade. Plant in early spring from flats. Space plants 10 to 12 inches apart. Very susceptible to rust disease in some areas. Fertilize and mow to discourage it.

Growth of wineleaf cinquefoil is fairly slow so space plants about 10 inches apart. Spring or early fall planting is best, usually from 1-gallon containers. Any soil is acceptable but it prefers slightly acid conditions.

PRATIA ANGULATA

Pratia angulata is a choice, small-area, evergreen ground cover, a

Potentilla tabernaemontanii spreads by runners, but is not invasive.

native of New Zealand. It grows fast with rooting, creeping runners, twining its way into cracks and crevices or around stones and taller plants.

It grows 2 to 6 inches high and spreads about 10 inches wide. Leaves are 1/2 inch long and almost round. Flowers are white, 1/2 inch long and similar to *Lobelia*.

Planting and care—Plant in rich, moist soil for best growth. Spring is best planting time, usually from flats or individual plastic packs. Space plants 6 to 10 inches apart. Does well in sun or light shade. Mow or trim back spring or fall.

Hardy to 10F (−12C).

PRUNUS LAUROCERASUS 'ZABELIANA'
Zabel cherry laurel

Zabel cherry laurel is a low, somewhat spreading type of cherry laurel, one of the most popular and reliable landscape shrubs. It grows higher than most ground covers, but because of an unusual, upward-outward growth habit, it is easily pegged or trained to grow horizontally. Makes an unusual and beautiful mounding bank cover.

Ultimate height is 6 feet but when pegged, 2-1/2 feet high is common. Evergreen leaves are dark green, 3 to 5 inches long.

Planting and care—Plant in early fall if possible. Nurseries keep plants available in 1-gallon containers. Morning sun with afternoon shade is best but plant is adaptable to many situations. Plant in well-drained soil and provide regular amounts of water. Space plants 3 to 4 feet apart.

Hardy to about −15F (−26C).

PYRACANTHA
Pyracantha, Firethorn

Pyracanthas are common, reliable shrubs. Several low, spreading forms are used as ground covers. All are evergreen with bright, glossy green leaves. Flowers appear in spring. Berries follow in fall and sometimes remain through winter.

Use them on banks, for low barriers or hedges and in similar small areas.

Here are *Pyracantha* species useful as ground covers:

'Walderi Prostrata', Walder's pyracantha, grows 1-1/2 to 2 feet high with a wide spread. Berries are bright red. Prune out occasional upright shoots. Space plants 4 to 5 feet apart.

P. koidzumii 'Santa Cruz', Santa Cruz pyracantha, grows 2 to 3 feet high and sends up an occasional branch to 4 feet. Red berries. Space plants 4 to 5 feet apart.

'Leprechaun' is 24 to 30 inches high and grows in a more rounded and dense fashion. Berries are crimson color. Space plants 3 to 4 feet apart.

'Tiny Tim' is a dwarf selection from Amfac Select Nurseries. It is dense and compact, normally reaching less than 3 feet high. Branches are nearly thornless. Cinnamon-red berries. Space 2 to 3 feet apart.

Planting and care—Fall is best planting time, usually from 1-gallon containers. Plant in full sun and any well-drained soil. Drought tolerant when established.

Pyracantha is subject to few diseases and pests, but is occasionally afflicted with the following. Fireblight disease kills whole branches, leaving scorched, hanging leaves. Sprays containing copper are effective when plants are in flower. Avoid overhead sprinkling. Prune and dispose of dead branches, cutting several inches into healthy

Polyantha roses are low growing, hardy, colorful and require little maintenance once established.

wood. Disinfect clippers between cuts in undiluted household bleach.

Apple scab will defoliate pyracanthas in cool, moist climates. Use recommended fungicides such as captan as the label directs.

Scale and woolly aphids can be controlled by oil sprays in winter. Use diazinon during growing season if infestation is serious. Controls containing dicofol will control spider mites.

Hardy to about 0F (−18C).

RANUNCULUS REPENS
Creeping buttercup

Creeping buttercup is an excellent, vigorous ground cover for moist, shady sites. It grows 8 to 12 inches high and spreads with above-ground runners. Roots are thick and strong. Leaves are dark green, slightly mottled and deeply toothed. Yellow, 1-inch flowers may be single or double and appear in spring. The variety 'Pleniflorus' has double flowers and is slightly less vigorous.

Planting and care—Set out transplants in spring or fall. Soil should be moist for best growth. Water regularly if soil tends to dry. Very fast spreading when conditions right.

Hardy to 5F (−15C).

Redwood sorrel. See *Oxalis*

Ribbon grass. See *Phalaris*

RIBES VIBURNIFOLIUM
Evergreen currant

Evergreen currant is native to islands near southern California. It is adaptable, drought tolerant, attractive and one of the few ground covers that will thrive in the dry shade under native oak trees.

Grows to about 2 feet high. Branches arch and sprawl to 8 feet wide. Dark green leaves are leathery, nearly round and almost 1 inch wide. They are fragrant when moist or crushed. Flowers are pink or purple but not showy. Red berries follow flowers.

Planting and care—Plant in fall to take advantage of winter rains. Any soil is acceptable. Grow in full sun or in partial shade near the coast. No summer water is necessary with coastal plantings after establishment. Give inland plantings some shade. Supply with occasional water or leaves will yellow. Prune out upright shoots.

Hardy to about 15F (−9C).

Rockrose. See *Cistus*

ROSA
Rose

Roses are such a large and varied group that listing all that have ground cover possibilities becomes a voluminous task. For instance, the most vigorous climber may be a large-area ground cover if canes are pegged and trained along the ground. At the other end of the scale, several miniatures, polyanthas and floribundas are beautiful and hardy ground covers. You will find complete information in *ROSES: How to Select, Grow and Enjoy,* published by HPBooks.

The four following roses are most useful and commonly grown as ground covers.

'Max Graf' is low and spreading, reaching 3 feet high and 4 feet wide. Pink flowers have gold centers and are about 3 inches in diameter. It is hardy, handsome and should be more widely grown. Try it on banks, around rocks or draped over walls. It is also an excellent barrier plant.

Hardy to −10F (−24C).

'Red Cascade' is a miniature rose with double, 1-inch, red flowers. Canes are pencil-thick and wide

Rosmarinus officinalis drapes over this low, concrete retaining wall.

Rosmarinus officinalis, trailing form, is shown at upper left. Upright form is at top right.

spreading to 5 feet in each direction. It is a modern rose and popular as a hanging basket plant. Leaves are moderately susceptible to mildew.

Hardy to 15F (−9C).

Rosa wichuraiana, memorial rose, is the species with greatest ground cover potential. It is one of the parents of 'Max Graf' and 'Red Cascade'. It is often trained vertically then allowed to cascade. Natural growth is prostrate and spreading, 12 to 18 inches high and 6 to 15 feet wide. Rooting, trailing stems have small, dark green, evergreen leaves. Flowers are small, white and fragrant. They appear late spring and summer. Where winters are colder, some leaves will drop.

Hardy to about −10F (−24C).

A fourth ground cover rose, 'Sea Foam', is endorsed by mountain-area gardeners. It has shiny leaves and sparkling white flowers. Spread is 8 to 10 feet wide.

Hardy to −10F (−24C).

Planting and care—Most roses are available in bare-root form in late winter or early spring. Soak roots in a bucket of water when you get plants home and plant as soon as possible. Miniature roses are available in containers throughout the year. Plant any time. All roses are adaptable plants, but all are best in full sun and rich soil. Drought tolerance is relatively good, but deep watering permits best growth. Fertilize spring and fall. Prune out old, dead branches each fall or early spring.

Rose moss. See *Portulaca*

ROSMARINUS OFFICINALIS
Trailing rosemary

Trailing rosemary is one of the premier ground covers of the West and all Mediterranean climates. Flowers and leaves are equally handsome. The plant's trailing and draping habit is always striking. Culture is very easy.

Upright varieties such as 'Tuscan Blue' may reach 4 to 6 feet high at maturity. But trailing and dwarf forms of rosemary grow only 1 to 2-1/2 feet high. Some will spread as wide as 8 feet. They are excellent as bank covers or spilling over planter or container edges.

Needlelike leaves are shiny dark green and white underneath. These are the same culinary rosemary leaves sold as an herb in markets. Use them freely in the kitchen or for flavoring barbecues. Flowers are lavender-blue, and bloom mostly in spring. Bees love the flowers.

Leaves have highest oil content just before flowering. This is the time to pick and dry them for kitchen use.

The best ground cover kinds are:

'Collingwood Ingram'—Grows to 30 inches high and spreads 4 to 5 feet wide. Showy blue flowers.

'Huntington Carpet'—Lowest-growing rosemary, only 12 inches high. Spreads to 4 feet wide.

'Lockwood de Forest'—Grows 24 inches high and 4 to 6 feet wide. Leaves are shiny light green. Flowers are dark blue.

Planting and care—Plant from containers or flats any time. Plant in full sun and in any well-drained soil. Drought tolerance is excellent, but occasional water is necessary in summer in hot, dry areas. Generous fertilizer and water promotes lush, woody growth. Pinch tips of new growth to promote compact, dense growth.

Hardy to 10F (−12C).

Rumohra. See Ferns

Rupturewort. See *Herniaria*

Santolina chamaecyparissus shows off with many yellow flowers in midsummer.

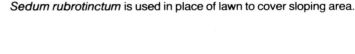

Sedum rubrotinctum is used in place of lawn to cover sloping area.

Ruschia. See Ice Plants

Sagina. See Moss

Salal. See *Gaultheria*

SANTOLINA
Lavender cotton

Lavender cotton is an excellent ground cover for all Mediterranean climates. It loves hot, dry weather, does not require particularly good soil and is drought tolerant. Two species are commonly used as ground covers. One is silver-gray and the other is deep green. Leaves of both are aromatic and bring striking, contrasting colors and textures to the landscape. In their natural form plants are low and mounding but they can be sheared into neat, geometric hedges. Both offer some fire resistance.

Santolina chamaecyparissus, lavender cotton, has silver-gray leaves divided into numerous, needlelike leaflets that have a woolly feel. It grows 18 to 24 inches high and 24 to 30 inches wide.

Yellow, buttonlike flowers are borne on slender stems above the plant in midsummer. *S. c.* 'Nana' is an 8- to 10-inch high dwarf form.

Hardy to −5F (−21C).

S. virens, green lavender cotton, grows 18 to 24 inches high. Leaves are similar to its gray cousin, but more narrow and dark green. It grows faster and is more tolerant of frequent watering.

Hardy to 5F (−15C).

Planting and care—Plant any time but best in spring. Nurseries have plants in 1-gallon containers or smaller plastic pots. Both species require full sun. They are tolerant of any soil as long as it is well drained. Prune plants severely in spring to remove any winter-damaged stems and to force new vigorous growth. Remove flowers as they fade.

SARCOCOCCA
HOOKERANA HUMILIS

This is one of the best ground covers for heavily shaded locations. Excellent under the dense shade of trees, sarcococca is neat and clean in appearance. A rich, moist soil is its only definite requirement.

Plant grows 18 to 24 inches high and spreads by underground runners to 6 feet or more. Leaves are shiny, dark green and 1 to 3 inches long. Flowers are tiny, white, fragrant and appear in spring. Black berries follow.

Planting and care—Plant in early fall or spring from 1-gallon containers. Plant in shade in organic-rich soil. Water regularly. Feed with general-purpose fertilizer in spring and fall. In cool-summer areas more sun is acceptable.

Hardy to −10F (−24C).

Scotch moss. See Moss

SEDUMS

This large and varied group of plants includes many useful ground covers. All have fleshy, succulent leaves. They actually prefer occasional drought and poor soil. Plants propagate easily and fast. Leaves that are broken from the mother plant will quickly root and spread. Footsteps crush leaves and stems, but sedums are otherwise hardy, low-maintenance ground covers.

Ground cover species and varieties are:

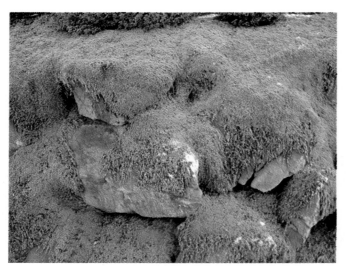

Sedum dasyphyllum is mosslike in appearance and texture.

Sedum spurium 'Dragon's Blood' derives its name from the flower color.

Sedum anglicum—Excellent covering for low banks and mounds. Grows 2 to 4 inches high. Leaves are small and dark green. Flowers are small, yellow and star shaped. Plant 6 to 10 inches apart for a fast cover.

Hardy to −34F (−36C).

S. brevifolium—Grows fast to 2 or 3 inches high. Leaves are bright green and covered with white, star-shaped flowers through spring and early summer. Needs good drainage.

Hardy to −34F (−36C).

S. confusum—Grows 6 to 10 inches high and spreads as wide. Leaves are 1 inch long, light green and clustered at branch tips. Yellow flowers are abundant and bloom in spring. This sedum is best in cool seasons. It is a native of Mexico and adapts naturally to long, hot summers by becoming dormant. Accepts the summer dormant period. Moisture during that time usually causes plant to die back.

Hardy to 10F (−12C).

S. dasyphyllum—Grows 2 inches high to make a mat of blue-gray, mosslike leaves. Flowers are small and white. Attractive, small-area ground cover.

Hardy to 5F (−15C).

S. lineare, frequently listed as *S. sarmentosum*—Grows 6 to 10 inches high and spreads with trailing, rooting stems. Leaves are chartreuse-green and about 1 inch long. Flowers are yellow and abundant in spring. This is one of the showiest of all sedums when in full flower. Space plants 12 inches apart.

Hardy to −35F (−37C).

S. oaxacanum—Grows 6 to 8 inches high and spreads fast, making an excellent ground cover. Leaves are light green and appear mostly in rosettes at stem ends. Flowers are yellow and abundant. Space 10 to 12 inches apart.

Hardy to 5F (−15C).

S. rubrotinctum, also listed as *S. guatemalense*, is one of the most dependable and useful ground cover sedums. It grows 6 to 8 inches high and spreads wide. Leaves are 3/4 inch long and fat like jellybeans. In full sun, leaf tips or entire leaf is bronze-brown, but in shade leaves are green. Recommended as a low bank cover, edging and in planters. Some homeowners in mild climates have replaced their front lawns with this sedum, although it does not tolerate foot traffic. Space 10 to 12 inches apart.

Hardy to 10F (−12C).

S. spathulifolium—Grows only 2 to 3 inches high. Silvery leaves are packed into rosettes. Spreads by trailing stems. An improved selection is 'Cape Blanca', which has more distinct leaf color. Flowers are light yellow and bloom in spring. Space 6 to 8 inches apart.

Hardy to −10F (−24C).

S. spurium—Grows 3 to 4 inches high, making a tight mat. Bronze-tinted leaves are 1 inch long. Pink flowers are borne on top of tall stems in summer. 'Dragon's Blood' has rose-red flowers. Space 6 to 10 inches apart.

Hardy to −35F (−40C).

'Utah'—A rapid grower 3 to 6 inches high. Leaves are dark green and small. Bright yellow flowers are abundant in spring. Space plants 6 to 12 inches apart.

Hardy to −35F (−40C).

Planting and care—Spring or fall are most favorable planting times, but any time is okay. Plants are normally available in flats. All ground cover sedums are best grown in full sun and dry, well-drained soils. In isolated areas of dry soil, they may be ideal. Plantings tend to be short-lived near sidewalks or where children or dogs play.

Soleirolia soleirolii, green and golden forms, are interesting to touch and view.

Spirea japonica 'Alpina' produces a pink flower display in spring.

SEMPERVIVUM TECTORUM
Hen and chickens

Hen and chickens are perfect plants to tuck into any empty garden spot. They are tolerant of soil quality and can even grow tucked in rock crevices. They are very hardy and long-lived.

Plants grow about 4 inches high and 4 to 6 inches wide. Leaves are 2 to 3 inches long, broad at the tip, usually with a tip-spine. Star-shaped flowers are white, pink, red, green and yellow. They bloom on long stalks in summer. After flowering and setting seed, parent plants die, but offshoots usually survive in quantity.

Planting and care—Hen and chickens are easy to grow. Plant any time in full sun and any well-drained soil. Plants are often passed neighbor-to-neighbor. Also look in the nursery for plants in 1-gallon containers. Afternoon shade is recommended for plants in desert areas. Drought tolerant, but plants are much better with water in summer.

Hardy to −10F (−24C).

Silver bush morning glory. See *Convolvulus*

Silver lace vine. See *Polygonum*

Silver spreader. See *Artemisia*

Snow-in-summer. See *Cerastium*

SOLEIROLIA SOLEIROLII
Baby's-tears

This is a cool, appealing, mosslike plant. It is damaged easily by footsteps or cold but recovers fast. In fact, when conditions are right, baby's-tears becomes an invasive plant. Use it under ferns, along borders, over bulbs—wherever soil is moist and shaded.

Height is 1 to 6 inches. It grows tallest in shady, protected locations. Tiny, round leaves are light green or golden green.

Planting and care—Plant from flats in spring or fall. Rich, moist, cool soil is ideal. Top growth is perennial in mild climates. In cold climates, plants come back in spring from roots and seed.

Leaves are hardy to 20F (−7C).

Speedwell. See *Veronica*

SPIREA JAPONICA 'ALPINA'
Daphne or creeping spirea

This is the most dwarf form of the long-favored spirea. Height is rarely more than 12 inches and spread is 2 to 3 feet. Leaves are lance shaped, about 1 inch long. Branches are stiff like wire. Pink flowers bloom in spring in clusters at branch tips. 'Little Princess' is very similar to 'Alpina' but it grows slightly taller and has rose-crimson flowers.

Planting and care—Early fall is best planting time, second best is spring. Plants are normally available in 1-gallon containers. Plant in full sun in dry or sandy soil. Space plants 12 to 18 inches apart for a fast cover. Water regularly to establish plants as necessary. Drought tolerance is good. Prune out older wood at end of bloom.

Hardy to −20F (−29C).

Star jasmine. See *Trachelospermum*

Strawberry. See *Fragaria*. Also see *Duchesnea* and *Waldsteinia*

Sunrose. See *Helianthemum*

Sweet alyssum. See *Lobularia*

Teucrium chamaedrys 'Prostratum' makes an excellent low border.

Thymus forms a low-growing, dense mat.

Sweet fern. See *Comptonia*

Sweet woodruff. See *Galium*

TAXUS BACCATA 'REPANDENS'
Spreading English yew

Taxus baccata 'Repandens', spreading English yew, is a low and spreading form of English yew, the popular hedge plant. It is a good, hardy, evergreen ground cover or low foundation plant that produces a neat and formal effect. Use it individually rather than in massed plantings.

Plant grows to 2 feet high but in an irregular form. Growth rate is slow but in time plant will cover an area 10 feet or more in diameter. Leaves are shiny dark green on top and white underneath. Red berries follow tiny flowers. Both leaves and fruit are poisonous.

Planting and care—Plant in early fall from 1-gallon containers. Plant in full sun or some shade. Any soil is okay. Drought tolerant once established. High heat combined with dry air will burn leaves, so avoid reflected heat. Relatively problem-free.

Hardy to −10F (−24C).

TEUCRIUM CHAMAEDRYS 'PROSTRATUM'
Germander

Germander is an outstanding, low-growing, spreading ground cover. It is ideal for poor soils and hot, sunny exposures. Plant also has moderate fire resistance.

It grows 8 to 10 inches high and spreads fast, making a 36-inch wide mat. Leaves are bright green and about 3/4 inch long. Lavender flowers appearing on spikes bloom spring and summer and are loved by bees.

Planting and care—Plant any time, but preferably in fall or spring. Shop for bushy plants in 1-gallon containers. Plant in full sun about 12 to 18 inches apart. A little shade is acceptable, but growth will be slow. Any soil will do, even if it is thin and rocky, but it must be well drained. Shear plants once a year.

Hardy to −10F (−24C).

THYMUS
Creeping thyme, Woolly thyme

Two thymes are particularly valued as ground covers. One, *Thymus praecox arcticus*, also known as *T. serpyllum*, is commonly known as creeping thyme or mother-of-thyme. The other is *T. pseudolanuginosus*, also *T. lanuginosus*, commonly known as woolly thyme. Both are very low creepers and perhaps the best ground covers for planting between paving stones. Both make striking and unusual lawns, or can be interplanted into existing lawns. Creeping thyme also makes a fun cover for an outdoor bench. It will trail nicely over edges.

Creeping thyme grows 2 to 6 inches high and spreads with creeping, rooting stems. Dark green leaves are about 1/4 inch wide. Flowers come in mid to late summer. They may be white or rose, depending on variety. Many varieties are available, distinguishable only by minor characteristics such as flower color or shade of green leaves.

Woolly thyme makes a more undulating but generally lower mat—to 3 inches high. Leaves are similar to creeping thyme but gray and woolly. Flowers are pink but rarely seen. It is dense growing and perhaps the best thyme for ground cover.

Planting and care—Plant in full

Trachelospermum jasminoides is well adapted as a low border.

Trachelospermum asiaticum serves as transition between bermudagrass lawn and *Ilex cornuta* 'Dwarf Burford'.

sun, spring or fall, in relatively dry soil. Plants are available any number of ways—1-gallon containers, flats or small plastic pots. Water regularly to establish. Space plants about 6 to 10 inches apart. For a lawn, control weeds first, then plant creeping thymes of various flower colors. Weeds will continue to be a minor problem requiring regular attention.

Both creeping thyme and woolly thyme are hardy to about −35F (−37C).

TRACHELOSPERMUM
Confederate vine and Star jasmine

Star jasmine is one of the most popular ground covers where it is hardy. It is also a useful vine, climbing to 20 feet or more if given room. It is easily trained by tip pruning to cover banks, border lawns and grow over tree roots.

Two species are used as ground covers:

Trachelospermum asiaticum is slightly more hardy and is popular in the southern United States. It is commonly known as confederate vine.

T. jasminoides, star jasmine, is slightly taller growing and leaves are glossier. It is popular in the West and Southwest.

When trained as a ground cover, confederate vine grows about 1 foot high and spreads 3 to 4 feet wide. Dull green leaves are about 2 inches long. Fragrant flowers are creamy white or sometimes yellow. Space plants 2 feet apart.

Star jasmine grows about 18 inches high and spreads 4 to 5 feet wide. Leaves are glossy, dark green and 3 inches long. Small, pinwheel-shaped flowers are white and sweetly fragrant. They appear late spring on new growth. Space plants 1-1/2 to 3 feet apart.

Planting and care—Plant early fall or spring. Typically available in 1-gallon containers. Full sun is best but some shade is acceptable. Plants prefer a quality loam soil. Improve poor soil with organic amendment before planting, then mulch after planting. Iron chlorosis is a possible problem in soils that have a higher pH. Use an iron chelate or ferrous sulfate to correct. Shear off upright shoots when they appear in spring.

T. asiaticum is hardy to 0F (−18C). *T. jasminoides* is hardy to 10F (−12C).

Trailing fuchsia. See *Fuchsia*

Trailing indigo bush. See *Dalea*

Trailing rosemary. See *Rosmarinus*

VANCOUVERIA HEXANDRA
American barrenwort, Vancouver fern

Vancouveria is a woodland plant native to the coastal mountains of California north to British Columbia. It is a close relative of *Epimedium* species and much of its culture and habit is similar. See page 113. *Vancouveria* spreads fast with underground runners. It is deciduous in fall. It is excellent in shade and persists under native oaks. Try it mixed with ferns, *Campanula* species or azaleas.

Plants grow to about 12 inches high. Leaves are apple-green and divided into three leaflets. They have a dainty, fernlike appearance that has led to the common name used by some gardeners—Vancouver fern. Leaves rise directly from

Verbena peruviana is colorful and drought tolerant.

Vinca major covers and protects slope.

underground runners. White, drooping flowers rise above leaves on stalks in spring.

Planting and care—Spring is best planting time. Plants are normally available in 1-gallon containers. Plant in partial shade 12 to 18 inches apart. Ideally, soil is rich, moist and well drained. Use a mulch if soil tends to dry out rapidly. Give new plants plenty of water. Give established plants deep, infrequent waterings.

Hardy to −10F (−24C).

VERBENA PERUVIANA
Garden verbena, Perennial verbena

Verbena is one of the most colorful, drought-tolerant ground covers, especially in Southwest gardens. Planted in full sun and well-drained soil, it spreads fast to make a permanent cover.

Height is 3 to 6 inches and spread is 24 to 30 inches. Leaves are small and closely set, making a dense, nearly weed-proof mat. Brilliant red flowers appear spring through fall in large, flat-topped clusters. Most nurseries offer taller-growing hybrids that vary in flower color. Most are shades of pink. 'Starfire' is a solid red selection.

Planting and care—Plant in spring, in full sun and in well-drained soil. Tolerates reflected heat of west and south walls and dry, hot slopes. Growth is superior in loam soils. Space plants 2 feet apart for a solid cover in one year. Drought tolerant once established. Clip plants in fall to remove dead flowers and to promote dense growth. Fertilize once a year in spring or fall.

Hardy to 10F (−12C).

VERONICA REPENS
Speedwell

Speedwell is a vigorous, creeping plant, often used between paving stones or as a bulb cover. It produces an effect similar to moss. Speedwell accepts considerable foot traffic so it makes a good lawn substitute.

Plant grows 2 to 6 inches high, varying with climate and exposure, with a spread to 1-1/2 to 2 feet wide. Leaves are rich, shiny green and about 1/2 inch long. Blue flowers bloom in late spring on 4-inch spikes.

Hardy to −10F (−24C).

A related species, *V. latifolia*, is known as Hungarian speedwell. It grows 4 to 8 inches high to 2 feet wide. Light blue flowers appear on 3- to 4-inch spikes in spring.

Hardy to 0F (−18C).

Planting and care—Plant in spring, in full sun or some shade. Space plants 1 to 1-1/2 feet apart. Tolerant of soil quality. Water as for a lawn.

VINCA
Periwinkle

Periwinkle, especially *Vinca minor,* is one of the best, most reliable and most popular of all ground covers. For large, shady areas, cool banks and under trees, it is outstanding. Another plant known as periwinkle is described under *Catharanthus,* page 101.

V. major is larger, less cold hardy and a more open, rampant grower. Use in large, rough areas.

Plant grows 18 to 30 inches high and spreads by trailing stems to form new plants. Leaves are dark green and 2 to 3 inches long. Lavender-blue, 2-inch flowers

Vinca minor is low growing and adapted to shade as well as sun. It's perfect as a living mulch under tree basins.

When neatly trimmed, *Vinca minor* is unsurpassed for a formal, refined effect.

appear intermittently throughout the season. It is tough and easy to grow. Accepts considerable drought but is better with some shade and some moisture. Mow every two or three years to keep beds neat and within bounds. Mowing also forces attractive new growth. Use under trees that drop large quantities of leaves; they disappear under periwinkle foliage. A gold, variegated form is available.

Hardy to 10F (−12C).

V. minor is more versatile in the landscape. It grows about 6 inches high or less, and spreads widely, making a nice and even mat. It is basically a smaller, refined version of *V. major*, but somewhat less adaptable and requiring more water and fertilizer. 'Alba' has wider leaves, white flowers and is wide spreading. 'Bowles' is a favorite variety. Flowers are larger and more showy. Plant is less spreading and suitable for smaller gardens. 'Miss Jekyll' also has white flowers and grows to about 4 inches high.

Hardy to −15F (−26C).

Planting and care—*Vinca major* grows in sun or shade. *V. minor* will grow in full sun but does best with filtered shade. Accepts any soil. Water regularly. Cut back or mow periodically to force more vigorous, attractive growth.

VIOLA
Sweet violet, Australian violet

Sweet violet, *Viola odorata*, is the wonderful, old-fashioned perennial violet, so characteristic of older gardens. It produces a lush, charming cover under shrubs and trees or bordering a lawn.

Height varies between 3 and 12 inches, depending on variety. It spreads by runners that root at joints. Dark green leaves are thin and heart shaped. Sweetly fragrant flowers are purple, white or sometimes pink. They appear in late spring. 'Royal Robe', with deep purple flowers on long stems, is the most popular variety. 'White Czar' is similar but with white flowers. 'Rosina' produces fragrant pink flowers in spring and fall.

Hardy to −10F (−24C).

Australian violet, *V. hederacea*, forms a tight carpet of soft green foliage that is attractive through all seasons. Height is 1 to 4 inches. Roots as it spreads to 10 inches wide.

Violet flowers are profuse in spring and summer.

Hardy to 20F (−7C). Tops are deciduous at 30F (−1C).

Planting and care—Plant in spring from flats, 1-gallon containers or individual plastic packs. Plant sweet violets in full sun in cool or coastal climates, in shade inland. Space plants 8 to 12 inches apart. Soil should be well amended with organic matter. Give average or more water. For greatest flower quantity, trim back severely in fall and fertilize in spring. If spider mites attack plants, mist frequently with dilute soap solution of 1 teaspoon per gallon of water.

WALDSTEINIA FRAGARIOIDES
Barren strawberry

Barren strawberry is related to common strawberry, but is much lower growing, more dense and does not bear fruit. It is native to North America as far north as New Brunswick and south to Missouri. It is an excellent, but rarely used ground cover. It is ideal for wooded, partially shaded locations.

Viola odorata has a sweet fragrance.

Zoysia tenuifolia is self-mounding and never requires mowing.

Plant grows 2 to 5 inches high and spreads 1 foot or more with above-ground, rooting runners. Leaves are glossy, bright green, turning copper colored in fall. They are divided into 3 leaflets, each about 2 inches long. Yellow, 3/4-inch flowers appear in spring, but do not produce fruit.

Planting and care—Spring or fall is the best time to plant, but any time is okay if a sprinkler system is available. Plants are usually available in flats. Plant in sun or shade, 6 inches apart, in moist, average-to-rich soil. Supply with ample water.

Hardy to −30F (−35C).

Wall rockcress. See *Arabis*

Wild ginger. See *Asarum*

Wintercreeper. See *Euonymus*

Wintergreen. See *Gaultheria*

Wire vine. See *Muehlenbeckia*

Woolly yarrow. See *Achillea*

XANTHORHIZA SIMPLICISSIMA
Yellow-root

Yellow-root is a special-purpose ground cover. It excels at covering wet soil. It will control weeds and mud along pond or creek shores. Try yellow-root wherever soils are wet enough to discourage most ornamentals.

Plant grows to 2 feet high or less and spreads to 24 inches within a season. Deciduous leaves are 1 to 3 inches long and toothed. They turn yellow-orange in fall. Both stems and roots have yellow bark.

Planting and care—Plant clumps 2 feet apart in spring, in sun or shade. Accepts any soil. Needs regular to ample amounts of water. Tolerates excessively wet soils.

Hardy to −30F (−35C).

Yellow archangel. See *Lamiastrum*

Yellow-root. See *Xanthorhiza*

Yew. See *Taxus*

Zabel cherry laurel. See *Prunus*

ZOYSIA TENUIFOLIA
Korean grass

Korean grass is a relative of zoysia-grass, which is used for lawns. See page 29. But it is very slow growing and makes a bumpy, mounding, yellow or dark green surface. Use it between paving stones or on banks, mounds and slopes. It tolerates some foot traffic, and gives an intriguing, Asian-looking effect.

Korean grass grows 2 to 8 inches high and spreads very slowly with both roots and above-ground runners. It has a fairly long dormant season, during which it is brown. In the most temperate climates the dormant season is short or nonexistent.

Planting and care—Plant clumps or plugs from flats in full sun or partial shade. Zoysia likes heat so late spring is the best time to plant. Space clumps 6 inches apart. Accepts any soil. Little water is needed when roots are established. Mowing is not necessary.

Hardy to 5F (−15C), but grows better where temperatures do not drop much below 20F (−7C).

Glossary

Acid—A pH reaction below neutral (7.0). Acid soil is in the pH range 4.0-7.0.

Acid forming—Fertilizers that tend to increase acid content of soil. Examples: Ammonium nitrate and ammonium sulfate.

Actual nitrogen—The amount of nitrogen in a fertilizer, regardless of the brand or formula. Three pounds of 20-7-14 contains same actual nitrogen as six pounds of 10-1-5. The chart on page 52 shows how much various ratio fertilizers it takes to equal 1 pound of actual nitrogen per 1,000 square feet.

Aeration—Increasing air movement into soil by removing cores of soil with hand tool or powered machine.

Alkaline—A pH reaction above neutral (7.0). Alkaline soil is in the pH range or 7.0 to 9.0.

Amendment—Any material, usually organic, added to soil to improve its properties.

Annual—A plant that germinates, matures, produces seed and dies within a year or less.

Biennial—A plant with a two-year life cycle. It dies after flowering and fruiting or seeding in the second year.

Blend—A combination of several grass varieties of the same species. Popular blends often combine shade-tolerant, disease-resistant and wear-tolerant Kentucky blue-grasses. See Mix.

Bract—A leaflike structure often found at the base of flowers. Bracts are usually small and green. Large, brightly colored bracts are commonly mistaken for flowers. The "flowers" of *Bougainvillea* species are bracts.

Broadleaf—A plant with netted leaf veins and usually prominent flowers. Leaves of grasses have parallel veins. See Narrowleaf and Dicot

Certified seed—A crop improvement society *certifies* the quality, variety and purity of lawn seed.

Chelates—Organic chemicals that hold minor nutrients such as iron or manganese until plant is able to absorb it.

Chlorosis—A loss of chlorophyll in plant leaves. Condition is indicated by yellowing leaves.

Clay soil—A soil made up of very small, flat particles that compact readily. It has a sticky feel when wet. Absorbs water slowly but retains it well.

Compaction—A soil condition that makes penetration of air and water difficult. Soil particles are forced together, sealing the soil surface.

Complete fertilizer—Contains a balanced formula of the three most essential nutrients for plant growth—nitrogen, phosphorus and potassium.

Contact herbicide—Destroys plant tissues it contacts. Is not systemic.

Cool-season grass—Any grass that grows best in cool climates. Example: Kentucky bluegrass.

Cold hardiness—See Hardy.

Coring—Method of lawn cultivation by removing *cores* of soil. See Aeration.

Cultivar—Plant variety bred for certain characteristics. From the words *cultivated variety*. Usually more expensive than standard varieties but worth the price. Names of cultivars are capitalized and enclosed in single quote marks.

Cutting—Plant section from stem or branch that will develop roots and grow into a new plant. A vegetative or asexual propagation method. Also called a *slip*.

Deciduous—Leaves of plants are shed all at one time at a certain season. Not evergreen.

Dethatching—Reducing thatch buildup, usually with mechanical tools. See Thatch, Vertical mower.

Dicot—A plant that emerges from its seed with two leaves. Develops netted veins. Broadleaf plants are dicots.

Division—Separating the rooted base of perennials, shrubs or bulbs to extend and multiply plantings.

Dormancy—Period when plant rests. Characterized by slow growth during winter, drought, or time of extremely high temperatures.

Dormant seeding—Sowing seed in late fall or winter when temperatures are too low for germination. Seed germinates the following spring.

Double—Flower with more than the minimum number of petals for flowers of that family. Usually has a full, frilly appearance.

Espalier—To train a tree or shrub to grow flat against a surface such as trellis frame or wall. Espaliers may be patterned informally or formally.

Evergreen—A plant that is always in leaf. It does not lose all its leaves at any one season, as a *deciduous* plant, but drops them gradually over a period of time.

Fertilizer burn—Occurs when moisture is pulled out of plant, dehydrating it. Fertilizers with high salt index, such as ammonium nitrate, are most likely to cause fertilizer burn.

Fumigant—Pesticides that are active in a vapor form.

Fungicide—Chemical product that kills or slows the growth of fungus diseases.

Fungus—Parasitic life form that feeds on many plants. Often referred to as a disease. See Fungicide.

Genus—A classification between the levels FAMILY and SPECIES; includes one or more species that share characteristics.

Germination—The sprouting of a seed.

Hardy—A horticultural term referring to a plant's ability to withstand low temperatures. Does not mean "toughness."

Heaving—Swelling or raising of soil caused by freezing.

Herbicide—Chemical product used to kill plants—usually used on weeds. *Contact* herbicides destroy plants on contact; *systemic* herbicides enter the plant's system, killing perennial roots as well as tops.

Humus—Decomposed, stable form of organic matter.

Hybrid—The result of a natural or man-made cross of two parent plants that differ in character from the parents.

Inorganic fertilizer—Produced from nonliving sources—such as chemicals.

Insecticide—Product that kills insects by contact or when it is eaten.

Iron chlorosis—See chlorosis.

Leaching—The downward movement of minerals, nutrients, salts and other materials through the soil, moved by percolating water.

Lime—An alkaline material often applied in the form of ground limestone to soil to reduce acidity.

Loam—A desirable, moisture- and nutrient-retaining soil type composed of a balance of sand, silt and clay particles.

Microclimate—Variations in climate—temperatures, sunlight, precipitation—on a very small scale. Different microclimates can often occur within a suburban-size yard.

Mix, mixture—A combination of several grass species. Provides greater tolerance to growing conditions compared to a single species. Popular mixes combine perennial ryegrasses with fine fescues. See Blend.

Monocot—A plant that emerges from its seed with one leaf. Develops parallel veins. All grasses are monocots. See Narrowleaf.

Mowing strip—A band of concrete, brick or other material bordering a lawn. The mower wheel is able to travel on the strip, speeding mowing jobs and reducing edging chores.

Mulch—A material used to cover the soil surface. Mulches are used to protect seedlings, improve water intake, preserve moisture, prevent erosion, modify soil temperatures and aid in weed control.

Narrowleaf—Typically identified by parallel leaf veins. Grasses are narrowleaf. See Broadleaf.

Nitrogen—The most important plant nutrient supplied by fertilizers. Used by plants to manufacture amino acids and protein. Necessary for healthy, green color. Chemical symbol is N.

Nonselective herbicide—Kills most kinds of plants when it contacts green, leafy parts. Example: glyphosate.

N-P-K—Chemical symbols for nitrogen-phosphorus-potassium, in that order. The ingredients of complete fertilizers and the three most important plant mineral nutrients.

Organic—Generally, things that are living or had once lived. As opposed to *inorganic*.

Overseeding—Sowing seed over thin spots in existing lawns to make a complete cover. Or, grass is sown over winter-dormant lawns such as bermudagrass for green lawn during the dormant period.

Perennial—A plant that lives for more than two years.

Pesticide—A product used to destroy pests. Fungicides, herbicides and insecticides are all pesticides.

pH—One of most important soil qualities determined by a soil test. A symbol used to express acidity or alkalinity. pH 0 to 7.0 is acid. pH 7.0 is neutral. pH 7.0 to 14.0 is alkaline. Optimum soil pH for plant growth is between 5.5 and 8.3. Test acidity-alkalinity of soils with pH tests kits or use the services of a soil-testing lab. See Acid and Alkaline.

Phosphorus—One of the three most important plant nutrients. Phosphorus is responsible for promoting root growth and is particularly useful in new plantings. Component in fertilizers. Chemical symbol is P.

Post-emergent herbicide—Destroys plants or weeds after they have emerged from the soil.

Potassium, potash—One of the three most important plant nutrients. A component in fertilizers. Chemical symbol is K. Often called potash.

Pre-emergent herbicide—A chemical applied to the soil that kills weed seed during germination, before plant emerges from soil.

Rejuvenate—Improving a lawn by removing thatch, deep coring and top dressing with organic amendment.

Renovate—Revitalize or improve an existing lawn. Method used to convert existing lawn of weeds or mixed grasses into lawn of more desirable quality. Frequently, undesirable grasses and weeds are removed using a herbicide, then Kentucky bluegrass or perennial ryegrass is replanted.

Rhizome—A horizontal, underground stem that produces new plants.

Rolling—Accomplished with a large drum. Ensures proper seed-to-soil contact in newly seeded lawns, or achieves root to soil contact in newly sodded lawns.

Runner—See Stolon.

Salinity—Saltiness of soil, water or fertilizer. See Fertilizer burn.

Scalping—To cut lawn to the soil level by mowing very close. Cutting into crowns of grass plants.

Selective herbicide—A product capable of destroying certain plants, such as broadleafed weeds, without damaging other plants, such as lawn grasses.

Self-sow—The tendency of a plant to reproduce itself by scattering seed that sprout and root readily. Example: African daisy *(Dimorphotheca sinuata)*.

Sepal—One of the outermost flower structures that usually encloses the bud. Found at the base of the petals after flower blooms.

Single—Flower with the minimum number of petals for flowers of that family. Example: Roses with 5-petaled flowers.

Slip—See Cutting.

Slow-release fertilizer—Makes nutrients available to plants over a long period of time. May be water soluble granules, plastic-coated pellets or organic.

Species—A specific plant distinguished from others in the same genus. See Genus.

Sprig—Tuft of grass plant used for propagation.

Stolon—Creeping, aboveground stems capable of rooting at joints. Used for propagation.

Strain—A cultivated line of plants similar in form but different in one aspect, usually flower color.

Surfactant—See Wetting agent.

Systemic—A chemical absorbed into a plant's system, passing with the sap into all parts of plant. Depending on product, a systemic can kill the plant, protect the plant from attacking fungi organisms or make the plant toxic to insects.

Taproot—The tapering, main root of a plant. It produces smaller, lateral root-hairs. Example: the weed curly dock.

Thatch—A strawlike layer of dead plant parts that accumulates between lawn grass and soil. Prevents water and nutrient penetration by acting like a "thatch roof." Lawn must be dethatched with a vertical mower.

Tiller—A side-shoot that forms at the base of a plant and produces new leaf blades.

Top dressing—Spreading a thin layer of weed-free soil, sand or organic matter on turf after aeration.

Variegated—Leaves are marked with white, silver or yellow colors.

Variety—A naturally occurring subdivision of a species. Similar to cultivars except cultivars are created by man.

Vertical mower—Machine that slices through lawn thatch and removes it. Also called a *dethatcher* or *lawn comb*.

Vegetative planting—Asexual propagation method. A means by which plants are reproduced by plant parts, rather than seed. Sprigs, stolons or plugs are used to reproduce grasses. Cuttings, slips or divisions reproduce ground covers.

Warm-season grass—Any grass that grows best in warm or semitropical climates. Example: bermudagrass.

Weed—Any plant that grows where it is not desired.

Well drained—Description of soil that allows water to move quickly into and through the soil and the root zone.

Wetting agent, surfactant—A chemical that changes the physical property of water by breaking it into molecular "pieces," which allows it to slip through hard-to-penetrate soils or thatch.

Whorl—A circle of flowers, flower parts or leaves.

Mail Order Sources of Ground Covers

Alpenglow Gardens
13328 King George Highway
Surrey, BC
Canada V3T 2T6
Rock and alpine plants. Dwarf shrubs and conifers. Catalog $1.

Bluestone Perennials
7211 Middle Ridge Road
Madison, OH 44057
Many perennials and ground covers.

Carroll Gardens
P.O. Box 310
Westminster, MD 21157
Many kinds of perennials and rock garden plants. 68-page catalog also includes a selection of ground covers.

Conley's Garden Center
Boothbay Harbor, ME 04538
Hardy wildflowers, ferns, native perennials, bulbs, orchids and ground covers. 50¢ for descriptive listing.

Far North Gardens
15621 Auburndale Avenue
Livonia, MI 48154
48-page catalog $1. Primrose and rare flower seed specialists. Several hardy ground covers.

Gardens of the Blue Ridge
P.O. Box 10
Pineola, NC 28662
Many ground covers including *Gaultheria* and *Phlox subulata*.

Garden Place
P.O. Box 83
Mentor, OH 44060
Perennial specialists. 56-page catalog includes many ground covers. Catalog $1.

Greer Gardens
1280 Goodpasture Island Road
Eugene, OR 97401
8½ by 11, 80-page color catalog for $2. Azalea and rhododendron specialists that also offer many ground cover plants.

Henderson's Botanical Gardens
Greensburg, IN 47204
Hardy ferns, vines and ground covers.

Lamb Nurseries
E. 101 Sharp Avenue
Spokane, WA 99202
Free catalog includes many choice ground cover plants.

Powell's Gardens
Route 2
Princeton, NC 27569
New varieties of bearded irises and daylilies, numerous perennials and dwarf conifers. Visit their demonstration garden. Catalog $1.

Russell Graham
4030 Eagle Crest Road NW
Salem, OR 97304
Many hardy perennials and Pacific Northwest native plants.

Sharp Bros. Seed Co.
Healy, KS 67850
Seed of many North American native grasses. Write for information.

Sheppard's Gardens
Burlington Road
Harwinton, CT 06790
8-page catalog includes many hard-to-find ground covers. Cost $1.

Siskiyou Rare Plant Nursery
2825 Cummings Road
Medford, OR 97501
Large collection of alpine plants. Many Pacific Northwest natives. Visitors by appointment. Catalog $1.

Sunnybrook Farms Nursery
9448 Mayfield Road
Chesterland, OH 44026
Many herbs, succulents and perennials. Catalog $1.

The Bovees Nursery
1737 S.W. Coronado
Portland, OR 97219
Rhododendron specialists that offer many companion shrubs and ground covers. Catalog $1.50.

The Garden Spot
4032 Rosewood Drive
Columbia, SC 29205
Many rare and unusual ivies. Stamped, self-addressed envelope brings descriptive price list of more than 100 varieties.

Wayside Gardens
Hodges, SC 29695
Wide selection of perennials, trees, shrubs and ground covers. Catalog $1.

Well-Sweep Herb Farm
317 Mt. Bethel Road
Port Murray, NJ 07865
Catalog lists many unusual herbs, many of which are good ground covers. Catalog 50¢.

Acknowledgments

Wayne Austin, Horticulturist, Orinda, CA

David Benner, Horticulturist, New Hope, PA

Buchart Gardens, Victoria, British Columbia, Canada

Evert O. Burt, Agricultural Research Center, University of Florida's Institute for Food and Agricultural Sciences, Ft. Lauderdale, FL

Kelly Cole, Camarillo, CA

Robert Cowden, Horticulturist, Walnut Creek, CA

Barrie Coate, Horticultural Director, Saratoga Horticultural Foundation, Saratoga, CA

David Loring, Soils Specialist, San Luis Obispo, CA

Michael Macauley, Irrigation Specialist, Menlo Park, CA

Dr. W. B. McHenry, Extension Weed Scientist, University of California, Davis, CA

Dr. William Meyer, Vice-President Turf-Seed, Inc., Hubbard, OR

Robert A. Moore, President, Aquatrols Corporation of America, Pennsauken, NJ

New York State College of Agriculture and Life Sciences at Cornell, Ithaca, NY

Dr. Harry Niemczyk, Professor of Turfgrass Entomology, Ohio Agricultural Research and Development Center, Wooster, OH

Brooks Pennington, President, Pennington Seed Inc., Madison, GA

Paul Sander, Camarillo, CA

Ron Stacy, Amfac Garden Perry's, Fremont, CA

Theodor Thompson, Camarillo, CA

John Traverso, Landscape Gardener, Walnut Creek, CA

David Vought, Camarillo, CA

University of California Division of Agricultural Sciences

Van Winden Landscaping, Napa, CA

Index

aron's-beard, 132
belia grandiflora 'Prostrata', 84
cacia redolens, 84
chillea tomentosa, 84, 85
cid, 172
cid-forming fertilizer, 53, 172
ctual nitrogen, 52, 172
diantum pedatum, 115, 116
egopodium podagraria 'Variegatum 85
eration, 68, 70, 172
erator, 67
frican daisy, 86
gapanthus species, 85, 90
gropyron cristatum, 30
grostis species, 18
ir-cushion mowers, 51
juga reptans, 90, 91
kebia quinata, 91
lgerian ivy, 126
lkaline, 172
lleghaney pachysandra, 155
mendment, soil, 172
merican barrenwort, 168
mmoniacal nitrogen, 53
mmonium nitrate, 53
mmonium sulfate, 53
nemone hybrida, 91
ngel's hair, 94
nnual, 172
nnual bluegrass, 58, 68, 70
nnual grasses, 79
nnuals, 92
ntisiphon device, 38
rabis alpina, 92
rabis caucasica, 92
rabis procurrens, 92
rctostaphylos hookeri, 83
rctostaphylos uva-ursi, 92, 93
rctostaphylos species, 92-93
rctotheca calendula, 86, 87
rctotis hybrids, 86
renaria species, 150
rmeria maritima, 94
rmyworm, 62
rtemisia species, 94
rundinaria species, 97
sarum species, 95
sparagus densiflorus 'Sprengeri', 95
sparagus fern, 95
stilbe japonica, 95, 96
thyrium goeringianum, 115, 116
triplex semibaccata, 96
ubrieta deltoidea, 96
urinia saxatilis, 96
ustralian saltbush, 96
ustralian violet, 170
utomatic sprinkler systems, 39
utumn fern, 116
xonopus affinis, 30

by cyclamen, 111
by's-tears, 166
accharis pilularis, 97
hiagrass, 15, 68
ja primrose, 153
mboo, 97
rberry, 98
rk mulch, 10
rren strawberry, 170
rrenwort, 113
sket-of-gold, 96
llflower, 100
ntgrass, 18
erberis verruculosa, 98
erberis species, 98, 99
ergenia species, 98
rmudagrass, 16, 58, 68
hybrids, 16, 17
ennial, 172
illbug, 62
rdsfoot trefoil, 148
shop's hat, 113
end, 172
ue cape plumbago, 159
ue fescue, 118

Blue grama, 30
Blue marguerite, 114
Blue star creeper, 145
Bougainvillea species, 99
Bouteoua gracilis, 30
Bract, 172
British Columbia, adapted lawn grasses, 14
British Columbia, adapted ground covers, 83
Broadcast spreader, 44
Broadleaf, 172
Broadleaf weeds, 55
Brooms, 99
Brown patch, 64
Bruckenthalia spicuifolia, 122
Buchloe dactyloides, 30
Buckhorn plantain, 58
Buffalograss, 30
Bulb covers plant list, 82
Burclover, 58

C
California lilac, 102
California poppy, 113
Calluna species, 123
Calluna vulgaris, 122, 125
Campanula species, 100, 101
Candytuft, 132
Cape marigold, 87, 89
Cape weed, 86
Care schedule for lawns, 68-71
Carissa species, 101
Carmel creeper, 102
Carolina jessamine, 120
Carpet bugle, 90
Carpetgrass, 30
Carpobrotus species, 133
Catharanthus roseus, 101, 102
Catmint, 153
Catnip, 153
Ceanothus species, 74, 102, 103
Centipedegrass, 19, 68
Central South, adapted lawn grasses, 14
Centranthus ruber, 103
Centrifugal spreader, 67
Cephalophyllum 'Red Spike', 133
Cerastium tomentosum, 103, 104
Ceratostigma plumbaginoides, 104
Certified seed, 172
Chamaemelum nobile, 104, 105
Chamomile, 104
Chelates, 172
Chewing fescue, 20, 21
Chinch bugs, 55, 62, 68
Chinese holly, 136
Chinese juniper, 140
Chlorosis, 172
Christmas fern, 117
Chrysanthemum parthenium, 104, 105
Cinquefoil, 160
Circuits, 38
Cistus species, 105
Clay soil, 172
Climates, lawn grass, 14
Clippings, 51
Clover, 68, 70
Coastal regions, recommended ground covers, 83
Cold hardiness, 172
Common aubrieta, 96
Common thrift, 94
Compaction, 172
Complete fertilizer, 172
Comptonia peregrina, 105
Confederate vine, 168
Conifers, 10
Contact herbicides, 55, 172
Controller, sprinkler system, 39
Convallaria majalis, 106
Convolvulus cneorum, 106
Cool-season grasses, 13, 47, 172
  care schedule, 70
  fertilizer needs, 52
Coprosma kirkii, 106, 107

Coreopsis auriculata 'Nana', 107
Coring, soil, 172
Coronilla varia, 107
Corsican mint, 149
Cotoneaster dammeri, 109, 110
Cotoneaster horizontalis, 108
Cotoneaster microphyllus, 108, 109
Cotoneaster species, 108-110
Cottonseed meal, 52
Cotula squalida, 107
Crabgrass, 59, 68, 70
Cranesbill, 120
Creeping barberry, 148
Creeping buttercup, 162
Creeping coprosma, 106
Creeping fescue, 21
Creeping forget-me-not, 154
Creeping Jennie, 148
Creeping juniper, 142, 143
Creeping mahonia, 148
Creeping oregano, 154
Creeping red fescue, 20
Creeping saltbush, 96
Creeping spirea, 95
Creeping St. John's wort, 132
Creeping thyme, 167
Creeping wire vine, 152
Crown vetch, 107
Cultivar, 172
Curly dock, 59
Cutting, for propagation, 77, 172
Cutworm, 62
Cyclamen hederifolium, 111
Cymbalaria muralis, 111
Cynodon dactylon, 16
Cyrtomium falcatum, 115
Cytisus species, 99

D
Daboecia cantabrica, 123
Dahlberg daisy, 112
Dalea greggi, 111
Dallisgrass, 59
Dandelion, 59
Daphne, 166
Davallia trichomanoides, 115
Daylily, 128
Dead nettle, 144
Deciduous, 172
Delosperma 'Alba', 133
Desert regions, recommended ground covers, 83
Dethatching, 66, 68, 70, 172
Dianthus species, 111
Dichondra, 30, 118
Dicot, 172
Dimorphotheca species, 87, 89
Diseases, 55, 64
Division, 77, 172
Dormancy, 172
Dormant seeding, 172
Double flower, 172
Drain valves, 38
Drape and trail plant list, 81
Drip watering, 76
Drosanthemum floribundum, 133, 134
Drosanthemum species, 134
Drought-tolerant plant list, 80
Dryopteris erythrosora, 116
Dryopteris species, 117
Duchesnea indica, 112
Dwarf coreopsis, 107
Dwarf coyote brush, 97
Dwarf plumbago, 104
Dwarf spruce, 157
Dyssodia tenuiloba, 112

E
Eastern Canada, adapted lawn grasses, 14
Eastern Canada, recommended ground covers, 83
Electric nylon line mower, 51
Elemental nitrogen, 53
English daisy, 54, 60

English ivy, 78, 127
English juniper, 141
Epimedium species, 112, 113
Equivalents, liquid measure, 56
Eremochloa ophiurides, 19
Erica species, 123
Erosion control, 78, 79
  plant list, 80
Eschscholzia californica, 113
Espalier, 172
Euonymus fortunei, 113, 114
Evening primrose, 153
Evergreen, 172
Evergreen candytuft, 132
Evergreen currant, 162

F
Fairway crested wheatgrass, 30
Fairy ring, 64
Fallowing, 35
False spiraea, 95
Fast-release fertilizer, 52, 53
Felicia amelloides, 114
Ferns, 115-117
Fertilizer, 34, 51, 52
  burn, 52, 172
  how to read a label, 53
Fertilizing cool-season grasses, 70
Fertilizing ground covers, 77
Fertilizing warm-season grasses, 68
Fescue, 70
Fescue, fine, 20
Fescue, tall, 21, 22
Festuca arundinacea, 21
Festuca longifolia, 20
Festuca ovina glauca, 118
Festuca rubra, 20
Feverfew, 104
Fire-retardant plant list, 81
Firethorn, 161
Five-finger fern, 115
Five-leaf akebia, 91
Flail mower, 51
Fleeceflower, 159
Florida, adapted lawn grasses, 14
Forage-type tall fescue, 22
Forget-me-not, 152
Forsythia intermedia 'Arnold Dwarf', 118
Fragaria species, 118
Freeway daisy, 88
Fuchsia procumbens, 119
Fumigant, 172
Fumigation, 35
Fungicides, 54, 172
  list of, 56
Fungus, 172
Funkia, 130
Fusarium blight, 64

G
Galium odoratum, 119
Gallons per minute (GPM), 37
Garden verbena, 169
Gardenia augusta 'Radicans', 119
Gardenia jasminoides 'Radicans', 119
Gaultheria species, 120
Gazania species, 87
Gelsemium sempervirens, 120
Genista lydia, 100
Genista pilosa, 100
Genista species, 99
Genus, 172
Geranium sanguineum prostratum, 121
Geranium species, 120
Germander, 167
Germination, 172
Glyphosate herbicide, 34
Golden fleece, 112
Goutweed, 85
Greenbug, 62
Grevillea tridentifera, 121
Ground covers, 73-171

encyclopedia, 84-171
  introduction and basics, 73-77
  lists, 80-83
  selection, 4, 5
Grubs, 55, 63, 68, 70
Gulf Coast, adapted lawn grasses, 14
Gypsum, 34

H
Hall's Japanese honeysuckle, 147
Hard fescue, 20, 21
Hardy, 172
Heads, sprinkler, 38
Heath, 122, 123, 124
Heather, 122, 124, 125
Heavenly bamboo, 153
Heaving, 172
Hedera canariensis, 126, 127
Hedera colchica, 126
Hedera helix, 126, 127
Hedera species, 126-127
Helianthemum nummularium, 128
Helminthosporium, 65
Hemerocallis species, 128
Hen and chickens, 166
Herb lawn, 11
Herbicides, 54, 55, 172
  list of, 57
Herbs, 129
Herniaria glabra, 129
Heuchera sanguinea, 129
Holly fern, 115
Hoses, watering, 48
Hosta species, 130, 131
Hottentot fig, 133
Humus, 172
Hybrid, 172
Hydromulching, 78
Hypericum calycinum, 132

I
Iberis sempervirens, 132
Ice plant, 133-135
Ilex cornuta, 136, 137, 138
Ilex crenata, 136
Ilex species, 136-138
Ilex vomitoria, 137, 138
Indian mock strawberry, 112
Inorganic fertilizer, 172
Insect pests, 55, 68, 70
Insecticides, 54, 172
  list of, 56
Irish heath, 123
Irish moss, 150, 151
Iron, 53
Iron chlorosis, 172
Irrigation consultants, 37
Irrigation plan, 40
Isobutylidene diurea (IBDU), 53
Ivy, 126
Ivy geranium, 156

J
Japanese anemone, 91
Japanese beetle grubs, 70
Japanese garden juniper, 143
Japanese holly, 136
Japanese painted fern, 115
Japanese spurge, 155
Junipers, 139-143
Juniperus chinensis, 140
Juniperus chinensis 'Pfitzerana', 124
Juniperus communis, 141
Juniperus conferta, 141
Juniperus davurica, 141
Juniperus horizontalis, 142
Juniperus procumbens, 143
Juniperus sabina, 143
Juniperus species, 74, 127, 139-143
Juniperus virginiana 'Silver Spreader', 143
Jupiter's beard, 103
Jute netting, 78

Index

K
Kenilworth ivy, 111
Kentucky bluegrass, 23, 24, 25, 70
Kikuyugrass, 31, 60
Kinnikinnick, 92
Knotweed, 159
Korean grass, 171

L
Lamiastrum galeobdolon 'Variegatum', 144
Lamium maculatum, 144
Lampranthus species, 134
Landscape design, 3, 4
Lantana montevidensis, 144
Large areas, plant list, 81
Laurentia fluviatilis, 145
Lavender cotton, 164
Lawns, 13-67
 alternatives, 8-11, 83
 care, 47
 climate adaptations, 14-29
 clippings, 51
 fertilizers, 53
 insecticides, 55
 problems, 54
 renovation, 66
 selection, 4, 5, 14-29
Layering, 77
Leaching, 172
Leadwort, 104
Leatherleaf fern, 117
Legume, 79
Lily-of-the-Nile, 85
Lily-of-the-valley, 106
Lily turf, 145
Lime, 34, 52, 172
Lippia, 157
Liriope 'Gold Band', 145
Lirope muscari, 117
Liriope species, 145
Loam, 172
Lobelia, 146
Lobelia erinus, 146
Lobularia maritima, 146, 147
Lolium multiflorum, 26
Lolium perenne, 27
Lolium x hybridum, 26
Lonicera japonica 'Halliana', 147
Lotus species, 148
Low-maintenance landscaping, 6-8
Lysimachia nummularia, 148

M
Madagascar periwinkle, 101
Mahonia repens, 148, 149
Maintenance, 7
Malephora species, 135
Mallow, 60
Manzanita, 92
Mazus reptans, 149
Melting out, 65
Mentha requienii, 149
Microclimate, 172
Milorganite, 52
Miniature gardenia, 119
Mix, 172
Mixture, 172
Moisture sensors, 39
Mondo grass, 145
Moneywort, 148
Monocot, 173
Moss, 9, 150
Moss pink, 157
Mountain states, adapted lawn grasses, 14
Mountain states, recommended ground covers, 83
Mowing, 50
 cool-season grasses, 70
 correct height, 50
 safety, 51
 strip, 6, 173
 warm-season grasses, 68
Muehlenbeckia axillaris, 152
Mulch, 8, 9, 44, 78, 79, 173

Myoporum parvifolium, 152
Myosotis species, 152
Myosotis sylvatica, 152

N
NPK, 173
Nandina domestica, 152, 153
Narrowleaf, 173
Narrowleaf weeds, 55
Natal plum, 101
Native moss, 150
Nepeta faassenii, 153
Nepeta mussinii, 153
Nephrolepsis cordifolia, 116
Netting, 79
New Zealand brass-buttons, 107
Nitrate nitrogen, 53
Nitrogen, 173
Nonselective herbicides, 55, 74, 173
North, recommended ground covers, 83
Northeast, adapted lawn grasses, 14
Northeast, recommended ground covers, 83
Northwest, adapted lawn grasses, 14
Northwest, recommended ground covers, 83

O
Oenothera berlandieri, 153
Oenothera species, 153
Omphalodes verna, 154
Ophiopogon japonicus, 145
Ophiopogon species, 145
Oregon boxwood, 155
Oregon intermediate ryegrass, 26
Organic, 173
Organic matter, 74
Origanum vulgare 'Compacta nana', 154
Oscularia species, 135
Osteospermum ecklonis, 87
Osteospermum fruticosum, 86
Osteospermum species, 88
Overseeding, 66, 173
Oxalis, 60
Oxalis oregano, 154

P
PVC fittings, 39
PVC pipe, 38
Pachistima, 155
Pachysandra terminalis, 73, 155
Pacific Northwest, recommended ground covers, 82
Pacific Northwest, adapted lawn grasses, 14
Parrot's beak, 148
Paspalum 'Sweet Adalayd', 31
Paspalum notatum, 15
Paspalum vaginatum, 31
Paxistima species, 155
Peat moss spreader, 44
Pelargonium peltatum, 156
Pennisetum clandestinum, 31
Perennial, 173
Perennial verbena, 169
Periwinkle, 169
Pernettya, 156
Pernettya mucronata, 156
Persian ivy, 126
Pesticides, 54, 173
Pests, 62
pH, soil, 173
 how to adjust, 35
Phalaris arundinacea picta, 156
Phlox subulata, 83, 157
Phosphorus, 53, 173
Phyla nodiflora, 157
Picea species, 123, 157
Pinks, 111
Pinus species, 158
Pipe, 38

Pittosporum tobira 'Wheeler's Dwarf', 158
Plantain lily, 130
Planting cool-season grasses, 70
Planting ground covers, 75
Planting lawns, 33, 47, 68, 70
Planting slopes, 75, 77
Planting warm-season grasses, 68
Plugs, 33, 37
Plumbago auriculata, 159
Plumbago capensis, 159
Poa pratensis, 23
Poa trivialis, 31
Polyantha roses, 162
Polygonum species, 159
Polystichum acrostichoides, 115
Polystichum species, 115, 117
Portulaca grandiflora, 160
Post-emergent herbicides, 55, 173
Potash, 53, 173
Potassium, 173
Potentilla species, 123, 160
Prairie grass, 10, 11
Pratia angulata, 160
Pre-emergent herbicides, 35, 55, 74, 173
Prepare soil, 34
Propagation, 77
Prostrate abelia, 84
Prostrate myoporum, 152
Prostrate pigweed, 61
Prunus laurocerasus 'Zabeliana', 161
Pyracantha species, 161
Pyrethrum test, 55

R
Ranunculus repens, 162
Red fescue, 20
Red thread, 65
Red valerian, 103
Redwood sorrel, 154
Reel mowers, 50
Rejuvenate, 173
Renovate, 67, 173
Renovating a lawn, 66
Rhizome, 173
Ribbon grass, 156
Ribes viburnifolium, 162
Rock rose, 105
Rockscaping, 8
Roller, 44, 45
Rolling, 173
Roman chamomile, 104
Rosa species, 162
Rose, 162
Rose moss, 160
Rosea ice plant, 134
Rosmarinus officinalis, 163
Rotary mowers, 50
Roughstalk bluegrass, 31
Rumohra adiantiformis, 117
Runner, 173
Rupturewort, 129
Ruschia species, 135
Rust, 65
Ryegrass, 70
Ryegrass, annual, 26
Ryegrass, perennial, 27

S
Sagina species, 150
Salal, 120
Salinity, 173
Santolina species, 164
Sarcococca hookerana humilis, 164
Savin juniper, 143
Scalp, 50, 66, 173
Scotch heather, 122
Scotch moss, 150, 151
Sea fig, 133
Sedum dasyphyllum, 165
Sedum species, 164-165
Sedum spurium, 165
Seed, 33
Seed mix, 33

Seed, sowing, 44
Seedbed preparation, 34
Selective herbicides, 55, 173
Self-sow, 173
Self-sowers plant list, 82
Sempervivum tectorum, 166
Sepal, 173
Shade-tolerant plant list, 80
Shore juniper, 141
Showy flowers plant list, 81
Shutoff gate valve, 38
Sickle bar mower, 51
Silver bush morning glory, 106
Silver lace vine, 159
Silver spreader, 94
Single flower, 173
Slip, for propagation, 173
Slope planting, 77
Slope-stabilizing chemicals, 78
Slow-release fertilizer, 52, 53, 173
Snow-in-summer, 103
Sod, 33
 installation, 37, 45
Sod cutter, 45
Sod webworm, 55, 63, 70
Soil, 33
 amendment, 35
 coring machines, 66
 fumigants, 74
 moisture, 48
 pH, 74
 preparation, 36
 salts, 52
 test, 34, 74
Soleirolia soleirolii, 166
South, recommended ground covers, 83
Southern California, adapted lawn grasses, 14
Southern grasses, 33
Southwest, adapted lawn grasses, 14
Sowing seed, 35, 44
Spacing ground covers, 76
Specialty grasses, 30
Species, 173
Speedwell, 169
Spike heath, 122
Spirea japonica 'Alpina', 166
Spotted spurge, 61
Spreading English yew, 167
Sprenger asparagus, 95
Sprigs, 33, 37, 173
Sprinklers, 48
Sprinkler systems, 39, 41
 components, 38
 cutting into water supply, 41
 design, 37
Squirrel's-foot fern, 115
St. Augustinegrass, 28, 68
Star jasmine, 168
Steer manure, 52
Stenotaphrum secundatum, 28
Stolons, 37, 173
Strain, 173
Sulfur, 34, 52, 53
Sulfur-coated urea (SCU), 53
Sun rose, 128
Surfactant, 173
Sweet alyssum, 147
Sweet fern, 105
Sweet violet, 170
Sweet woodruff, 119
Sword fern, 116
Systemic, 173
Systemic herbicides, 55

T
Tall fescue, 61
Taproot, 173
Taxus baccata 'Repandens', 167
Teucrium chamaedrys, 167
Thatch, 173
Thymus pseudolanuginosus, 11
Thymus species, 82, 167
'Tifway' bermudagrass, 13

Tiller, 173
Top dressing, 173
Trachelospermum asiaticum, 168
Trachelospermum jasminoides, 168
Trachelospermum species, 117
Trailing African daisy, 88
Trailing fuchsia, 119
Trailing indigo bush, 111
Trailing lantana, 144
Trailing Rosemary, 163
Translocated herbicides, 55
Turf-type ryegrass, 70
Turf-type tall fescue, 21

U
Underground irrigation system installation, 37, 42, 43
Urea, 53
Ureaformaldehyde (UF), 53

V
Valves, 38
Vancouver fern, 168
Vancouveria hexandra, 168
Variegated, 173
Variety, 173
Vegetative planting, 173
Verbena peruviana, 169
Veronica repens, 169
Vertical mower, 67, 173
Vinca, 101
Vinca major, 169, 170
Vinca minor, 169, 170
Viola odorata, 171
Viola species, 170

W
Waldsteinia fragarioides, 170
Wall rockcress, 92
Warm-season grasses, 13, 47, 173
 care schedule, 68
 fertilizer needs, 52
Watering, 48
 ground covers, 76
 established lawn, 49
 hoses for, 48
 new lawn, 35
Weeds, 54, 58, 68, 70, 82, 173
 control, 35, 74
Well-drained soil, 173
West, recommended ground covers, 83
Western sword fern, 117
Wetting agent, 49, 173
White trailing ice plant, 133
Whitestem filaree, 61
Whorl, 173
Wild ginger, 95
Wild strawberry, 118
Windflower, 91
Winter creeper, 113
Wintergreen, 120
Wood chips, 8
Wood fern, 116
Woolly thyme, 11, 167
Woolly yarrow, 85

X
Xanthorhiza simplicissima, 171

Y
Yaupon, 138
Yellow archangel, 144
Yellow-root, 171

Z
Zabel cherry laurel, 161
Zoysia tenuifolia, 171
Zoysiagrass, 29, 68, 171